Hoover Institution Publications

Rulers of Empire:
the French Colonial Service
in Africa

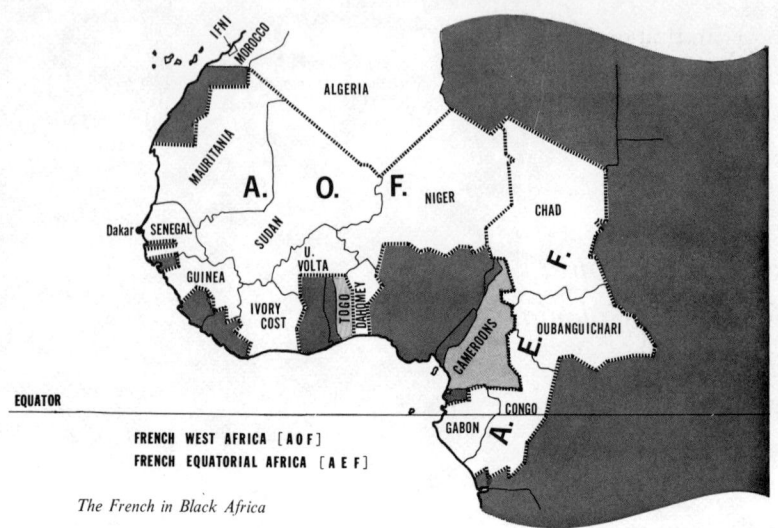

FRENCH WEST AFRICA [AOF]
FRENCH EQUATORIAL AFRICA [AEF]

The French in Black Africa

Rulers of Empire: the French Colonial Service in Africa

William B. Cohen

Hoover Institution Press
Stanford University
California 1971

The Hoover Institution on War, Revolution and Peace,
founded at Stanford University in 1919
by the late President Herbert Hoover,
is a center for advanced study and research
on public and international affairs in the twentieth century.
The views expressed in its publications
are entirely those of the authors
and do not necessarily reflect
the views of the Hoover Institution.

Hoover Institution Publications 95
© 1971 by the Board of Trustees of the Leland Stanford Junior University
All rights reserved
Library of Congress Catalog Card Number: 76-137405
Standard Book Number 8179-1951-1
Printed in the United States of America

For R.D.

Contents

	Preface	xiii
	Abbreviations	2
	Introduction	3
I.	Founding an Overseas Administration	6
II.	The Years of Experimentation	18
III.	Beginnings of the *Ecole Coloniale*	37
IV.	The Locus of Power	57
V.	The Colonial School and the New Generation	84
VI.	The Era of Lost Opportunities	108
VII.	The ENFOM, 1940-1959	143
VIII.	The Corps in an Era of Change	158
IX.	The Legacy	194
	Appendices	
	I. Undersecretaries and Ministers in Charge of Colonial Affairs	209
	II. Letter and Questionnaire Sent to Former Administrators	211
	III. Average Number of Years Spent by Administrators in the Colonies	217
	IV. Map of Geographic Origins of Administrators Serving in 1940	219
	V. Map of Geographic Origins of Administrators and Governors Having Graduated from the *Ecole Coloniale* 1909-1941	221
	Notes	223

Bibliography	249
Index	273

Illustrations and Maps

Illustrations
- Louis Faidherbe — 10
- Maurice Delafosse — 50
- Fresco at the *Ecole Coloniale* — 54
- Joost Van Vollenhoven — 66
- Georges Hardy — 88
- Henri Labouret — 96
- Robert Delavignette — 99
- Marius Moutet — 136
- Félix Eboué — 164
- Charles de Gaulle Opening Brazzaville Conference — 168

Maps
- The French in Black Africa — frontispiece
- Geographic Origins of Administrators in the Corps in 1940 — 219
- Geographic Origins of the Graduates of the *Ecole Coloniale* 1909-1941 — 221

Tables

1. Correlation between source of recruitment and success within the Corps of administrators appointed 1887-1914 — 29
2. Number of men entering the Corps, 1887-1913 — 32
3. Evaluation of administrators by their governors — 34
4. Educational background of 694 administrators recruited between 1887 and 1914 — 35
5. Correlation between educational level and administrative ability of administrators entering the Corps between 1887 and 1914 — 36
6. Percentage of applicants admitted to seven *grandes écoles* — 90
7. Percentage distribution of fathers' professions of students admitted to the *Ecole Coloniale* — 91
8. Fathers' professions of 138 former administrators who had attended the *Ecole Coloniale* — 92
9. Application of the *indigénat* code in the Sudan in the 1930s — 119
10. Percentage distribution of fathers' occupations of students admitted to the ENFOM and the ENA — 152
11. Attitudes toward the timing of reforms of 1945-1946 — 176
12. Attitudes toward reforms of 1956-1957 — 186
13. Attitudes toward decolonization — 189
14. The prime cause for decolonization as seen by different age groups in the Corps — 192

Preface

This work was begun at Stanford University in 1965 initially as a dissertation; it developed from an interest in the history of French bureaucratic organizations, and was further stimulated by Alexis de Tocqueville's affirmation that French colonial administration was a kind of caricature of the metropolitan bureaucracy.

It is true that the men sent out to Africa from the late nineteenth into the middle of the twentieth century, who had been recruited and trained in France, were imbued with values they often shared with their metropolitan colleagues, and many of the assumptions and rules under which they operated had their counterpart in metropolitan bureaucratic organizations. But as the study developed I became less certain that Tocqueville's generalization was a useful tool of analysis. For the problems which the overseas bureaucracy faced in the tropical milieu were unique, in that only in the most general way could the colonial service be viewed as a paradigm of the metropolitan administration.

The study thus originally intended only as an illustration, developed into a history in its own right of the Corps of men who commanded in the century to half century—depending on the areas—the French possessions in sub-Saharan Africa and Madagascar. The book emphasizes administration in French West Africa both because that region was the largest and most populous administered by the Corps, and because of the extensive published and archival material available in Paris and in Africa. Nevertheless, since administrators were rotated to the federation of French Equatorial Africa and to Madagascar, the study also illuminates the functioning of the entire Corps.

The service numbered approximately 4,000 members from the time of its inception in 1887 until its demise in 1960, and it ruled nearly a third of the African continent. To write about a bureaucracy of that size which administered such a large area is clearly a hazardous venture, but perhaps the study will encourage further in-depth regional histories of French rule and lead others to write biographies of individual administrators. Such histories would undoubtedly teach us much about French colonial rule.[1]

Imperial history has rightly been castigated because it assumed to be African or Asian history, when in fact it was little more than a history of European activity in those continents. Nevertheless, imperial history has its value in helping understand the origins and development of the dominant relationship that Europeans established and maintained over non-Europeans in the nineteenth and twentieth centuries. While taking into account the African setting, the book is also intended as a contribution to the history of French imperialism.

The sources for the study include published material, archival and oral sources, as well as respondents' answers to the questionnaire (see Appendix II) sent out to most of the former administrators living in France. Unfortunately, only a few biographies and autobiographies of French overseas administrators exist. Compared with members of the British colonial service who left a rich published record of their thought and action, the French have been taciturn.

Monographs on colonial administration and colonial policy provide some fragmentary information. Official publications such as the *Bulletin officiel des colonies* and the *Journal officiel* of the French government and of the various French possessions give useful details on regulations concerning recruitment and promotion. Those publications also include some of the circulars sent out by ministers of colonies and governors to their administrative subordinates. Other regulations and circulars not published are available in the archives of the former ministry of overseas France and in the archives of the colonies.

The most important archival sources for the study were the former administrators' personnel files, of which approximately 1,000 were examined. Of these, 250 relating to administrators who finished their overseas service before 1915 were available in the French national archives and the rest were in the archives of former French West Africa in Dakar, Senegal. In both archives official reports written at all levels of the administration give important information on the administration and at the same time reveal the attitudes of those in the colonial service.

The research and writing of the dissertation were made possible by grants from the French Ministry of Foreign Affairs, Stanford University, the Hoover Institution, and the Foreign Area Fellowship Program. Preparation for publication was facilitated by a grant from the Indiana University West European Studies Program and the Research and Advanced Studies Program. I should like to express my appreciation to all of them for their generous assistance.

I owe several individuals also a debt of gratitude. Professor Gordon Wright as dissertation adviser always gave thorough and helpful criticism, in spite of his heavy duties at the United States Embassy in Paris. Professor G. Wesley Johnson, of Stanford University, acted as second reader and also gave invaluable advice. Mr. Robert Lumsden of Evanston, Illinois, offered many useful suggestions for the improvement of the manuscript. Professor Rémi Clignet of the Northwestern University Sociology Department permitted me to draw on his ideas and French overseas experiences during pleasant weekly luncheons in the academic year 1966-1967.

In Paris, Governor-General Robert Delavignette gave unselfishly of his time and offered many useful suggestions. He answered innumerable questions both in personal conversations and in correspondence. Other former members of the French colonial service were also most helpful—notably Pierre Alexandre, Robert Cornevin, Hubert Deschamps, and Pierre Gentil. Governor-General Louis Pignon, president of the *Association des anciens élèves de l'Ecole nationale de la France d'outre-mer* in 1965, contributed an introduction to the questionnaire. I also wish to express my thanks to those members of the association who responded to the questionnaire, and to *Editions à la page,* Montreal, Canada, for permission to reproduce passages from Jacques Kuoh Moukouri, *Doigts noirs: Je fus écrivain-interprète au Cameroun*, 1963, pp. 28-30.

I am grateful to Mlle. Antoinette Ménier and M. Jules Laroche of the *Archives nationales, Section outre-mer*, and MM. Jean Francois Maurel and Oumar Ba of the *Archives de Sénégal* for their help. The final stages of the manuscript received the useful criticisms of Lewis Gann, Hoover Institution, and of my colleague, David Pletcher, Indiana University. And finally, a word of thanks to my reliable typists Mrs. Mary Jane Gormley and Mrs. Mary Anne Fugelso.

*Rulers of Empire:
the French Colonial Service
in Africa*

Abbreviations

AAOF	Archives de l'AOF, Dakar
AEF	Federation of French Equatorial Africa
ANS	Archives nationales, Sénégal, Dakar
ANSOM	Archives nationales, France, Section outre-mer
AOF	Federation of French West Africa
BAPAC	*Bulletin de l'Association professionelle des administrateurs coloniaux*
BOC	*Bulletin officiel des colonies*
BSAEC	*Bulletin de la Société des anciens élèves de l'École Coloniale*
ENA	Ecole nationale d'administration
ENFOM	Ecole nationale de la France d'outre-mer
IHEOM	Institut des hautes études d'outre-mer
J.o.	*Journal officiel*

Introduction

Forts and trading posts acquired in the seventeenth century on the coast of West Africa became the springboard for French territorial conquests in Senegal in the mid-nineteenth century. From Senegal, a generation later, French explorers and military adventurers began a remarkable advance inland into the Western Sudan and southward toward the Gulf of Guinea. In the 1880s, after the French naval officer Savorgnan de Brazza had laid claims to parts of the Congo for his country, the French at the same time began a push northward which culminated at the turn of the century in the connection of the sub-Saharan empire with the colony of Algeria. That accomplishment fulfilled a dream which several generations of French officials had entertained. And in 1895 a French military expedition seized the island of Madagascar.

In France several ministries and several colonial services administered the French overseas possessions. By 1914—a convenient date since the French had by then acquired virtually all their empire—the French ruled their possessions through three different ministries: the ministry of colonies, the ministry of foreign affairs, and the ministry of interior. These divisions of authority were not along functional lines; they had been determined by particular historical circumstances. For example, the protectorates of Tunisia and Morocco had been put under the authority of the ministry of foreign affairs because the international situation had made it undesirable to declare them outright colonies. But Laos and Cambodia, also protectorates, were administered by the ministry of navy and later transferred to the ministry of colonies when it was established in 1894. Algeria, although considered a colony when its conquest began in the 1830s, was first administered by the ministry of war and later was transferred to the ministry of interior. Finally, the large European population in that country had succeeded in having it integrated with metropolitan France, thus placing it, like any other metropolitan department, under the responsibility of the ministry of interior. Various proposals were made to combine the administration of all the different dependencies into a single ministry of overseas France, but until its disintegration the empire remained divided among the three separate ministries: colonies, foreign affairs, and interior.

French control of the overseas possessions was further decentralized through five colonial services. Tunisia and Morocco were each administered by a Corps of Civil Controllers, while Algeria had a Corps of Administrators of Mixed Communes; later, prefects sent out by the ministry of interior administered Algeria. The ministry of navy employed two corps to administer the areas under its jurisdiction—the Civil Services of Indochina, established in 1887, and the Corps of Colonial Administrators, founded in the same year, which administered the remainder.

The naval ministry transferred its responsibilities of colonial rule to the ministry of colonies when it was established in 1894, so that both the Corps of Civil Services and of Colonial Administrators were under the jurisdiction of the ministry of colonies after that year.

This study is the history of the Corps of Colonial Administrators, the great bulk of which served in Africa; only a small number were dispatched to the minor French possessions in India, the Pacific and Indian oceans, the Antilles, St. Pierre and Miquelon, and Guiana. But the emphasis of the book is on the vast majority of the Corps—the men who served in Black Africa and Madagascar.

Since French colonial administration was in actual practice a decentralized system giving nearly full authority to the men in the colonies, the understanding of French rule requires a study of the men who exercised that authority overseas. Their class background, geographical origins, formal training, and ideological outlook had a bearing on the manner in which the French overseas bureaucracy functioned. In its turn, of course, the nature of the overseas administrative structure set a framework within which the French administrators could perform.

Methods of recruiting and training French colonial officials developed gradually after a number of experiments. When, finally a regularized method had been instituted on the very eve of World War I, the French continued to be faced with the problem of attracting men into the colonial service who would accomplish the tasks which the mother country had set for its colonial mission. The increased stress on recruiting men with a certain bureaucratic training ensured that after 1920 a more pliable service than had existed before developed. Nevertheless, the factors of distance and the relative lack of interest which both government and Parliament evinced in overseas problems meant that until 1945 only a minimum of external control was exerted on the colonial service.

While the first generation of colonial administrators did much to destroy the traditional political structures overseas, the generation that followed in the interwar period was often reluctant to create that full assimilation of the colonies with the motherland which was often proclaimed as the colonial program in Paris; so that French colonial rule, like its other European counterparts, while destroying much of the traditional fabric of the colonial world, did not form it into a Western image.

The colonial service did not operate in a vacuum. Colonialism, which was an example of the global nature of modern history, was profoundly affected by the two world wars which succeeded each other within a generation. And the rise of nationalist movements created a new challenge to colonialism and changed the very context within which colonial rule could be regarded. The Corps of Colonial Administrators perhaps reached its nadir of power in 1920 when the numerous reforms and changes had streamlined it into an efficient arm of French control. But the profound social and political changes unleashed by World War I, the spread of education, and at least rudimentary economic growth transformed the colonial service into something of an anachronism on the eve of the second global war.

In spite of constitutional and administrative adjustments the French after 1945 never completely regained control over their empire. The last fifteen years of colonial rule found the Corps challenged by a growing opposition both at home and in the colonies and it no longer possessed the kind of authority it had had in the pre-1939 era. Independence opened yet another chapter for the activity of the members of the Corps—a phase of the final pages of their history.

I Founding an Overseas Administration

French colonization in the seventeenth and eighteenth centuries achieved domination over land but usually not over the indigenous populations. Upon the arrival of the first settlers in North America, the French established an administration, but though it maintained close control over the settlers' lives, it made no attempt to establish administrative control over the Indians, with whom its relations were limited to trade and quasi-diplomacy.

By the beginning of the nineteenth century, France had lost its continental empire in North America. Its remaining overseas possessions were now modest in size and sparsely populated; they consisted of plantation colonies such as the Antilles, which were inhabited by white plantation owners and their imported Negro slaves, and small trade forts on the coastline of West Africa and India, which were occupied by a small number of French traders and officers. As in North America, relations with the indigenous populations in these regions were usually limited to trade and the establishment of some form of diplomatic relations with the local states.

Only Britain and Holland, the two powers that emerged with empires at the end of the Napoleonic era, administered the indigenous populations of their empires. In the northeastern part of India the British East India Company had begun as early as 1772 to assume the direct collection of revenue and the administration of justice. Britain increasingly limited the prerogatives of the private company, and by the middle of the nineteenth century the government took over the responsibility of administering most of the Indian subcontinent. The Dutch in the East Indies were the second European power to follow this procedure. In the seventeenth and eighteenth centuries, the Dutch East India Company had established a few posts which conducted trade relations with the surrounding populations. In 1798 the company lost its administrative control to the Dutch government, which in turn lost the islands to the British during the Napoleonic Wars. When the Dutch government regained the colony in 1816, it attempted to establish effective rule over the countryside by sending Dutch officials into the interior of the colony. Like the British, these functionaries ruled indirectly, that is, they controlled the local populations through existing political and social institutions.

Once the British and the Dutch had founded an administration over their empires, they began to establish regular methods of recruiting colonial officials. In 1806 a college was founded at Haileybury, near London, which anyone who wished an appointment to the Indian service was required to attend. In 1853 the Macaulay Commission introduced entrance examinations for the Indian Civil Service, with the main emphasis on classical studies; those who passed the examinations were also trained in Indian and Oriental affairs before being sent abroad. In Holland, the Dutch appointed officials from among the men who had passed the required courses in Javanese affairs at the Royal Academy of Delft. In 1864 attendance at the school ceased to be a prerequisite for appointment to the Dutch East India Service, and a rigorous examination on the history and the institutions of the Dutch possessions was substituted. Most candidates, however, still prepared for the examination by attending the school at Delft.[1]

The British and Dutch established a fairly elaborate system of recruitment and training of officials for India and Indonesia, but they found no pressing need to establish such methods for their other colonial possessions, which at the time were small and insignificant. Both countries had established territorial control by appointing functionaries overseas to administer specific regions, for which they were accountable to a central authority, the colony's governor. The French did not need to imitate their imperial competitors, for in France itself, of course, this kind of administration had a long history: under the *ancien régime* the monarchy had dispatched its intendants to the various provinces, and from the time of Napoleon the new territorial divisions, the departments, were administered by prefects.

Only when French control began to extend over larger areas overseas was it necessary to establish a full-scale administrative system and to devise methods of recruiting and training colonial officials. The first French territorial administration overseas appeared in Algeria, a direct by-product of the attempt to secure military control over the colony. In 1830 the first French soldiers landed in that country, but by the following decade, in spite of several difficult military campaigns, they had not achieved mastery over the North African territory, because of Algerian resistance.[2]

The year 1840 brought a turning point for Algeria and important innovations in the field of colonial administration. The newly appointed governor, General Thomas Bugeaud, was determined to strengthen the precarious French position by decisively putting down the Algerian opposition. He was a tough-minded soldier who had gained a fearsome reputation for crushing the popular uprising of 1834 in Paris. Bugeaud achieved military victory over the Algerians, but realized that successful battles were less important than was permanent control over the local population. As long as that control was not assured, groups or individuals might foment an uprising at any time against the French and challenge their rule. In every occupied region Bugeaud established an administrative unit, the *bureau arabe,* which had previously existed at the military headquarters in Algiers from 1832 to 1835; it was made up of officers advising the French military leaders on policy toward the local inhabitants. The various *bureaux* simultaneously attempted to maintain control over the local population by supervising the activities of the local chiefs. The original *bureau arabe* had collected Arab documents, translated them, and attempted to exercise some control over the chiefs in the conquered areas; its responsibilities had covered the entire colony. In resurrecting this institution, Bugeaud made an important innovation—he established an individual *bureau* for each region.

The officers belonging to Bugeaud's *bureaux* knew Arabic, they had made some study of the local customs, and were supposed to maintain close relations with the populations whose affairs they were administering. Traveling around their military districts, the officers gave orders to the chiefs and supervised the collection of taxes raised to help defray the costs of the colonial administration. The somewhat limited functions of the *bureaux arabes* were soon extended to include, in the words of an ex-member, responsibility for fulfilling "all the needs, all the demands, all the initiative which a conquering race has in a conquered territory."[3]

The military imprint of French rule long remained in Algeria; several decades later, for example, the officers of the *bureaux* were being selected as before from among the infantry officers serving in the colony. At first they seem to have been relatively satisfactory as administrators, but in the 1850s the officers became notorious alike for brutality toward the local populations and for insubordination toward their administrative superiors.[4]

The small French possessions in West Africa, considered as little more than convenient bases for French naval power, were originally administered by the ministry of the navy, a control which was to last, with minor exceptions, until the creation of a ministry of colonies in 1894. In the meantime the West African possessions had grown to the extent that they became the base for further territorial expansion, both in Senegal and beyond—an advance that created problems similar to those that had existed in Algeria. The French therefore had to develop a system that permitted them to exercise unchallenged control over their new acquisitions. The first stage was the establishment of a territorial administration in Senegal, France's first West African colony. The French experience in Senegal was to be of great significance, for it influenced subsequent administration in all of Black Africa under French control. It was largely the work of Louis Faidherbe, who had served as an officer under General Bugeaud in Algeria.

Faidherbe, with his steel-rimmed glasses, gave the impression of a dour authoritarian. A convinced republican and the son of a volunteer in the revolutionary wars, he was to win his renown in the service of Emperor Napoleon III. In Senegal, the thirty-six-year-old officer found an outlet for the ambivalence he felt between his personal authoritarianism and his republican ideals. Like the Jacobins of his father's generation, he believed that through conquest he could impose more enlightened and humane institutions on the subjugated regions. "Our intentions are pure and noble, our cause is just; the future cannot fail us,"[5] he proclaimed at the end of his mission.

Mediocre as a garrison officer in France, Faidherbe demonstrated in Senegal remarkable skills as an officer and as an administrator. In 1854 he was appointed governor of Senegal, a post he occupied longer than had any of his predecessors (there had been eighteen during the fourteen years prior to his appointment). Except for an interval between 1861 and 1863 he served continuously until 1865. During his governorship Faidherbe made sizable new territorial acquisitions. In 1854 the West African colony had included only the Island of Gorée, Saint Louis, the capital, and some fortified posts farther up the Senegal River. Until Faidherbe's appointment the French position in Senegal was relatively precarious; in Saint Louis, for instance, the French were required to pay annual tribute to the Moors. Faidherbe destroyed much of the Moorish control over Saint Louis, and through his successful military conquests, he secured the base from which a unified contiguous colony could later be established. With remarkable foresight the young governor also anticipated by more than half a century the French domination of the Niger River and set out to create in Senegal the territorial base from which his successors could spread their conquests over the land that later became French West Africa.

Faidherbe's conquests brought under French control relatively large expanses of territory inhabited by a variety of peoples. Permanent French authority over these areas required some sort of control over the local populations, which, according to Faidherbe's estimate in 1856, numbered 50,000 people.[6] The governor assigned three officers from the *Bureau des affaires extérieures*—the office in charge of maintaining diplomatic relations with the nearby African states—to keep an eye on the newly

LOUIS FAIDHERBE

annexed regions. The officers were expected to tour the countryside and to supervise the activities of the local chiefs, but they always seemed to find more pressing desk work at the *Bureau* in Saint Louis, and generally neglected their travels.

In 1857 Faidherbe created an alternative system which would permit more effective control over the annexed regions, drawing on his experience in Algeria, always his model. Senegal, he wrote, needed an administration modeled after that of the North African colony: "In Algeria and Senegal the aim is the same: to dominate the country at as low a cost as possible and through commerce get the greatest advantages; the difficulties to be overcome are analogous—the means to reach them the same."[7] Like Bugeaud in Algeria, Faidherbe established a territorial administration, a system whereby officials were permanently assigned to specific regions and charged with supervising the local chiefs. The function of the French officials, he declared, was to "maintain tranquility so that the natives may work and produce in all security to feed our posts with their products and so that they may recognize the advantage of our domination."[8]

Faidherbe divided the colony into regions known as *arrondissements*; these divisions varied in number between two and seven. Over each *arrondissement* he placed a military officer known as a *commandant d'arrondissement*. In the first years following 1857, there seem to have been no clear guidelines determining the duties and responsibilities of the officers. Guidelines were first established in 1862 when Faidherbe's successor, Governor Jauréguiberry, defined the functions of the *commandants d'arrondissements* in a special decree, which declared that each officer was entrusted with "the safety and tranquility of the *arrondissement*" and instructed him to make sure that the inhabitants of his territory demonstrated "the fidelity and obedience that they owe France." The officer was to report regularly to the governor all incidents that "might disturb the peace of his *arrondissement*." He was to listen to the complaints and grievances of the local populations and to inform the governor of all actions taken to redress those grievances.[9] The decree was influenced by traditional rules of military hierarchy, which tended to limit the powers of the local field commanders and leave the ultimate responsibility for all actions to the superior officer behind the fighting lines, for it circumscribed the powers of the *commandants* by requiring them to consult the governor prior to acting "on all important questions which do not need an immediate decision."[10]

In the system that Faidherbe established, an important administrative role was assigned to the local rulers, the *bracks, burs* and *damels*. He subdivided the *arrondissements* into *cercles*, each of which was headed by a traditional ruler known as *chef de cercle*. These chiefs transmitted orders to the local village chiefs. Obedience was ensured by the fact that the village chiefs often owed traditional allegiance to their superior rulers, who had now become *chefs de cercles.* This system of administration was built in a pyramidal shape; at the apex was the governor, at a lower echelon two to seven *commandants,* under each of these four or five regional chiefs, and finally the village chiefs; it was the system that was to be characteristic of French rule in West Africa, as the *cercle* itself was to become the unit of French territorial administration in West Africa.

Originally the regional chiefs were entrusted with rather extensive power. They were of course assigned the responsibility of executing in their own regions all orders received from their *commandant,* but in their own right they were also left with important responsibilities. At the outset the *chefs de cercles* had full judicial and police powers over their *cercles,* and they were also ordered to encourage trade and agriculture in their districts.

Faidherbe, faced with the immediate problem of establishing control over large areas, had originally used the existing local political structures when he had transformed the *burs, bracks,* and *damels* into *chefs de cercles.* He initiated the process, later completed by his successors, of transforming the chiefs from independent political forces into subordinate instruments of the French administration. He did not hesitate to dismiss those who failed to perform effectively; in 1857 he deposed a chief who was a drunkard. Also, he purposely appointed submissive chiefs who would comply with French orders. In one case he appointed a chief solely because the latter was "an agreeable man without initiative who will act only according to our instructions."[11]

In 1863 Faidherbe significantly reduced the powers of the *chefs de cercles* by transferring their administrative, judicial, and police powers to French officers who now became known as *commandants de cercles.* These *commandants de cercles,* placed under the supervision of the *commandants d'arrondissements,* supervised the regional chiefs who, now endowed with fewer powers, also found their authority restricted to a smaller region known as a *canton.* These regional chiefs, called *chefs de cantons,* in their turn commanded and supervised the village chiefs. In yet another change, the office of *commandant d'arrondissement* was abolished, and the *commandant de cercle* became the principal territorial representative of the French administration. Although the administrative units in French Equatorial Africa and Madagascar were given different designations, territorial administration within the two areas was closely patterned after the Senegalese model.

Once the basic organization of territorial administration was established, the French faced the far more difficult problem of finding qualified men to serve in the colonies. Each governor handled the recruitment of administrators for his own colony; it was only after 1887, when all the administrators serving in the various colonies were pooled into a single corps, that a central administration in Paris took over recruitment.

When studying the recruitment of administrators prior to 1887, one should examine the practices of the governors in the individual French possessions. Most colonies faced problems similar to those of Senegal. The administrative system in that colony is the best documented and the logical example of early recruitment practices, since it was to have the greatest impact on the development of colonial administration as a model for the rest of Black Africa under French control.

All the colonies faced the difficult problem of attracting qualified men to distant and unhealthy regions which had gained the reputation of being the white man's grave. Shortly after becoming governor of Senegal, Faidherbe expressed concern over the manpower situation. He informed his superior in Paris that even the highest officials in the colonies, the governors, were usually incompetent men. He therefore advised the minister of the navy in 1856 to discontinue the habit of appointing

by chance and for personal convenience, without considering the needs of the country, an officer from such and such a service; and have him occupy for a year, eighteen months, or two years the government of Senegal, [a colony] which he has never seen, just in the same manner as one would give him the command of a naval vessel, a frigate or a regiment.[12]

His predecessors, Faidherbe asserted, had not only arrived unprepared and totally ignorant of colonial affairs, but they had also shown so little zeal for their work that they left the colony as ignorant as they had been on the day of their arrival. In addition to improving the quality of the governors, he went on, the ministry would have to find for the governors worthy subordinates who could act as advisers and fill administrative posts in the interior of the colony—"six or eight young men who will adopt this country, decide to make their career here, work with ardor to understand it and be well-informed about the conduct of native affairs."[13] These men, Faidherbe suggested, should be recruited from the young military officers who were already stationed in the colony and thus had at least a rudimentary knowledge of the situation. In order to encourage these officers to enter and remain in the territorial administration, he advised "rewards and promotions, for the profession is tough, and hardly attractive."[14]

Three years later, in 1859, Faidherbe wrote the minister of Algeria and colonies that "it is time seriously to introduce the civilian element into the government of the colony."[15] But civilians were not appointed; instead naval personnel continued filling administrative posts in Senegal, and second-rate officers at that. An admiral later claimed that he reserved these positions in Senegal and Gabon for those of his officers who *"are needy and without a future."*[16] As a result, Faidherbe's successor, Governor Jauréguiberry, wrote of his administrative staff:

The *commandants d'arrondissements* are generally far from possessing the rich knowledge and special qualities indispensable to the positions with which they are entrusted. Many among them have lost the habit of work and have no inclination to study, and as a result fail to perform at their best. In short, they are only good enough to command a company.[17]

As early as 1855 two writers, Frédéric Carrère, a minor French official, and Paul Holle, the mulatto explorer and soldier from Saint Louis, had remarked on how unsuitable the naval personnel was for administrative positions. Neither the officers' studies nor their practical experience, they wrote, prepared them to be administrators.[18] Even though himself a naval officer, Governor Jauréguiberry demonstrated the same lack of confidence in the military administrators. "As far as I know," he wrote, "the love of order, the respect for law, education, ... agriculture and commerce have never been propagated by the power of bayonets."[19] An additional disadvantage of naval personnel was that often shortly after arriving in the colony they could be commandeered back to ship service. Civilians, Jauréguiberry thought, would be less brutal than the military, would remain for longer periods in the colony, and would carry on a more enlightened administration.

But the naval ministry ignored Jauréguiberry's advice to recruit civilians; in any case it would have been most difficult to attract qualified civilians to posts in the African bush. As a memorandum of the naval ministry stated in 1869,

Who then is the intelligent man with good education and liberal ideas ... who would consent to exile himself to Saldé or Matam [in remotest parts of Senegal], with ten black soldiers under his orders and a village of a hundred huts to survey; and how will he find the occasion to apply his intelligence?[20]

Then in 1879 Jauréguiberry became minister of the navy, and in his new role was able to encourage the replacement of military by civilian officials overseas. He ended the "regime of the admirals" in Cochin-China by appointing civilian governors. In Senegal on his insistence governors appointed only civilians to the territorial administration, and by 1880 eight out of ten *commandants de cercles* in that colony were civilians. But although the origin of recruitment may have changed, the colonial administration was by no means improved. If the civilians did not have the particular vices which Jauréguiberry thought characteristic of military officers, most of them were as brutal toward the local populations and as negligent of orders from their superiors as the military had been. Many civilians who entered the colonial administration were men with questionable pasts who for various reasons had decided to leave France and seek their fortunes elsewhere.

The unhealthy and uncomfortable life in the colonies did not attract the best Europeans of any nationality. In 1837 Sir George Cornwall complained that the scum of England was being "poured into the Colonies."[21] Twenty years later, while the British civil service sought to appoint only top Oxbridge men for service in India, the lack of candidates forced it "to be content with first any men from Oxford and Cambridge, and finally from any university at all."[22]

The French seem to have fared even worse; for their lack of candidates was so serious that they could impose neither educational nor character qualifications upon aspirants for the overseas service. The governor of Senegal noted in 1879 that the colony drew "persons who if not compromised at home were at least incapable of making a livelihood in it." The only men attracted into the colonial administration, he wrote, were "the lost children of the mother country."[23] For nearly half a century to come, the French colonial administration continued to attract the rejects of French society—those unable to pursue a promising career in France for lack of education or other handicaps. In some cases the recruits were men who had gone afoul of the law. One of the administrators serving in Senegal in 1879 was a "bankrupt who had spent considerable time in jail"; predictably, he was a poor administrator who did "only what he wished to do and even worked for policies contrary to those of his superiors."[24]

The poor quality of the *commandants* was noticed from the beginning, but complaints became especially marked in the 1880s. The administrators, it was said, tended to ignore their administrative superiors and ruled their *cercles* according to their personal whims. In 1885 the governor of Senegal noted that in spite of repeated instructions forbidding the *commandants* to impose penalties without seeking his prior consent, they were levying "severe fines on the natives without serious cause" and without the governor's permission.[25]

Administrators with initiative, struggling against red tape, may well have drawn upon themselves the criticisms of governors who preferred subordinates with bureaucratic habits and outlook. Thus not all of the criticisms should be taken at face value. But the governors were not always complaining that their subordinates were overactive. On the contrary, *commandants,* because of laziness, it was alleged, failed to maintain effective control over their regions; as early as 1874 a report declared that the *commandants* had ceased to administer their *cercles* and were leaving all important functions to the local chiefs.[26] A decade later, when Joseph Gallieni arrived in Senegal (which was to become the springboard for his military conquest of the area later known as French Sudan), he noticed the idleness into which the *commandants* had fallen:

> They never visited the surrounding villages, they limited themselves to accepting without verification the information of their interpreters, and thus permitted the neighboring chiefs and inhabitants to escape from our authority and join our enemies.[27]

Gallieni advocated the "method of Faidherbe" which had emphasized the need for remaining in constant touch with the local inhabitants.

From the middle of the 1850s until 1887, the date of Gallieni's observation, the Faidherbe method had remained only an ideal. To be sure, Faidherbe had managed to establish a workable administrative organization which remained unchanged and indeed lasted with few modifications until the very end of French colonization; but the problem of recruitment with which he and his successors had grappled still remained unsolved.

An examination of eighteen personnel files belonging to men who served overseas before 1887 reveals that their superiors rated only three as capable; eleven were described as definitely unreliable and even brutal functionaries; and four files give insufficient information. Senegal's problems in this respect were, however, not unique. An administrator who had entered the service in New Caledonia was sent away in 1886. His governor wrote: "This functionary has left nothing but bad memories; as incapable as some of his colleagues, he did not possess their honesty."[28] A man who had been administrator in the Comoro Islands in 1886 behaved so "strangely" that he was sent on leave. When he returned he was sent to administer another island, but according to his superior his "ridiculous and brutal behavior" made it necessary to transfer him again. This time he was to be sent to the Congo, but the governor of that colony heard about him in time to refuse his services. He went to Bénin instead, but he was also not wanted there. Finally he landed in Senegal, but soon after his arrival he was murdered.[29]

There were a few good officials, but they proved to be exceptional cases. A marine infantry officer in Gabon entered business and then the administration. A conscientious, hard-working, and popular official in his district, he stood out from his colleagues; and his governor wistfully remarked, "I wish Gabon had many functionaries like him."[30]

One of the most important causes for the poor recruitment of administrators can be found in the nature of the central administration of colonies. Until the 1880s it was an insignificant undersecretariat in the naval ministry, with little prestige and only limited authority over the growing empire. The absence of a strong central administration meant that there were few common bonds among the far-flung possessions of the empire. The individual governors, rather than the central administration in Paris, appointed the colonial administrators. Also only a few men were needed for each colony—in Senegal, perhaps three or four new *commandants* annually. For such a modest number it was obviously impractical to devise intricate methods of recruitment or training as had been done in England and Holland for the India and Dutch East India services.

It became possible to enlist more highly qualified French colonial personnel when a central institution began to recruit for the entire empire or at least larger parts of it; the undersecretariat of colonies assumed the task, and a turning point was reached. After that time the problems were not over, but at least an attempt could be made to recruit and train better officials for overseas service.

II The Years of Experimentation

Close observers of the French colonial administration were acutely aware of its shortcomings. In 1874 the famous French colonial theorist Paul Leroy-Beaulieu blamed the deficiencies in the French overseas administration on the poor recruitment of personnel and on the lack of a specific colonial service.

France more than any other country [he wrote] has committed grave errors in the recruitment of its colonial personnel; it has had no other law than chance and favoritism.... It is time for France to imitate England and Holland and to create a corps of colonial administrators, especially selected and trained....[1]

The essential prerequisite for establishing such a corps, in his judgment, was the establishment of a strong and relatively autonomous colonial office in Paris, for only such an office could effectively direct and shape the colonial services. Unlike the British, the Dutch, and—to Leroy-Beaulieu's consternation—even the Spanish, the French had not set up a colonial ministry.[2]

The colonies were not considered important enough for a single ministry to occupy itself exclusively with them; rather, until 1894, they remained the collateral responsibilities of ministries and services whose chief tasks lay elsewhere. Under Richelieu the colonies were administered by the *surintendance* of navigation and commerce; in 1669 Colbert assigned them to the ministry of the navy. Within that ministry the areas of responsibility were unclear, and not until 1710 was a special bureau of colonies created with a civil servant at its head.[3]

As a rule the ministry of the navy had little but strategic interest in the colonies. But in 1858, during the Second Empire, Napoleon III briefly established a ministry of Algeria and colonies as a sinecure for his cousin Prince Napoleon; after two years, however, Algeria was returned to the ministry of war, and the colonies to the ministry of the navy. In the

1870s, in the first years of the Third Republic, colonial affairs continued to be the responsibility of a civil servant with the title of director, who headed an office called the directorate of the colonies.

In November 1881 when Léon Gambetta, leader of the moderate republican forces, became prime minister, he wished to emphasize the peaceful rather than the martial aspects of French colonization. Accordingly he transferred the directorate of colonies from the ministry of the navy to the newly baptized ministry of commerce and the colonies,[4] but only three months later, when he fell from power, the directorate went back to the naval ministry. The colonies apparently assumed a higher status in 1882, when the Freycinet government appointed an undersecretary of state for colonies to head the office in the naval ministry dealing with colonial affairs. Adding to the power of the undersecretary was the fact that rather than being a civil servant, he was a political figure.[5]

Three outstanding figures served as undersecretary of colonies between 1881 and 1894 and helped to make the system increasingly independent of ministerial control. At the same time they strengthened the government's control over the colonies.

The first of these notable undersecretaries was Félix Faure, appointed in 1883. Faure was a businessman from Le Havre and had been one of Gambetta's early disciples. An able member of the Chamber of Deputies, Faure had political and administrative skills which distinguished him in his earliest years in politics: finally in 1895 he rose to the presidency of the republic. While undersecretary of colonies, Faure maintained friendly relations with the minister of the navy and won a large measure of initiative in the colonial field. After he left office the authority of the undersecretariat continued to grow; from 1886, for example, the undersecretary for the first time was authorized to sign payment orders for colonial expenses, and a *Bulletin officiel* was published for the undersecretariat of colonies separate from that of the naval ministry.

Eugène Etienne was the second undersecretary who contributed to the formation of an independent ministry and strengthened its authority over the empire. Like Faure, Etienne was a businessman and a disciple of Gambetta. In Parliament he represented the district of Oran in Algeria. Gambetta's influence, Etienne's own business interests, and his life as an Algerian settler had made him a dedicated empire builder. He became undersecretary of colonies for a few months in 1887 and again during three eventful years from 1889 to 1892. Later he occupied several key cabinet posts and in the Chamber of Deputies led a large group of parliamentarians known as the *Groupe colonial*, which was dedicated to the cause of imperial expansion. While undersecretary of colonies, Etienne played a crucial part in expanding the French empire in Africa. He zealously sent explorers to the black continent and thus gave "the world the impression that from the bulge of the Niger to the Mediterranean, everything was reserved for France."[6] His authority and prestige grew when he gained admission to the regular meetings of the cabinet. By 1892 the work of Faure and Etienne had been so successful that a deputy described the undersecretariat of colonies as a ministry in every aspect except that of name.[7]

Théophile Delcassé, the third of the outstanding undersecretaries, destroyed the last vestiges of the undersecretariat's dependence on another ministry. When he assumed the office in 1893, Delcassé demanded that his administration be transferred to a separate building. At that time the offices of the undersecretariat occupied a few poorly aired and dimly lit rooms in the ministry of the navy which in Napoleonic times had served as a guardhouse.[8] By having the offices moved to the Pavillon de Flore, a wing of the Tuileries, Delcassé gave it added prestige.[9] Physically separated from the ministry of the navy, the undersecretariat was less subject than before to ministerial control. This was especially true while Delcassé was undersecretary, for he was not one to take ministerial orders readily. Indeed, his personality reminded Faure of Julius Caesar.[10]

Increasingly independent in its administration, the undersecretariat had become a ministry in nearly all aspects but name. Already a century before, in the 1780s and 1790s, colonial publicists and officials had suggested the establishment of a separate ministry of colonies.[11] In the 1880s an increasing number of persons advocated such a ministry.[12] Overseas officials added their voices: Gallieni, campaigning in the Sudan, wrote Etienne of the necessity for a ministry of colonies which would give the empire a coherent policy and a colonial tradition separate from that of the naval ministry.[13]

Legally, the cabinet had the power by simple decree to elevate the undersecretariat to a ministry, but it hesitated to do so in the 1890s because the Chamber of Deputies was basically hostile to such a change. Many deputies opposed the action, because they feared it would mean increased expenses for colonial administration, others because they assumed a separate ministry would more effectively be able to sponsor what they considered an undesirable stress on overseas expansion. Feeling that a ministry was desirable but not wanting to risk the hostility of the Chamber, the relatively weak government of Charles Dupuy decided to forego its decree powers and submit the question to the legislators. The first reading of the bill occurred on May 15, 1893, but action was delayed on it until the following year. The undersecretary of state for colonies, Maurice Lebon, gave the bill new urgency when he resigned in March

1894, claiming that it was impossible to administer the empire with the existing administrative structure.[14] Delcassé spoke for a ministry of colonies, and his persuasive oratory seems to have finally ensured the passage of the bill by a vote of 260 to 239 in May 1894.[15]

Faure and Etienne, in addition to strengthening the undersecretariat, had instituted reforms which consolidated the undersecretary's control over colonial personnel. In 1883 Faure had established a standard uniform for civilian officials serving in the colonies;[16] this was an important step, symbolizing as it did, the subservience of the colonial administrations to the central administration in Paris. In 1887 Eugène Etienne took the crucial step: by decree he gathered territorial administrators under his authority into one body, the Corps of Colonial Administrators. The only administrators excepted were those of Indochina, who were assigned to a separate corps.[17]

By the decree of 1887 the *chefs de service* in the French possessions in India, the *commandants particuliers* in Porto Novo, the *résidents* of Grand Popo, Ogoué, Louango, the *commandants de cercles* in Senegal, and the *commandants d'arrondissements* in New Caledonia—all of whom represented French authority in the colonies—were now united into one corps. The roles of the colonial administrators continued to vary, as before 1887. In Grand Popo, for example (later part of the French colony of Dahomey), the *résident* was more of a diplomatic representative than a territorial administrator, while in New Caledonia the *commandant* exercised effective control over the local population. Nevertheless, as the French began to consolidate their positions and extend their conquests, the functions of the administrators grew somewhat more uniform, while recruitment, promotion, and salaries of the administrators were standardized after 1887.

During the quarter of a century between 1887 and 1912, the central administration in Paris employed various methods of recruitment, all aimed at improving the quality of the administrators being sent overseas. The decree of 1887 had been drawn up for that purpose, but its only requirement, so far as candidates were concerned, was that they must be government employees with an annual salary of 2,000 francs or more.[18] The stipulations of the decree did not in themselves necessarily ensure a better Corps; nevertheless the undersecretary, in establishing centralized authority over the colonial administrators, could now exert more rigorous control over their appointment. Within a year after the decree, some candidates for the lowest rank of administrators were required to take examinations for entrance into the Corps.[19]

In the early 1890s, as the areas under French control expanded and a bureaucracy developed, the administration in each colony began to hire officials for specialized functions. While the governor had administrators to rule over the local regions, in the colonial capital he acquired his own staff, the secretariat, which was separate from the newly founded Corps of Colonial Administrators. And to aid the administrators in the bush, either in performing clerical tasks in the administrative center of the *cercle* or in administering a subdivision of the *cercle* under the administrator, the governor appointed men with the title of agents. In French West Africa they were called *agents des affaires indigènes*, and in the other regions *agents des affaires civiles*. (After 1920 the latter designation was also used for those officials in French West Africa.) These agents filled subordinate positions for which the British were accustomed to use indigenous personnel. (Hereafter these functionaries will be referred to as "agents.")

The colonial administrators were civil servants of the French state, responsible to the local governor but hired and fired by the central administration in Paris. The agents, however, were civil servants of the colony who could be appointed or dismissed at the will of the governor. They formed a separate corps in each colony, but after the founding in 1904 of the French West African federation (Afrique Occidentale Française, AOF) and the erection of a similar federation for French Equatorial Africa (Afrique Equatoriale Française, AEF) in 1910, they constituted a corps within each federation, subject to appointment and dismissal by the governor-general.

Methods of recruitment, promotion, and salaries of agents varied from one colonial group to the next. French citizenship was the only requirement for appointment. As an impassioned critic of the colonial administration wrote:

A hairdresser, a chestnut vendor, a ditch digger, depending on his contacts (the *concierge* of an administrator on leave, the bath attendant, the friend, etc.), can be appointed *commis des affaires indigènes* without anybody caring about his capacities, his intelligence, his disposition, or his aptitudes.[20]

The agents usually secured their appointments through political patronage or other forms of favoritism. A young man who had only an elementary education and whose previous professional experience consisted in raising horses in the army was appointed as an agent in 1904 because he could claim important connections. The personnel bureau in Dakar which processed his application noted:

Seems very little educated. See his application. Recommended by M. Emile Chautemps [deputy] at the request of M. Le Gall, former secretary-general to the presidency, and by M. de Herissé, former director of the bank of Réunion. Proposal: [Appointment as] *Commis* fourth class.[21]

In France the *baccalauréat* was absolutely necessary for any kind of administrative career, and persons without a secondary school education were doomed to occupy low positions from which they could never rise. Because appointment as an agent before 1912 did not require any specific educational background, many young men without education but with aspirations toward joining the Corps of Colonial Administrators chose the post of agent. Only men in the most desperate circumstances, such as those who had failed in business overseas or who had extremely lowly positions in France, saw the post of agent as an end in itself.

The poor quality of the men entering the territorial administrations in the colonies before 1887 was plainly evident, but since it was impossible to find immediate replacements, Etienne had little choice but to integrate into the Corps the forty men who had belonged to those administrations. Thus his solution to the pressing manpower problem was mere makeshift.

The colonial vocation was generally not popular in France. A small minority of men were interested in an overseas career—men from the seacoast areas of France, the Bordeaux region, and the area around Marseilles—who could identify with the naval tradition of their regions. Nevertheless, and especially before 1900, the colonial administration was not considered attractive. In particular, health conditions were appalling. Nearly all the administrators suffered from frequent malaria attacks; a few unfortunate ones serving in Equatorial Africa contracted sleeping sickness. Most of those returning to France every two years on leave required prolonged hospitalization or rest cures. Tropical diseases took a heavy toll of the Corps; between 1887 and 1912, 135 out of 984 appointees (16 percent) died in the colonies.[22] If they did not die there, the administrators' lives were nevertheless dramatically shortened. Retired colonial officials died seventeen years earlier than their contemporaries who had occupied metropolitan posts. Even though sanitation and preventive medicine had improved by the 1920s, nearly a third of the 16,000 Europeans living in AOF in 1929 were hospitalized an average of fourteen days.[23] Because of the deplorable health conditions the administrators could not bring their families with them and few men were willing to accept a career involving nearly lifetime separation from their families. This state of affairs lasted until health risks had been reduced with the building of hospitals and roads, making it easier to transport the sick or to secure medical aid. These improvements came at an uneven pace—in Senegal in the 1890s, but in areas that were penetrated at a relatively later date (such as Niger and parts of the Ivory Coast) only in the 1920s.

To be sure, the salaries of the administrators were twice as high as those that civil servants in comparable positions might have earned in the metropole. This inducement, however, did not offset the high cost of living in the colonies and, for married men, the expense of keeping up two households, one in France and the other in the colonies. Although there were a few individuals who seem to have entered the Corps because of the relatively higher salaries, this was usually not a significant factor in the choice.

In general the prestige of overseas service was low, largely because some of the early administrators who were not socially accepted at home proved overseas to be brutal and dishonest. The passage of time did not immediately erase this negative image of the colonial service. A French settler described the colonies in 1894 as "the *refugium peccatorum* for all our misfits, the depository of the excrement of our political and social organism."[24] In 1909 Lucien Hubert, a senator friendly to the colonial administration, found it necessary in the face of adverse criticism, to deny "the odious legend which represents the colonial administrator holding in one hand the bottle and in the other the whip."[25]

As late as 1929 Georges Hardy, the director of the *Ecole Coloniale*, which had been founded in 1885 by Faure, then undersecretary of the colonies, complained that when a young man leaves for the colonies, his friends ask themselves, "What crime must he have committed? From what corpse is he fleeing?"[26] Even in the next decade, in spite of the significant improvements made in the recruitment of the Corps, the negative image of the colonial vocation seemed to remain. A newspaper article in 1931 claimed:

To leave the metropole and to go to the African or Indochinese jungle meant that one had a guilty conscience. Nobody can understand why an intelligent and active boy would be so imprudent as to disregard the good, quiet, and safe position of a bureaucrat at 3,500 francs a year with pension, in order to go and live in the tropics, get some dangerous fever and fool around [*s'accoquiner*] with colored people....[27]

Hubert Deschamps, who had then already served several years in the colonial service, claimed in 1931 that the colonial administrator was still considered "a little bit the bad boy of the past, the gentleman of adventure, and his name evokes...the specter of the pirate...the sadistic bureaucrat, the professional liar, and the drunkard."[28] Admittedly the members of the colonial service, or people connected with the French overseas venture, were prone to exaggerate the lack of appreciation they received from the homeland; nevertheless, it is clear that the French colonial service never enjoyed the high prestige that the British colonial service seems to have enjoyed in Britain.[29]

French civil servants in the pre-1914 era were highly motivated by the social prestige of their position, and by such dignities as elevation to the *Légion d'honneur*. Very few colonial administrators, however, received that decoration; indeed, the Corps was probably the least decorated branch of the higher governmental bureaucracy. This neglect stemmed from the fact that the minister of colonies was a junior member of the cabinet with few nominations allotted to him, most of which he usually awarded to his collaborators in Paris. Of thirty available to the colonial ministry, only an average of four a year went to the actual administrators.[30] Even though the Corps grew twentyfold between 1887 and 1910, its members received no more decorations in the latter year than in the former.

There were, then, a number of psychological and material reasons that discouraged many young Frenchmen from considering a colonial career. Until 1914, therefore, the undersecretariat or the ministry of colonies had only a limited number of applicants from whom to choose the colonial administrators. Although Etienne's decree of 1887 was an important first step toward improving the quality of the Corps, almost twenty-five years were to elapse before the ministry could cease heterogeneous recruitment and establish a uniform training program for all the administrators.

During his tenure in office, in 1889, Etienne had created an administrative section of the *Ecole Coloniale*[31] in which future administrators would receive special training in colonial affairs. All the administrators were supposed to be recruited from among graduates of the school. Such recruitment, by ensuring common training for all administrators, would have done much to improve the quality and morale of the Corps, but unfortunately the school was not equipped to train more than a few students each year—only a fraction of those needed in an ever expanding empire. Also, the school faced widespread opposition in France. Several chambers of commerce had considered beginning their own colonial training program in the hope that the government would appoint their students to the Corps. When the government chose to train its own civil servants rather than accept those specially trained to serve the interests of the Bordeaux merchants or the Marseilles shippers, the chambers of commerce angrily denounced the school.[32] Another self-interested critic was Emile Boutmy, the eminent director of the *Ecole libre des sciences politiques,* who had instituted a training program in colonial affairs at his school. When his students were not appointed to the colonial administration, he devoted an entire book to assailing the *Ecole Coloniale.*³³ Colonial officials attending the Colonial Congress of 1889 induced it to adopt a resolution attacking the practice of sending overseas young men whose comprehension of colonial affairs was limited to bookish learning.³⁴ Because of the opposition, by 1892 graduates of the *Ecole* had lost their monopoly of recruitment into the Corps, but the school was not abolished, as some of the more vocal critics had advocated.

After these experiences, the undersecretariat, in trying to fill the Corps and at the same time heeding its critics, returned essentially to the methods of recruitment employed in 1887. Although the *Ecole Coloniale* students provided some recruits, others continued to come from the ranks of the metropolitan civil servants or of those who had seen some form of government service in the colonies. The ministry's experience with the men coming from these different sources gradually shaped its recruitment policies, so that the period up to World War I was basically one of experimentation. It was on the eve of the war, in 1912, that the colonial ministry established methods of recruitment and training of colonial personnel which were to remain basically unchanged until 1945.

One important source of manpower during the early years was the armed forces. Colonial military officers had played a predominant role in building the French empire in Africa, and this role and their experience in colonial affairs made them likely recruits. But military men were a mixed blessing to the Corps. A number of them who were appointed as administrators often had, to be sure, an intimate knowledge of the people in their district—some of whom they had helped to subjugate. Often, however, they could not shake off unfortunate habits acquired during their military careers. One administrator who had formerly been a naval officer was described by his governor as "an old sea dog" who "finds it difficult to understand that one cannot run a *cercle* as if it were a ship."³⁵ Many former officers who became administrators established martial discipline in their territories and were often brutal or excessively harsh in their treatment of the local populations. Many within the Corps who came to oppose the continued recruitment of military officers—and with good reason—were the civilians;³⁶ for until 1905 officers with a captain's rank or higher were appointed to the upper ranks of the Corps, thus impeding the promotion of other administrators.

Between 1887 and 1900, 15 to 20 percent of the Corps consisted of former officers. Thereafter the colonial ministry became increasingly wary of appointing officers to the Corps, both because of their record of brutality and the civilian opposition to them. After 1905 the ministry abolished the provision that required one-sixth of the Corps to be appointed from among officers, and from that time only an occasional officer was admitted. In 1907 the Corps had only thirty-four military officers (twenty-seven former colonial military officers and seven naval officers) out of a total of 465 men,[37] or 7 percent of the Corps. As the older ex-officers retired, the proportion decreased still further.

A second group joining the colonial service consisted of functionaries employed by the government administrations in France. Whereas the German colonial service was nearly entirely staffed by civil servants from the mother country, the French Corps contained only a few. In 1907, for example, only fifty administrators out of 465 came from metropolitan administrations.[38] The type of man who would choose a comfortable career in the metropolitan civil service was unlikely to expatriate himself to the colonies, and those who did rarely adjusted well to the active life in the bush. A former chief clerk serving in Senegal was described by his governor in the following manner: "Since he has had the command of the *cercle* of Louga [one year] he has found it unnecessary to go any farther than twelve kilometers from his residence. Ignored by the natives, he ignores them. He has obviously made an error in entering the corps of administrators."[39] Ineffective as administrators, these officials were fit only to perform clerical tasks in the colonial capitals, and because of many unfortunate experiences with them, the ministry after 1905 virtually stopped recruiting metropolitan functionaries.

A third group from which the ministry selected administrators in the early years comprised the functionaries of the secretariats-general in the colonial capitals. After reaching a certain rank in the secretariat and serving a minimum of two years overseas, these functionaries were eligible for appointment to the Corps of Colonial Administrators. Unfortunately the experience they brought to the Corps was relatively worthless, for they had usually spent their time shuffling papers in the offices of a colonial capital just as if they had remained on the banks of the Seine. From this sterile regimen the members of the secretariats did not gain any particular insight into the life of the local populations; like the metropolitan civil servants, they were too much bound up in bureaucratic routine to make good administrators. A former member of the secretariat who had entered the Corps was condescendingly described by his governor as "only made of the stuff of a copyist."[40] The governor was probably correct. Increasingly, members of the secretariats were considered undesirable in the Corps, and indeed very few sought to enter. In 1907 the Corps contained only forty officials drawn from that source;[41] thereafter the number continued to decline.

A fourth source of recruits was the agents. Prior to 1914 this group supplied a majority of the administrators, and indeed until World War II half of them continued to be recruited from this source. Until approximately 1905 the ministry of colonies did not exercise sufficient care in allowing them to become administrators, so that incompetent, even brutal men were sometimes appointed to the Corps. In 1898 an agent in the Ivory Coast who had been ordered to "inflict a harsh punishment" on the assassins of two French officers annihilated a whole village to which the assassins belonged. He informed the governor, "I have ordered the following measures: the complete destruction of this people by killing all adult males and the assimilation of the women and children by the neighboring peoples." The governor reminded him that "if justice obliges us sometimes to shed blood, it never obliges us to bathe in it."[42] After thus severely rebuking his subordinate, the governor promoted him the same year, and three years later he was allowed to enter the Corps of Colonial Administrators. Another agent had been dismissed from a private French company for insubordination and general worthlessness and had then become one of the local pimps in the town of Rufisque; eventually he was made an administrator.[43]

A high proportion of agents, however, turned out to be effective functionaries. Their service as administrators' assistants gave them a sound practical knowledge of territorial administration and its intricacies. Even novices in the Corps might be men with long practical experience in overseas administration, since they served at least four years in a colony and sometimes as many as ten years before being appointed to the Corps.

As the agents were the only group of functionaries whose members all aspired to become administrators, they constituted a large human reservoir for recruitment. The main drawback, of course, was that they were generally uneducated; often they could neither keep proper accounts nor write a readable report. Their lack of general culture, according to some of the higher officials, brought with it a certain lack of restraint, of a sense of balance and moderation. To remedy these faults, beginning in 1904 the governors-general of AOF and Madagascar and the governors in the other colonies required aspiring agents to take examinations usually calling for both practical and theoretical knowledge. The examination given to prospective agents in French West Africa in 1913 consisted of copying a report, writing an essay on the consequences of the opening of the Panama Canal, and taking tests in dictation and arithmetic. In the beginning these examinations were not taken very seriously; one candidate was appointed as an agent in spite of having failed both the dictation and the arithmetic tests.[44] In general, however, the new procedure discouraged many uneducated men from trying to become agents and thus had the effect of raising their educational level. Gradually the standards of appointment were raised, and the advancement of agents to the rank of administrator became more selective.[45]

A growing number of ex-agents proved their ability as administrators after 1905, but graduates of the *Ecole Coloniale* had long since shown themselves to be the real elite of the Corps. They were conscientious, honest, and reliable, and treated the local populations in a gentler and more humane manner than did their colleagues. Governors unanimously praised them; for example, in 1904 Governor-General Gallieni of Madagascar wrote that "the best administrators are recruited from the *Ecole Coloniale*."[46]

Experience clearly showed that the most successful administrators were either ex-agents or graduates of the *Ecole Coloniale*. The success of administrators recruited from the various sources is summarized in Table 1, based on all available files representing slightly more than two-thirds of the total number entering the Corps from 1887 to 1914.

Table 1

Correlation between source of recruitment and success within the Corps of administrators appointed 1887-1914

	Functionaries of secretariats-general	Metropolitan officials	Military officers	Agents	Ecole Coloniale graduates	Other sources
Number of administrators considered capable	17 (33%)	12 (30%)	29 (46%)	260 (57%)	50 (68%)	1 (10%)
Number of administrators considered incapable	32 (63%)	21 (51%)	25 (40%)	113 (25%)	13 (18%)	8 (80%)
Number on whom insufficient information	2 (4%)	8 (19%)	9 (14%)	85 (18%)	10 (14%)	1 (10%)

While the *Ecole Coloniale* graduates and the ex-agents made the best administrators, as a group they still had certain deficiencies that needed correction. Many seasoned colonial officials were skeptical of the ability of the young *Ecole Coloniale* graduates, complaining that after two years of study they thought they knew everything about the complex art of administering a *cercle*. To be sure, the legal studies of the school tended to make its graduates excessively rigid, and they seemed shallow pettifoggers to the old bush administrators who had made the ignoring of regulations virtually an article of faith. In 1902 Hubert Lyautey, who was then Gallieni's assistant in Madagascar and later gained fame as the founder of the French administration in Morocco, wrote of the graduates of the *Ecole*:

> They ... seem to become increasingly bureaucratic; everything in their behavior takes on the form of a circular. ... Regulations have become dogma for them, and those which they themselves created seem after a few months to have the authority of divine revelation. Finally and primarily they think abstractly ... and it is only through our mentality that they understand the native. Certainly ... they are better morally and professionally than the first group of colonial functionaries; *they are irreproachable, but worse.*[47]

In spite of Gallieni's favorable remarks about the graduates of the *Ecole Coloniale,* he led a school of thought—in which Lyautey was the foremost disciple—emphasizing the importance of appointing men who already had practical knowledge of colonial affairs. Advice from the men in the bush discouraged the ministry of colonies from attempting to expand the *Ecole Coloniale* and giving its graduates sole access to the Corps. Before World War I, ex-students of the school constituted only a small proportion of the Corps—15 percent (seventy of 465) in 1907, 20 percent (170 of 861) in 1914.[48]

Experience showed that some graduates of the *Ecole Coloniale,* despite their superior training, were incapable of administering their districts when they first arrived overseas. A famous case which seemed to prove the inadequacy of purely intellectual training was the Toqué scandal of 1903. Emile Toqué was a graduate of the school; before leaving France he had demonstrated remarkable courage and presence of mind when he jumped into the Seine and saved a drowning person. He was sent to the Congo and put in charge of a large district. Baffled by the problems confronting him, Toqué resorted to terror and sadism. On the 14th of July 1903, he celebrated the national holiday by blowing up a prisoner with gunpowder. Shortly after the news of this act arrived in France, the brutal methods of exploitation used by the rubber companies in the Congo also came to light, and the administrators received some of the blame for not investigating or preventing the companies' actions.[49] The Congo scandal seemed to demonstrate the need to improve the administration, and the Toqué affair showed that even well-educated students from the *Ecole*

Coloniale needed a certain amount of practical experience in addition to their formal training.

In writing about the Toqué incident, Minister of Colonies Etienne Clémentel described it as "the affair which has so profoundly shaken public opinion in France." It seemed to him that the maladministration that had been discovered in the Congo was perhaps owing to the fact that authority had been entrusted to "officials who are too young or of uncertain mental stability, [who are] isolated and far from their superiors, and at the same time possess nearly unlimited powers."[50] To remedy in part the situation revealed by the Toqué incident, Clémentel issued a decree requiring that graduates of the *Ecole Coloniale* serve one or two years as probationers before being appointed to the Corps. During their probationary time they were not permitted to command a district but instead were assigned as assistants to older and more experienced members of the Corps. This expedient remedied some of the faults that Lyautey had found in the school's graduates and which the Toqué incident had presumably demonstrated. Many of the old bush administrators were tough authoritarians, and undoubtedly the new system of apprenticeship enabled them to transmit some undesirable methods to the younger generation of colonial officials. But many of them at least were excellent masters at showing the novices how to establish a tax roll, how to ride for days on horseback, and how to arbitrate a dangerous feud between two neighboring ethnic groups.

As the ministry attempted to improve the quality of the graduates of the *Ecole Coloniale*, it also tried to make better administrators of the colonial agents who were promoted to the Corps. What the latter needed, it contended, was some training in administrative law, accounting, ethnology, and other fields of knowledge in which the graduates of the *Ecole Coloniale* had received an effective preparation. Such training might help overcome the differences in educational background which had begun to divide the Corps. As the governor-general of Madagascar, Victor Augagneur, observed:

The administrators group themselves according to their origins: the graduates of the *Ecole Coloniale* form one Corps, those coming from the agents constitute another one. Rivalries ... if not jealousies are thus born.[51]

An efficient bureaucracy seemed to require standardized training, and the logical way to obtain it was to educate the agents further. In 1905 the ministry decreed that henceforth all agents wishing to be considered for appointment as administrators would have to undergo a one-year training program at the *Ecole Coloniale*. For years this decree was ignored, but in 1912 its provisions were repeated in a new decree, which was enforced. Thus the *Ecole* henceforth had a monopoly over the training of all administrators; no one could enter the Corps without previous attendance at the school. To gain admission into the school the agents were required to pass entrance examinations, which stressed theoretical rather than practical knowledge. For example, the examinations in 1914 for agents in AEF consisted of questions on the physical, social, and economic geography of Equatorial Africa, on regulations concerning native administration, and on the financial, political, and administrative organization of the colonial system.[52]

The decree of 1912 was suspended in 1914 for the duration of the war, and its real impact was felt only after 1920, when the agents were required to spend one year at the school, the cadets two years; nevertheless the two groups were brought closer together because of their similar training and the mutual contacts they had established in Paris.

In order to understand the relatively slow progress made in developing internal cohesiveness in the Corps and standard methods for training its members, one must keep in mind that the French empire was continuously in a process of flux. Although the French zones of influence had been relatively well delineated by 1900, they were still undergoing changes on the eve of the war. In general, the French empire in Africa was under control but not totally "pacified"; for example, in Niger, Mauritania, Chad, and the Ivory Coast, a struggle against the French continued into the 1920s.

The expansion of the empire brought with it a dramatic growth of the Corps of Colonial Administrators; within one generation it increased twentyfold (see Table 2).

Table 2

Number of men entering the Corps, 1887-1914
(figures in parenthesis indicate the number then serving in the Corps)

1887	40	(40)	1896	29	(105)	1905	74	(398)
1888	16	(54)	1897	34	(132)	1906	68	(444)
1889	2	(50)	1898	43	(163)	1907	51	(476)
1890	5	(50)	1899	22	(166)	1908	82	(549)
1891	14	(56)	1900	60	(214)	1909	50	(574)
1892	12	(63)	1901	3	(217)	1910	68	(604)
1893	13	(73)	1902	58	(268)	1911	169	(745)
1894	14	(80)	1903	28	(280)	1912	65	(795)
1895	7	(82)	1904	70	(338)	1913	97	(861)

The unbroken but highly uneven growth of the Corps must be kept in mind when one considers the difficulties the ministry had in attracting qualified officials. In 1899, twenty-two administrators were appointed; in 1900, sixty; but in 1901, only three. So long as the central administration in Paris could not anticipate the needs of the colonial service from one year to the next it could neither recruit systematically nor set up a proper training program. It was only when the French had completed their conquests and had established permanent administrative organizations in the colonies that the colonial office could estimate administrative needs and plan recruitment rationally. The problems of personnel planning and the lack of candidates for overseas service were not unique to the French; for similar factors forced the Germans in their East African empire to be content with the officials they could recruit. According to one writer, the German choice of officials lay—much as with the French—"between irresponsible adventurers, aggressive militarists, and civil servants trained in the rigors of the domestic bureaucracy."[53]

Yet in spite of heterogeneous recruitment and irregular procedures, the colonial ministry did manage to improve the quality of its administrators. In judging their quality, one must rely largely on the quarterly reports submitted by the governors. Obviously governors could often disagree in rating a subordinate. Also, of course, today's standards might lead us to reject the criteria they used. Initially, those administrators who could maintain order in their *cercles* were considered satisfactory, while low ratings went to those whose excessive harshness toward the local populations caused uprisings, who systematically left their governors ignorant of events in their *cercles,* who kept poor accounts, or who were unable to explain deficits in their treasury. All administrators, including the very best, were highly authoritarian, even highly arbitrary, and many governors were very lenient in judging their personnel. It was only the worst exercise of discipline—for example, flogging followed by death—that the governors invariably recognized as brutality.

In view of the toleration with which most governors regarded their subordinates, the governors' reports are not very reliable gauges by which to measure the quality of the administrators serving in the period 1887-1914. Still, with the passage of time, as the governors developed both a greater sense of the administrators' human responsibilities toward the local populations and more effective ways of checking on them, their reports became increasingly credible. That the quality of the administrators also improved is confirmed in personnel files of officials who entered the Corps between 1887 and 1914. A steadily growing proportion received ratings of satisfactory from the governors who reviewed their work (see Table 3).

Table 3

*Evaluation of administrators by their governors**

Year of recruitment	Total files examined	Number of administrators considered capable	Number of administrators considered incapable	Files with insufficient information
1887	18	3 (17%)	11 (61%)	4 (22%)
1888-1899	106	56 (53%)	33 (31%)	17 (16%)
1900-1909	318	156 (49%)	112 (35%)	50 (16%)
1910-1914	252	156 (62%)	52 (21%)	44 (17%)

*It may be that the files examined give a somewhat excessively negative image of the quality of the administrators in the Corps in the early years. The reports, especially in the 1880s, were sometimes unfair, since they reflected the political and personal animosities of the governors. These reports became more reliable as the Corps became increasingly homogeneous and the governors were to a greater degree recruited from among former administrators. I have tried to take this problem into account by classifying an administrator as "incapable" only if he received a poor rating from more than one of his superiors.

Several factors contributed to improvement of the Corps. One of the most important was the improvement in the quality of the agents, from whose ranks so many Corps members were chosen. Another was the rising prestige of the Corps, as the ministry raised salaries, increased slightly the number of decorations, and made recruitment more selective. After the turn of the twentieth century the colonial service was able to attract an ever growing number of secondary school and university graduates. Among the administrators appointed prior to 1900, only half had formal education through the *baccalauréat*, but from 1900 to 1905, 70 percent held that degree, and from 1906 to 1914, 75 percent (see Table 4).

Like the metropolitan bureaucracy, the colonial service increasingly attracted men with law degrees. Of the new recruits from 1900 to 1905, 23 percent had studied law; the proportion rose to 29 percent in 1906-1914. (These figures include the men who studied law as part of the curriculum of the *Ecole Coloniale*.) The study of law did not fully prepare men for colonial service, but it taught them to respect orders and follow regulations, both valuable assets for overseas service. Roman law, which

Table 4

Educational degrees of 694 administrators recruited between 1887 and 1914*

Year appointed	Total files examined	a	b	c	d	e	f	g	h	i	j	k	l	m	n
1887-1899	124	7	–	7	8	–	4	–	1	1	–	6	3	31	56
1900-1905	175	19	1	18	1	1	2	1	–	6	–	7	3	63	53
1906-1914	395	46	5	52	12	6	8	1	–	1	4	14	9	140	97

*Representing slightly more than two-thirds of the total number appointed to the Corps during this period.

a Ecole Coloniale graduates
b Docteur en droit
c Licence en droit
d Bachelier en droit
e Licence ès sciences
f Licence ès lettres
g Diplôme de l'Institut des langues orientales
h Diplôme de l'Ecole libre des sciences politiques
i Docteur en médecine
j Diplôme de l'Ecole de pharmacie
k Degrees from either Ecole navale or Saint-Cyr
l Brevet de l'Ecole des hautes etudes commerciales
m Baccalauréat
n Primary education

stressed the universality of law and the basic equality of man, may have given some administrators a certain sense of obligation and duty toward the local populations. In general, it was the most educated administrator who was inclined to be humane, whether his training had been in law or in some other area of knowledge.

An investigation of the educational background of the administrators suggests that there was a direct correlation between the rising educational level of the men in the Corps and their achievement. Some governors may have been overimpressed with the educational qualifications of some of their subordinates and may have judged them less on their administrative capacities than on their educational qualifications,[54] but this possibility does not obscure the correlation between the highly educated and highly capable officials.

Not surprisingly, the improvement in the administrators' educational level coincided with the French progress in "pacifying" the areas under their control. Obviously it was much easier for an administrator to be gentle and humane in a "pacified" area than in one in which French

Table 5

Correlation between educational level and administrative ability of administrators entering the Corps between 1887 and 1914

	Less than secondary school	Secondary education	Higher and university education
Number of administrators considered capable	103 (50%)	110 (47%)	158 (62%)
Number of administrators considered incapable	71 (34%)	76 (33%)	61 (24%)
Number of administrators with incomplete files	32 (16%)	48 (20%)	35 (14%)

authority could be constantly challenged.

For all the complaints that the governors had made of their early subordinates, it might be argued that these rough buccaneer types were probably just the sort of men who were necessary to break local resistance and assert French authority. When the primary stage of colonization—or conquest—had been accomplished the time had come to begin the secondary stage: the establishment of a regular functioning administration. The buccaneer vanished and was replaced by the bureaucrat. In the face of this change, which occurred during the decade preceding World War I, it was logical for the ministry of colonies to insist on a high educational level for its administrators. Drawing on its former experiences the ministry arrived in 1905 at two irresistible conclusions: education was necessary to produce the most desirable overseas officials, and the best education available was to be had at the *Ecole Coloniale*. Accordingly the ministry decided to appoint to the Corps only graduates of the school and the ex-agents trained there. With this decision to funnel all future administrators through the *Ecole*, the era of experimentation had come to an end.

III Beginnings of the Ecole Coloniale

Until 1914 the *Ecole Coloniale* played a very modest role in the training of colonial administrators, furnishing only one out of every five members of the Corps. Nevertheless, its development before World War I is important because the achievements of its graduates led the ministry of colonies in 1912 to restrict membership in the Corps to those who had been trained at the school.

The establishment of a specialized training program for French colonial administrators was begun in Indochina. The French had founded the *Collège des stagiaires* at Saigon in 1874 to train the administrators for Cochin-China. Admission to the school was open to all young Frenchmen possessing one of a series of diplomas; after taking a one-year course and passing an examination, they were eligible for the lowest rank of administrator. The students, however, seem to have learned little at the school, partly, it was said, because the torrid weather in Saigon discouraged them from studying, and partly because there was no library.[1]

The governor of Cochin-China discontinued the school in 1878, but many higher officials in Indochina favored special training to prepare future colonial administrators; they argued that a school similar to the college could be successful if it were established in a more benign and intellectual climate. Paul Bert, the anticlerical fanatic who was made governor-general of Indochina to get him out of France, became the spokesman of those officials. Bert proposed an *Ecole d'administration annamite*, located in Paris. No stranger to nepotism, he also suggested that his son-in-law, Joseph Chailley-Bert, the colonial publicist, be made the first director of the school. Undersecretary of State for Colonies Eugène Etienne rejected the son-in-law but favored Bert's general proposal relative to the location of the school.

Parliament also proved sympathetic to a training program for administrators for Indochina; during a tempestuous debate on colonial policy which broke out at the beginning of 1888, Félix Faure, then undersecretary of state for colonies, managed to calm parliamentary hostility for a time by promising to found an *Ecole d'administration indochinoise*. Faure, however, did not describe it as a separate institution, but simply as a curriculum of courses drawn from the law faculty, the *Ecole libre des sciences politiques*, the *Institut des langues orientales*, and a few new ones particularly concerned with colonial affairs.[2]

It was Etienne, however, who actually established a program of colonial studies. In this he was probably influenced by the experience of other colonial nations, especially the Dutch.[3] After the 1880s Leroy-Beaulieu's *De la colonisation chez les peuples modernes* introduced to his countrymen the subject of comparative colonization while Chailley-Bert, through newspaper columns and two travel accounts, publicized British and Dutch methods of administration in India and the East Indies.[4] In 1856 the British had closed their training school for men belonging to the Indian civil service, but the Dutch maintained a very active school at Delft.

Rather than found an *Ecole d'administration annamite*, as Bert had suggested, Etienne decided in 1889 to set up classes in colonial administration at the already existing *Ecole Coloniale*. The *Ecole Coloniale* had its roots in an informal school established in Paris during the 1880s for young Asians brought from the colonies to study French. In 1885 the French explorer Auguste Pavie, who had trudged barefoot through Laos exploring that country for France, returned to his homeland with thirteen young men, sons of mandarins and other important personalities in the French protectorate of Cambodia. The boys were housed in a hotel rented by the undersecretariat of state for colonies and were taught not only the French language but also French civilization. Félix Faure, then undersecretary of state for colonies, named the hotel and its inmates the *Ecole cambodgienne*. As one provincial paper put it, the aim of the improvised school was to bring young men of noble birth and high intelligence to France and thus "consolidate the ties" between France and her possessions in Indochina. The paper assumed that "the sight of the marvels of our nation and particularly of the capital . . . would inculcate in these young people an admiration that certainly would turn to our advantage."[5]

When Faure founded the *Collège cambodgienne* in 1885, he probably envisioned a worldwide role for the school, and intended that it should train sons of chiefs from all over the empire.[6] In 1886 the son of the king of Porto Novo (in later Dahomey) was admitted to the school. The following year Etienne changed the school's name to the *Ecole Coloniale*, as if to indicate the expanded role which he intended for it. No other Africans were admitted, but the *Ecole Coloniale* recruited many young men from French Indochina outside Cambodia. Approximately twenty Indochinese students attended yearly.

In establishing a training program for French colonial personnel, Etienne was primarily concerned with providing instruction for the men belonging to the Civil Services of Indochina, a colony which in the late 1880s was the largest and most important single French possession under his authority. Indochina had been recently conquered, and after 1879 naval personnel had been replaced by civilian officials and administrators. Etienne recognized that for a long time to come the administrative services would require a steady supply of able young Frenchmen and he hoped that his new training program would fulfill that need.

Etienne affiliated the training program with the *Ecole Coloniale* so that the Indochinese students of the *Ecole* could furnish language practice to the future administrators, who were required to learn Vietnamese and Cambodian. A further reason for the affiliation was that the school's director, Etienne Aymonier, was an experienced man who had run the former *Collège des stagiaires* in Saigon.

Etienne intended that the *Ecole Coloniale* should give courses in colonial administrative theory and in Indochinese languages which would prepare the young officials to take on important responsibilities as soon as they arrived in the colony. The old system, he declared, had two disadvantages. On the one hand, because the young administrators were ignorant about the colonial scene, they were required to serve in unimportant and subordinate positions until familiar with their regions, but by then they had become so enervated by the climate that they had to be repatriated. On the other hand, if they were given important posts immediately upon their arrival, "their inadequacy resulted in failures, [which] are sometimes deplorable for the work of colonization."[7] By giving the young men a sound grounding in principles of colonial administration before appointing them, Etienne hoped he would be able to make a substantial improvement in the quality of the colonial administrators.

Very quickly the *Ecole Coloniale* expanded its scope beyond training personnel for Indochina. An African training section was opened in 1892. For a time other sections were created to train French personnel as custodians for colonial penitentiaries, as naval pursers, and commercial agents, but these were soon discontinued. In 1905 a section to train colonial judges was established, in 1914 another, to prepare students for administration in North Africa and, after World War II, still another, to train labor inspectors for the overseas territories.

Indochinese students had originally constituted the entire student body of the *Ecole Coloniale*, but after 1889 they constituted only what was called the "native section." This section continued to enroll approximately twenty Indochinese students a year until the outbreak of World War I, but the school had become predominantly an institution to train Frenchmen for service overseas. It was so identified in the public mind after 1889 and so regarded by the administration of the school, which increasingly neglected the students of the "native section." For example, during the 1890s only two teachers were employed for their benefit—one in mathematics and the other in French. And the school came finally to serve the Indochinese students primarily as a place of residence while they pursued their studies elsewhere. Where before 1890 the Indochinese students had received an education very similar to that given in French secondary schools, thereafter their education was technical, and they were trained to become telegraph operators, accountants, engineers, or forest rangers. This change stemmed in part from the change in policy toward the Asian colony. In the 1880s control over Indochina had still been somewhat tenuous, and therefore French doctrine had stressed the benefit of indirect rule. By educating the sons of mandarins and other dignitaries in a metropolitan school, Etienne and his immediate predecessors had hoped to build up a pro-French party through which to tighten control over the country. As direct rule was consolidated in the early 1890s, the French administrators no longer needed friendly intermediaries and could concentrate on educating Indochinese as technical auxiliaries to their administration.

In the 1890s many colonial officials no longer favored giving the elite of the colonial populations a French education. At the International Colonial Congress of 1889 in Paris the well-known sociologist Gustave Lebon claimed that the British had transformed members of the Indian elite into agitators against colonial rule by giving them a European education. He predicted that if the British continued this practice they would probably lose their colony. Educating the native populations might similarly subvert French colonial rule.[8]

Ideas much like those held by Lebon were put forth in 1900 when the administration of the *Ecole Coloniale* considered whether it should continue the "native section." Its report asked:

Are there not more inconveniences than advantages in giving natives needs, tastes, and aspirations which they will find difficult to satisfy when they return to their country? Even more, is it not dangerous to mix them through everyday life with young Frenchmen in schools, in cities, in our discussions, in all our interior struggles?[9]

The report went on to say that the students from the colonies had become so absorbed into the stream of French life that they had "abandoned their native costumes and were wearing European clothes." As a result of this experience, young men from the colonies would acquire "sentiments which, if spread to a larger number of natives, might create a hindrance to our domination."[10] In spite of this negative judgment, officials of the school decided to retain the "native section," but with the outbreak of war in 1914, it was discontinued. The reservations which *Ecole Coloniale* officials were beginning to feel toward Western-educated Indochinese foreshadowed the ambivalence with which French overseas functionaries in the future viewed the emergence of a Westernized elite.

The founding of the administrative section of the *Ecole Coloniale* is a great milestone in the history of French administration. Except for the short-lived *Ecole nationale d'administration*, founded after the revolution of 1848, the administrative section of the *Ecole Coloniale* was the first government program specifically established to train men for civil service positions. Not until over half a century later was the prestigious *Ecole nationale d'administration* founded in Paris to train upper civil servants for metropolitan France.

When founding the administrative section of the *Ecole Coloniale*, Etienne did not ask Parliament for a budgetary appropriation. Realizing the chamber's hostility toward colonial expenditures, he chose to finance the training program from the proceeds of a private bequest to the government. Once the program had been in effect for a year, however, he could call for an appropriation on the grounds that the administrative section had proved its usefulness.

The funds were granted, but some legislators believed that Etienne had deliberately misled Parliament; the influential *Journal des débats* wrote of the government officials:

... from subterfuge to subterfuge they have managed to give a semblance of respectable existence to a hybrid institution which should be prevented from further development; it endangers the good order of our finances and the future of our colonial power.[11]

The journal was skeptical of the abilities of men who lacked practical experience in the field; the *Ecole Coloniale*, it feared, would be a costly means for producing inefficient administrators. One Radical paper claimed that it had been founded simply to provide employment for Louis Vignon, the son-in-law of Prime Minister Maurice Rouvier, who taught at the school.[12]

This skepticism and open hostility toward the school was in part justified, for the administration recruited students with no concern for their academic abilities. All young men between the ages of eighteen and twenty-five with a secondary school degree (*baccalauréat*) were eligible without any entrance examination. Only after attending the school for a year were the students required to take a test, which determined whether they should continue their studies. Presumably the officials of the school adopted this procedure because it allowed the poorly prepared students from the *lycées* to catch up with their more advanced comrades. An entrance examination would have favored the sons of the upper classes, who usually had a better secondary school training; in the words of the school's director, the procedure followed made it possible to recruit "from the mass of the public."[13]

Despite the general liberality which the school exercised in its admission policies, it tended to discriminate against some students because of their political beliefs. In the 1890s the republican regime still felt threatened and therefore wished to ensure that only men favorably inclined toward republicanism would be employed as government functionaries. Before admitting a student, the school checked on "the past political life of [the candidates'] families, their personal convictions, and morality."[14] This practice led a later critic to note that all that was necessary to enter the *Ecole Coloniale* in the 1890s was "to be a *bachelier* and a republican."[15]

The educational requirements were later to be raised, but there seems to have been continued interest in admitting republicans to the school. The applicants were required to have a certificate of previous good conduct from their local prefect; and until about 1905 the prefects, in addition to certifying that the candidate had no criminal record, would usually add a comment about the political beliefs of the candidate and of his family. Thus in 1904 a prefect wrote of one candidate: "The information gathered on M . . . is excellent from all points of view. He belongs to a family which is very devoted to the Republic."[16] The agents also were appointed largely as a result of political patronage and thus two of the main sources of recruitment to the Corps—the graduates of the *Ecole Coloniale* and the agents—were almost all reliable republicans.

The low standards of admission had been instituted to democratize the recruitment of the school, but there is little evidence that it attracted many candidates from other than middle-class families, which have traditionally served the French state. It is certain, however, that the absence of entrance examinations drew students unfit for academic studies. So many poorly qualified students attended the school that, in the words of a later school publication, they "gave their imprint and their original character to the *Ecole Coloniale.*"[17] Under pressure from a parliamentary commission headed by the reporter of the colonial budget, André Lebon (later minister of colonies), the *Ecole Coloniale* by decree adopted entrance examinations in 1896. The same decree also brought about curriculum changes. The training program was shortened from three to two years, and at the same time a one-year preparatory program was instituted. This preparatory year was needed because the school's entrance examinations were so specialized that it was very difficult to pass them without preliminary training. Between 1896 and 1914 approximately one out of three applicants was admitted to the school. And of those admitted, nearly all came from the preparatory section; of the ninety-seven students admitted from 1897 to 1899, eighty-two came from that section.[18]

The examinations were in the form of a *concours*, a competition for a restricted number of positions. They were divided into three stages. The first part of the *concours* dealt with the subject matter taught in the first two years of law school, with the exception of Roman law and the history of French law. Those passing the law examinations were then tested on the general history of French and foreign colonization, geography, and English or German. The final part was an oral examination in which the candidates were tested on their knowledge of road and building construction, hygiene, practical accounting, and a foreign language.

The oral examination was exclusively concerned with testing the candidate's knowledge; the French examiners, unlike those for the British colonial service,[19] made no attempt to judge a candidate's poise or personality. This was in line with the traditional French procedure for hiring civil servants, the *concours*. Designed primarily to test a candidate's ability to express himself in written French,[20] yet it was considered an objective and nearly infallible means for selecting capable men. While the British colonial service identified ability with the possession of certain character traits, such as leadership ability, sportsmanship, and self-reliance,[21] the French colonial service identified both professional ability and character with passing the *concours*. The French even now regard their education as a "formation," contributing to the shaping of the total individual. As W. R. Sharp observed, "To the Frenchman it is intelligence, or what is sometimes merely supposed to be intelligence, which marks off par excellence the elite from the rank and file."[22]

In passing his examination, an applicant not only was accepted in the school but was given access to the Corps of Colonial Administrators, for the cadets upon graduation were almost automatically appointed to it. To be sure, a slightly higher grade average was required for entrance than for simple graduation, but by 1914 only a few graduates had failed to qualify for the Corps.

Until the entrance examination was introduced in 1896, the *Ecole Coloniale* had not been regarded as a serious institution in France. Up to that time a relatively large proportion of the students (one-fifth) coming from the "old colonies," the West Indies, were either creole or colored.

Beginning in 1897, when entrance became more difficult, a smaller proportion of students than before applied from overseas.[23] When, after World War I, the school's graduates had sole access to the Corps, the number of administrators who were indigenous to the colonies diminished further (although there always were a few coming from the French Antilles). The decrease apparently occurred as an effect of raising the standards of the *Ecole*, rather than from deliberate government policy. It is of historic interest that, simultaneously with the French experience, in the British colonies there was also a decrease in the number of local inhabitants appointed to higher administrative posts. In both empires this change occurred as a result of the progress of pacification and the improvement of health standards, which increased the ability and willingness of white men to go overseas for longer periods of time. The change also reflected the increasing desire by the imperial powers to exercise full control over their colonies.

The new examinations which were reputed to be so rigorous did not immediately silence complaints about the poor quality of the cadets. A report of 1899 observed of the students that "one does not find among them minds accustomed to speculation and nourished by advanced studies." The future administrators needed such qualities, the report continued, because "they ... are called upon to spread out influence and to make our national genius loved."[24] Among those entering the school in 1899 none could read a map properly, and none was well prepared in foreign languages.[25] Two years later however the quality of the candidates had improved, for in 1901 the admissions committee noted that an increasing number of the young men seeking entrance were now proficient in English (except for pronunciation) and in highway and building construction. The candidates were generally ill-prepared in geography, but to the displeasure of their examiners they knew more about the geography of non-French colonies than about France's empire. By about 1905 the new entrants seem to have improved in quality so much that the examining committee no longer complained about them.

From its founding until 1931, the administrative council of the *Ecole Coloniale* was presided over by Paul Dislère, former head of the colonial department at the naval ministry and a noted expert in French colonial jurisprudence. Dislère was an important member of the prestigious *Conseil d'etat*; in 1905 he was the lawyer who received the delicate task of drafting the laws concerning the separation of church and state. Dislère's important political connections, together with his personal initiative and energy, assured the new school the necessary financial and moral support of government authorities. In his earlier career Dislère had opposed colonial expansion, arguing that it was an economic waste, but he gradually changed his mind and even became an ardent proponent of French imperialism.

Dislère also was an impassioned assimilationist; he believed that the colonies should be endowed with institutions identical to those in France and that the natives should be transformed into full-fledged French citizens.[26] Etienne Aymonier, a former administrator in Indochina and director of the *Collège des Stagiaires* in Saigon and then of the *Ecole Cambodgienne*, became the first director of the *Ecole Coloniale*. He concerned himself with the daily administrative problems of running the school, while Dislère as president of the school's administrative council was responsible for school policy; indeed, until the late 1920s Dislère tended to dominate each succeeding director. In both its organization and its curriculum the *Ecole Coloniale* reflected to a large extent Dislère's personal views, especially by its emphasis on legal studies.

While attending the school, students were expected to obtain a *licence en droit* from the law faculty in Paris. Traditionally the upper civil service in continental Europe has required legal training of its members.[27] In preparing men for the colonial service, the directors of the *Ecole Coloniale* saw no reason why they should receive substantially different education from that being given to higher government employees serving in France. Thus they trained the cadets in law, assuming that legal studies would transform them into effective civil servants who would respect government regulations and bureaucratic hierarchy. The study of law, it was also presumed, gave a certain sense of right and wrong and a respect for the rule of law.[28] In addition, of course, overseas functionaries would need legal training, since one of their main tasks was to administer and enforce law. In effect the student spent more time at the study of law than in attending the special courses of the *Ecole*.

The teachers at the school assumed that Roman law had universal validity and that its basic principles could be applied anywhere regardless of climate, topography, or inhabitants. M. Leveillé, a professor of colonial law at the *Ecole*, wrote:

law is ... a universal language.... He who has studied it will immediately recognize constant principles underlying superficial variations between different local laws.... There cannot be ten different ways to organize a family, to conceive of property or of a contract. For example, marriage, sales, borrowing, and salaries are not a question of [local] customs but are, rather, basic to life.[29]

In so reasoning, Leveillé showed his faith in the basic unity and equality of mankind, an idea common to his times. Based in part on generous universalist principles, this doctrine also evinced a certain naive ignorance

45

of colonial social and economic structures.

The formal structure of the curriculum at the *Ecole Coloniale* reflected the assimilationist trend; it neglected not only differences between France and her empire but also variations among the colonies themselves. Thus all administrators, regardless of where they were destined to serve, received identical training during the preparatory period and the first year at the school:[30] law, French and foreign colonization, administrative organization of the colonies, colonial policy, and accounting.

Only just before their last year of studies did the students indicate whether they wished to enter the Indochinese or the African section. A student's destination depended on his academic ranking. Until the 1920s, with a few notable exceptions, the top half of the class tended to choose the Indochinese section; the student at the bottom of the class invariably entered the African section. The Indochinese administration was more attractive—especially to those with families—because it offered higher salaries and faster promotion,[31] as well as better transportation, school, and hospital facilities. Interestingly enough, physical comfort was not the sole criterion for choosing a post, for the graduates of the *Ecole Coloniale* did not consider the positions in the central administration in Paris to be choice appointments.[32]

In the second year of studies, all the students took courses in colonial administrative law and topography and continued their study of foreign colonization policies, but they spent relatively few hours acquiring specialized knowledge pertaining specifically to either Indochinese or African administration. The cadets in the African section studied African geography and the administrative and legislative organization of North Africa and of French West Africa. A general ethnology course covering the entire empire was instituted in 1890, dropped five years later, and finally restored as colonial anthropology. The language requirements in the African section, as established in 1897, had very little relevance to existing fact. Both Malgache and Arabic were required—yet the first was spoken only in a portion of Madagascar and the latter virtually limited to the Islamized regions of French Africa.

Upon graduation from the school, the cadets of the African section were ranked by academic standing, and in that order they were permitted to choose the area to which they wished to be sent. The preferred region was sometimes AOF and at other times Madagascar; AEF was invariably considered the least desirable assignment. Within each federation certain colonies were preferred because they had more material comforts and a better climate than others; this was the case with Senegal in AOF and Gabon in AEF. The new officials, however, could not choose a particular colony within the federation and did not even learn their exact post until they arrived in Africa. British colonial officials knew where they would be sent and could prepare for service in a specific region, but the French graduates of the *Ecole Coloniale* were assigned at first only to a federation.

In many ways the school was divorced from the realities of colonial life, for it tended to stress a highly theoretical, rather than a practical knowledge of overseas affairs. Legal studies were overemphasized—indeed the students had to spend most of their three years at the *Ecole Coloniale* poring over legal treatises. They learned irrelevant minutiae to recite, instead of acquiring a well-rounded knowledge of the empire. Rather typical is a question from an examination in French administrative organization: "Describe the financial regime instituted in the Antilles and Réunion by the Senatus Consultus of 1866. Criticize it and discuss the reforms of 1900."[33] That kind of information was of little importance for the colonial administrators, very few of whom served in the Antilles or Réunion. None of the administrators served in North Africa, but they were all required to take courses concerning that region. The impracticality of the language training in the African section has been mentioned; the cadets in the Indochinese section also found their training in Cambodian and Vietnamese useless when they arrived in Indochina, for they had been trained in the classical variant.[34]

The organization and curriculum of the *Ecole Coloniale* continued to reflect many of the assimilationist attitudes, which had been supported by Dislère, but in the early 1900s, the school ceased to be an advocate of pure assimilation and instead adopted in part the doctrine of association. The latter doctrine advocated respect for local traditions and political structures, particularly the chief-system. The associationists stressed the uniqueness of colonial societies and their need for special institutions different from those of France, whereas the assimilationists favored the spread of French institutions overseas. The theory of association was especially strongly advanced by colonial officials, whose overseas experience impressed upon them the dissimilarity between France and the empire in terms of social, economic, and political developments.[35]

An element of humanitarianism in the doctrine of association was its announced desire to spare colonial societies from being forced into a French mold. But the theory of association never entirely freed itself from some of its racist origins. In the beginning the distinctions between the French metropolis and French overseas possessions had been entirely postulated on the inferiority of the overseas populations and the desirability of preserving an indefinite French domination over the colonies.[36] It was not only a tender regard for local institutions that converted so many French colonial officials to the policy of association; just as important was the fact that by stressing the differences between colonial societies and France, they hoped to prevent the introduction of locally elected political officials who would—as in France—exercise control over administrative rule.

After 1900 the many colonial officials who taught at the *Ecole Coloniale* made it the main—indeed, almost the only—intellectual center advocating the policy of association and denouncing that of assimilation. The school introduced its logical correlative—courses on the colonial societies; obviously, if colonial institutions were to be respected, they would have to be understood. Since its foundation, the administrative section of the *Ecole Coloniale* had offered such courses but, at least in the beginning, it had failed in its aims. The noted publicist Chailley-Bert observed in 1901 that the graduates of the *Ecole Coloniale* "have an imperfect knowledge of the customs and institutions of the peoples they administer ... and they do not speak their languages fluently."[37]

Until about 1905 Chailley-Bert's criticism of the *Ecole Coloniale* was valid, for much of the training was useless and even scientifically inaccurate, and many of the courses seemed to reflect the current anthropological racism. A Paris newspaper reported in 1894, for example, that the instructor in administrative methods, Vignon, told his students that "the black races are backward races which should be treated like wild animals" and that "these races are stagnant."[38] In 1905 a student received eighteen out of twenty points on an examination about the peoples of Africa in which he had stated, "The young Negro is quite intelligent, but his brain ceases growing at an early age, and thus stops developing."[39] The student was only repeating an assertion that the sociologist Gustave Lebon had made at the international colonial congress meeting in Paris in 1889.[40]

After about 1905, the curriculum at the school underwent serious change, and despite slim scientific resources, it soon began to give impressive training in African customs, institutions, and history. In addition, by 1910 Manding languages were taught at the school. Arabic ceased to be required of the students in the African section, although special credit was given to those who knew it.

These curriculum improvements compare favorably with special courses that other colonial powers instituted for their colonial personnel. The Dutch trained their overseas officials in Javanese affairs, while the Germans required that candidates for administrative service in German East Africa study African languages, geography, ethnography, hygiene, tropical agriculture, and trade—courses that were offered at the *Seminar für Orientalische Sprachen* of Berlin, founded in 1887. The British lagged behind; it was only in the 1930s that they instituted special courses for their colonial personnel assigned to Africa.

The *Ecole Coloniale* was especially well served by those of its professors who were former colonial officials. In teaching courses on methods of administration and history and institutions of the overseas empire, they drew on their own experiences and research. Not only did they reinforce the new curriculum in giving a more accurate picture of the colonial societies; they imbued the school with a new spirit.

One of the best known officials, whose course was later remembered as the highlight of every cadet's education at the *Ecole Coloniale*, was Maurice Delafosse. First a bush administrator and later a governor, he taught courses in African customs, language, and history. He was one of the greatest ethnologists of his time, and his teachings were far ahead of any others then taught in France. As Robert Delavignette has remarked:

[While] Seignobos at the Sorbonne was declaring that the blacks were mere children and had never formed nations ... Delafosse at the *Ecole Coloniale* was teaching his students that they were men and in pre-colonial times had even founded empires.[41]

By teaching the future administrators that Africa had had its own history and political and social institutions, the teachers were imparting a certain respect for indigenous African ways and they denounced complete assimilation. Louis Vignon, who was presumed to have made the unfortunate comment about the inferiority of the black races, although he still believed in the superiority of Europeans, now declared that the colonial societies had their own unique value and had to be respected by the French administrators. In 1904 the outline of his course on French colonization read:

The policy to follow toward native societies: Necessity of studying the religion, customs, traditions, laws, social and administrative organization of the conquered native societies.

Profound differences between the mentality of Europeans and that of Africans and Asians. ... Opposition between the principles of 1789 and the conservatism of non-European populations. The advantage gained by respecting their ideas and social forms.[42]

As the viewpoint of the colonial officials had influenced the school's curriculum, it was also to affect the attitude of the *Ecole Coloniale* toward physical fitness. Ever since 1890 the school had offered riding classes and fencing lessons. Indeed, the school's fencing team was one of the finest in the nation. From the beginning physical education was stressed, but proficiency was not required. But in 1909, influenced by the old bush

MAURICE DELAFOSSE

administrators, the school officials decided that since the importance of physical fitness "for colonial administrators is beyond doubt" students would not be allowed to graduate if they did not have a passing grade in physical education.[43] In 1910 three students of the *Ecole Coloniale* received their air-pilot licenses, even though only one of them was to find practical use for his training.[44]

Until World War I and even later, the *Ecole Coloniale* did not enjoy the prestige of the *grandes écoles* like *Saint-Cyr* or *Polytechnique*.[45] In fact, it remained a relatively unknown institution, for in 1909, during a debate on the colonies, a senator proclaimed that what France needed for its colonial officials was a colonial school, whereupon the minister of colonies explained that such a school had existed for twenty years.[46]

To some people, however, the *Ecole* and careers in the colonies had become sufficiently well known by 1900, so that some considered the colonial service an acceptable alternative to the metropolitan civil service or to liberal professions in France. A graduate of the *Ecole Coloniale* described how his father chose a career for him; the father called him into his office and addressed him in the following terms:

You are eighteen years old, you have your *baccalauréat*. You must now choose a profession and start a career. I know you would like to be a journalist and enter politics. But this is not a profession—especially at the age of eighteen. We must think of something else. You are blind as a bat, which rules out a military career. You have told me you dislike medicine and teaching. That is your right. You are neither stupid enough nor elegant enough to be a diplomat. You haven't the disposition for business . . . that limits the possibilities rather narrowly. There's still the colonies.[47]

The colonies attracted a class of men who found career opportunities in France too limited. Since overseas service—despite its obvious hardships—offered quick promotions, it made an admirable career for ambitious young men who wanted a government post without the drudgery and slow promotion of the metropolitan administration. The Corps was still new, the top positions readily accessible. In 1904 a newspaper advising parents to send their children to the *Ecole Coloniale* wrote:

. . . in a society like ours, so ancient and so exceptionally complex, a young man is caught like a cog in a machine. . . . Years and years may pass before he can have a position of responsibility. Everyone knows how slow promotion is in administrative careers, both military and civilian. That is not the case in the colonial service.[48]

Many of the young men entering the *Ecole Coloniale* had brilliant expectations. Joost Van Vollenhoven, while a student at the school, wrote his uncle:

If one distinguishes himself in this post [of colonial administrator] one can ... eventually be named governor-general. The administration has a future, as you can see. Add to this that the French colonies are hardly explored and you will understand immediately the future there is in such a position for an active and ambitious man.[49]

By his drive and brilliance Van Vollenhoven was to fulfill his goal of becoming governor-general within ten years of entering the administration. Even after the 1920s, when the top posts of the Corps were no longer so easy to attain, the myth remained that colonial service provided a quick means of rising to the top.

Patriotism—a desire to strengthen France by spreading her civilization abroad—was also influential in drawing men to the Corps. One of the abiding ironies of the colonial venture was that many of the men who went overseas to spread European rule and civilization were tired of Europe. Thus, while the overseas areas had their own charm, the interest in the colonies was to a significant degree an outcome of the dissatisfaction that many Europeans felt with their own culture and society. Lyautey fulminated against French parliamentarism and bureaucracy. France's salvation, her hope of rejuvenation lay overseas, he declared. The colonies were "the most glorious school of energy in which our race is being retempered and recast as if in a crucible."[50]

The colonial literature which emerged at the turn of the century—writings by Pierre Loti, André Demaison, Robert Randau—presented imperialists as "brimming over with life, will, intelligence, and, of course, heroism."[51] The literature was filled with examples of white men performing noble tasks among primitive peoples. But the French novelists were less influential in this respect than was Rudyard Kipling. The British author's preeminent influence was best described by André Maurois:

From 1900 to 1920 Kipling influenced French youth as few French writers have been able to do. His mannerisms became French mannerisms; his legends and stories (*Just So Stories*, *The Jungle Book*) inspired the games and shaped the thoughts of French children.

Kipling's impact, Maurois thought, lay in the message that he and other novelists sought to convey, and which the lives of the French colonial figures embodied:

I found above all in his books (*Kim, Stalky & Co.*, and *The Bridge Builders*) a heroic conception of life. It was neither exclusively British nor exclusively imperial. His heroes, no matter what their nationality or their job, conquered disorder by overcoming laziness, envy, ambition, and desires.[52]

The influence exerted by this heroic conception of the colonial life was reinforced at a more philosophical level by the writings extolling the life of action and the cult of energy, such as those of Nietzsche, Charles Péguy, and Ernest Psichari, Renan's grandson. Psichari, a young mystic who served as colonial officer in Mauritania before his premature death on the battlefield in World War I, was especially popular.

J. F. Reste, who entered the *Ecole Coloniale* in 1900 and was to reach the very highest ranks within the colonial service, reminisced over half a century later on the spirit that dominated his youth, influencing him and his classmates to choose a colonial career. With his classmates, Reste was stirred by the need for action which was the result of "a mystique of poetry, exoticism, and humanism." The exoticism which was reflected in the world of art, music, poetry, and fiction influenced a large stratum of French youth. "We, the young, we lived as in a dream; we abandoned ourselves to the gentle reveries of the poems of Leconte de Lisle, José Maria de Heredia, Baudelaire, Arthur Rimbaud." The humanist approach played an equally strong role in attracting Reste and his comrades overseas. They were inspired by both Tolstoy and Henri Poincaré; the colonies seemed to provide a place to experiment the marriage of humanism and science. By technical feats human societies could be improved. The great colonials—Garnier, Savorgnan de Brazza, Ballay, and Gallieni—were symbols of French national rebirth, examples of heroism that these young men wanted to emulate.

The colonial experience seemed a method by which France might renew her youth. "France has doubted in its destiny," but the colonial heroes had created an "unvanquished generation ready to reestablish our country on its eternal foundations." Reste and his contemporaries at the *Ecole Coloniale* looked forward impatiently to service in Asia and Africa, where awaited the "promise of a free and independent life, devoted to the accomplishment of tasks to which we can give the best of ourselves. We lived in emotional times and we were ready to leave for these distant countries, impatiently awaiting the unknown and the marvellous."[53]

Reste's reminiscences were supported by the survey that André Tarde and Henri Massis (writing under the pen-name "Agathon") made of French youth before World War I. The prewar generation was preoccupied with the need for heroic action, and some of its members saw overseas a particular opportunity for personal fulfillment. One member of that

FRESCO AT THE *ECOLE COLONIALE*

generation wrote, "We all felt our young blood boil with the fever of departure; we were all drunk with new horizons and unknown oceans."[54]

Most of the young men entering the *Ecole Coloniale* came from middle or even lower middle class background, from the group that the French traditionally call the *classes moyennes*.[55] Few sons of the French nobility entered the *Ecole Coloniale* prior to World War I; usually the only aristocratic names in the Corps of Colonial Administrators belonged to former military officers. In serving the republican regime the French nobility as a rule restricted itself to the diplomatic service and the officer corps. Generally speaking, aristocrats opposed colonial expansion. Undoubtedly the initial custom of rejecting young men of royalist families also discouraged sons of the nobility from applying to the school. The relatively low prestige of the colonial career and of the preparatory training was a further deterrent.

Because of the school's educational requirements, members of the lower classes did not enter it. Few children either of the working class or of the peasantry had a *baccalauréat*, the minimal diploma required for entrance. This was due in part to a certain disinclination of the lower classes to give their children a higher education, and in addition, of course, to the material fact that until 1931 secondary schools charged fees. If, in spite of these difficulties, some lower-class children did receive a secondary education, lack of funds and limited ambitions made it unlikely that they would decide to continue their studies. Also, the cost of studying at the *Ecole Coloniale* must have been prohibitive to many. One administrator estimated that the cost of living three years in Paris (two-year curriculum and an additional preparatory year), together with the tuition fees at the school and at the law faculty, was eight to ten thousand francs.[56] Before World War I this sum approximated a common laborer's full salary for three years, and two years' earnings for the average government employee.[57] It is true that some of the neediest and best students were not required to pay fees, but the school provided very few scholarships, and these were meagre.[58] Unless the students' families lived in Paris their education would be so costly that only the middle classes could afford it; and even for them it represented a substantial sacrifice.

After 1900, the widespread use of colonial officials as teachers marked a definite improvement in the school. The adoption of the doctrine of association indicated a desire to relate more concretely to the colonial reality. A graduate of 1913 undoubtedly overstated the case when he wrote of his education at the *Ecole Coloniale*, "It gave me a solid theoretical foundation which needed only to be applied practically."[59]

Of course the personnel needs of the colonies underwent significant changes as the administration in the early 1900s became increasingly regularized, needing fewer of the "buccaneer" types and more bureaucrats. The students from the *Ecole*, ingrained with a sense of duty and prepared for bureaucratic routine by their legal studies, now became invaluable to the new type of service that was evolving overseas. The ministry of colonies recognized that these men were indeed best fit for the Corps; during a parliamentary debate in 1909 on the colonial service, Minister of Colonies Milliès-Lacroix stated that "the best functionaries come from the *Ecole Coloniale.*"[60] Until World War I the school trained only a small proportion of those entering the Corps (15 percent) but as a result of the changing needs of the colonies, and the progress that the school had made in the generation after its founding, the ministry of colonies made it the only avenue for entrance into the Corps.

IV The Locus of Power

Robert Delavignette entitled his work on the career of colonial administration *Les Vrais chefs de l'empire*. No title could have been more aptly chosen, for until World War II the colonial administrators were the men who shaped the empire, its almost undisputed masters. Their role until 1914 will be discussed in this chapter.

The importance of the administrators stemmed from three factors: the decentralized nature of the colonial administration, overseas French administrative doctrine, and the extensive powers given the *commandants de cercles*. All three ensured them a central position in the formation of the empire while in effect minimizing the influence of their superiors in the administrative hierarchy.

On paper the French overseas administration seemed a highly centralized organization. A very clear hierarchy of authority had been established: the minister of colonies in Paris; the governors-general who presided over the colonial federations in Dakar, Brazzaville, and Tananarive; the governors of the individual colonies; and finally the *commandants de cercles*. The reality, however, was quite different. Delavignette best summed up the situation when he wrote that in the colonial administration "there was none of this bureaucratic centralization that saps the energy. The *commandant* did not wait for orders from the governor of Zinder, [and] the governor of Zinder for those coming from the governor-general in Dakar."[1]

A number of factors disrupted the administrative pyramid. One of these was the geographic distance that separated the various levels of the hierarchy. Slow communications before World War I often made it difficult for authorities to see that their policies were executed by their subordinates. The higher an official stood on the hierarchical ladder, the less he knew about specific problems and the less capable he felt of solving them.

Colonial ministers in Paris were most helpless of all—they were not only separated from the colonies by the ocean, but also seldom technically equipped to handle the problems that arose. Not until the 1920s did any ministers have colonial experience.[2] At least two ministers had been avowed anticolonialists before taking office. Etienne Clémentel, who served in 1905, won a certain notoriety for his naiveté in colonial matters. It is said that when Clémentel took over the ministry of colonies, the sight of the French possessions on a world map inspired him to say, "The colonies—I did not know there were so many of them!"

Some ministers, of course, made serious attempts to acquaint themselves with the colonies, even going so far as to visit them. But these official tours were usually limited to the colonial capitals and of little use in educating the ministers to their tasks. And even though a minister acquired some competence in colonial questions, he might lose office at any time; the instability of French governments meant that on the average his term of office was barely more than one year.[3]

The central administration in Paris had been organized to prevent the development of strong centralized authority. In fact, the law of 1894 which had established the ministry of colonies had declared that it should be an administration sufficiently decentralized not to strangle official initiative in the colonies or to stunt the development of the colonies.[4] On the contrary, the law had stipulated that the ministry should establish institutions that would be suitable for each colony.[5] As a result, rather than being organized along functional lines, the central administration was divided into regional bureaus. These bureaus did not keep close control over the colonies, and their responsibilities and powers were rather unclear. In 1910 Adolphe Messimy, reporter of the colonial budget and future minister of colonies, described the ministry as "a grouping of confused services."[6]

Six years later, Gratien Candace, reporter on the colonial budget and deputy from the Antilles, complained that the officials in Paris had to deal with such diverse problems that they had no expertise in any field and were forced therefore to leave full responsibility to the governors. Candace favored dividing the ministry of colonies along functional rather than geographical lines, so that officials might develop expertise in a given field. For example, he blamed the regional organization for the haphazard development of public instruction overseas: "for several years nobody [in the ministry] has had any interest in the spread of primary and professional education in the colonies."[7]

The personnel in the central administration were poorly equipped to advise the ministers on colonial policy, since few officials in the ministry had ever been in the colonies. Although a decree of 1896 had required two years of service in the field for all officials serving in the ministry, this provision was not enforced. A ministerial order in 1907 suffered the same fate; the staff members of the ministry at Rue Oudinot had no inclination to go to the tropics.

It is difficult to explain how the officials managed to flout the regulations of the ministry. General Messimy, who had been one of the most efficient ministers of colonies before World War I, observed in the 1930s:

> The French functionaries do not want to go to the colonies; believe me, I ... tried everything ... but without success. I tried to introduce at Rue Oudinot the principle that all functionaries of the ministry would have to go overseas. The repugnance [to this order] was so lively that some of these gentlemen would have resigned rather than leave Paris, even for only six months.[8]

In 1917 Governor-General Van Vollenhoven of AOF suggested a possible remedy for the split between the functionaries in Paris and those in the field—that the Corps of Colonial Administrators and the higher bureaucracy be merged to form a single unit, and that the ministry be run by administrators temporarily serving in Paris. That method, he believed, would confront the central administration with the realities of colonial life.[9]

After 1919 a small number of administrators were called to serve in Paris, thus bringing some direct knowledge of the colonies to the ministry. But not until a quarter of a century later was Van Vollenhoven's scheme implemented; in 1942 the Corps was merged with the higher bureaucracy of the central administration. Although slow in coming, the integration of the ministry personnel with that of the overseas officials—when it finally occurred in 1942—compares favorably with the British practice, which until the end of colonial rule continued to divide the men in the field strictly from the Colonial Office.

As in most other branches of the French bureaucracy, a corps of colonial inspectors was personally responsible to the minister of colonies and reported to him on the overseas administration. The Corps of Colonial Inspectors, founded in 1887, was an elite organization recruited through an extremely difficult examination; a number of its members were former administrators. The inspectors were the *missi dominici* of the ministers; their integrity and fairness were generally recognized. They were few in number; twenty-six in 1905, thirty-three in 1917, twenty-nine in 1935.[10] Because of the immensity of the empire and the multifarious activities on which they were required to report they could visit only a limited number of colonies each year. The more remote colonies were often neglected; in 1930, for example, Niger was inspected for the first time—only partially—and Mauritania had never been inspected at all.[11] As a result, the inspectors were of limited use in ensuring centralized control. At the most, they supplied the central administration with information for the exercise of the only function that Van Vollenhoven had thought necessary for the metropole: a veto over any action in the colonies that might "not be worthy of France or which might threaten her sovereignty."[12]

Even this function was sometimes too difficult for the metropole. When Brazza inspected the Congo in 1905 on a special mission, he discovered examples of severe maladministration about which Paris knew nothing. He wrote the minister of colonies:

> During my voyage I have acquired the definite impression that the ministry has been kept ignorant of the real conditions of the natives and the manner in which they have been treated.[13]

Personal limitations and the nature of the administrative structure made it impossible for the ministers of colonies to keep themselves well informed about the colonies. In their ignorance they could scarcely formulate intelligent policy. The functionaries of the ministry complained in a collective letter that there was no long range direction; rather, colonial affairs were being handled on a day-by-day basis.[14] Charles Regismanset, who served as director of political affairs of the ministry of colonies, was even more definite: "It is abundantly clear that France has no colonial program, and in maintaining this negative attitude, she is faithful to a tradition. She has no program and has never had one."[15]

Planning of overseas policies might have developed through the interchange of information among the colonial powers, but this scarcely existed. Although comparative colonization was taught at the *Ecole Coloniale* and French officials participated in international colonial conferences, the ministry of colonies seems to have had little interest in the overseas experiences of other colonial powers. The association of functionaries of the ministry of colonies claimed in 1911:

> The minister is completely uninterested in foreign colonial policy: England, Belgium, Holland, Germany, Italy, Spain, Portugal, the United States, and Japan can conquer, administer, [and] lose half the globe without arousing his curiosity. He ignores the Anglo-Indian empire, the greatest colonial achievement in the world.[16]

In addition to his lack of interest, it was difficult for a minister to procure information about other colonial powers because the ministry lacked translators. Every time it sought to learn the content of a document published by another imperial power, it had to send the document to the ministry of foreign affairs for translation—a tedious process which thoroughly dampened curiosity.[17]

The ministry of colonies was not a highly desirable post; when cabinets were formed it was usually one of the last ones filled and usually fell to a time-server or a mediocrity. The personal qualities of the ministers, together with the structure of the administration at Rue Oudinot, made it unlikely that the ministry would closely control overseas officials.

Rather than being made in Paris, colonial policy tended to be made in Dakar, Brazzaville, or Tananarive. In their letter of 1911, functionaries of the ministry of colonies complained that "the minister avoids giving orders to the governors-general and the governors as much as possible." Also—and this they found intolerable—the overseas officials were giving the minister orders.[18] Fifteen years later the journalist Robert Doucet described the ministers as only rubber stamps for the governors-general.[19] A former governor who served in the interwar years confirmed Doucet's description:

In my thirty years in the colonial administration, I never received an instruction from the ministry of colonies. We were the real rulers of the empire; no one told us what to do. In theory, the ministry of colonies had control over everything, but in practice, it did not care to exercise this authority. Its only real function was to receive our requests and recommendations and transform them into decrees. Besides, the minister of colonies was a rather weak character; no one really cared what he thought or what he did. We were the ones who had the authority.[20]

In terms of experience, the governors-general were better equipped than were the ministers to supervise the administrative hierarchy beneath them. Of the nine governors-general serving in AOF between 1904 and World War II, for example, all except Ernest Roume (1902-1908) had previously served overseas, and even he had acquired some knowledge of the colonies as director of political affairs at the ministry. All the other governors-general, in fact, with the exception of Joost Van Vollenhoven (1917), had at some time served in a *cercle*.

But the staff officers of the governors-general were as a rule less well prepared than were the governors-general to handle colonial problems. Until 1913 the governor-generals' staffs consisted of a separate corps, that of the secretariat-general; its tasks were exclusively bureaucratic, and its members received no experience in bush administration. But after that time, the secretariat in the French colonies was merged with the Corps of Colonial Administrators. German and British colonial administration, on the other hand, retained the division between the secretariat and the men in the field. In theory the merger of the secretariat with the Corps meant that the members of the secretariat received experience in the bush while the administrators served some time as desk officers. The members of the secretariat, however, made such deplorable bush administrators that the governors preferred to keep them at desk jobs. When Van Vollenhoven became governor-general, he tried to have all his desk officers serve in the bush; such an experience, he thought, would "renew their ideas, would make them more effective."[21] But others did not follow his procedure, and it was to be several years after World War I before desk officers and bush administrators were interchanged with any regularity.

Surrounded as they were by an inept staff, the governors-general found it difficult to supervise closely the work of their subordinate colonial governors, to say nothing of the individual *commandants*. Instead they spent most of their time coordinating the administration of the colonies that constituted the federation and acting as intermediaries between the individual governors and the ministry of colonies. Engrossed in these bureaucratic tasks, even the most experienced governors-general often had only a vague idea of what was going on in their colonies.

One might assume that the governors could supervise the *commandants de cercles* closely, for they were almost exclusively recruited from the top rank of the Corps of Colonial Administrators. Frequent inspection tours within the colony would have ensured close control over their subordinates, but for the most part the governors were tied down to the colonial capitals writing reports and compiling statistics and, thus like the governors-general, had little control over their subordinates. In any case, travel was difficult; many of the colonies were so large or their roads in such poor condition that during the rainy season some regions were virtually inaccessible. At the turn of the century, it took three months for officials appointed to Oubangui-Tchad during the rainy season to reach their destination. As a rule, the governor regularly supervised only the *cercles* located closest to the administrative capital.

The lack of control by their superiors led the administrators to practice various subterfuges. Eager to win fast promotion by mounting ambitious projects and fearful that these might be vetoed in advance by a cautious governor or an official in Paris, the administrators often kept their superiors ignorant of what they were doing until they had finished whatever project they had begun. One of the main explorers and conquerors of the Sudan, Borgnis-Desbordes, told Leroy-Beaulieu: "When I am on an expedition, my first concern is to cut the telegraph line."[22] Some civilian administrators also adopted this attitude; a number of them deliberately failed to report to their superiors for long periods of time. The commissioner-general of the Congo noted in the late 1880s that one subordinate "hardly writes to me and does not inform me of anything."[23] A few decades later, Governor-General William Ponty described "the old school of administrators" as being composed of those who know "little about official regulations"; and, he could have added, nor care less.[24]

During this early period some administrators took on the airs of proconsuls. The governor of the archipelago of the Comores wrote in 1888 of one of his subordinates:

> He does not understand, and never will, that he is not the real chief, nor the sovereign of the island, but that he is dependent upon the governor of Mayotte. . . . He is just like M . . . who was surprised at not being given the gun salute when he came to Mayotte.[25]

In at least one instance an administrator personalized his authority to such an extent that when he was away from his post, he left his wife in charge, with authority to tax, judge, and imprison the local inhabitants.[26]

The experience of Gallieni in Madagascar at the turn of the century is worth recounting because it illustrates how little the governors could control their subordinates. More than almost any other French colonial official, Gallieni constantly moved around and supervised his own men. Later he described his method:

> In the Sudan I was constantly on horseback, stopping at the most ten days in important places in order to solve on the spot problems which were presented to me. Ten years later in Madagascar I also passed the greatest part of my time travelling by *filanzane* [a chair carried by porters] and later, when the roads permitted travel more easily, by coach, by car, and often by boat.
> "This is what has to be done. In one month I shall return to see if everything is executed." That was the phrase that I constantly pronounced during my long and numerous inspection tours. In this manner all my people were always forewarned, and everyone competed to show me the progress accomplished when I returned.[27]

Yet in spite of all his activity, Gallieni failed to detect and to prevent some of the worst abuses. He had abolished slavery, but his subordinates in Madagascar virtually re-established it disguised as a harsh system of labor dues. Gallieni had ordered that the members of forced labor gangs should be paid and fed regularly, but his orders were so badly executed that during 1896-1897 one-fifth of the local inhabitants employed in public works died.[28]

Governor-General Roume of AOF was dissatisfied with the limited control that the governors were able to establish over their *commandants*, and in 1906 he ordered each governor to appoint an inspector of administrative affairs in his colony who would tour each *cercle* within the colony and report on its administration. The Corps of Colonial Inspectors, under the direct orders of the minister of colonies, was charged with inspecting the whole overseas French establishment, while the local inspectors of administrative affairs were limited to inspecting the administration of the *commandants de cercles*. Roume's plan was sound but, limited by a shortage of personnel, the governors were often unable to spare an administrator as inspector of administrative affairs, or could appoint him for only brief spans of time. In the 1920s and even the 1930s several *cercles* within AOF had still never been visited by an inspector of administrative affairs. Thus, even within the individual colonies, establishing a centralized administration had proved impossible. A high official visiting the Ivory Coast in the 1930s noted the relatively limited control exercised by the governors over the *commandants*; in fact, it seemed to him that the colony "now resembles a federation of *cercles*, which the *commandants* rule according to their own whim."[29]

Accounts of two eminent bush administrators illustrate the relative freedom from their administrative superiors enjoyed by the *commandants*. Maurice Delafosse, who served before World War I, described how he was unable to keep up with the stream of regulations and decrees that were pouring out from the different bureaucratic offices. Finally he decided to ignore them:

I fall peacefully asleep on the growing pile of official journals and explanatory circulars, leaving it to chance to guide me. . . . I administer haphazardly. Sometimes by a lucky coincidence I make the decision which should have been made. Usually I make one that no text, new or old, could justify; then my error usually passes unperceived.[30]

Delavignette approvingly gives an example of an administrator in the 1920s who "stuck departmental circulars in his trouser pockets before he had read them" and then at the end of the day threw them together with his trousers into the linen basket.[31]

The attitudes expressed by Delafosse and Delavignette were by no means foreign to the spirit of the French colonial administration. Both Gallieni and Van Vollenhoven had by their example and writing instilled into the colonial administration a doctrine stressing a maximum of personal initiative by the men serving on the spot. The honor and respect in which both were held by their contemporaries and by later generations of French officials assured for their doctrines an important role in the shaping of French administrative practice. Gallieni first attracted attention by his successful military expedition to the Sudan. Later he effectively established French military domination over the northern part of French Indochina, and in 1896 he was called upon to organize the French administration in Madagascar. His unique personality inspired many anecdotes. In the heat of battle he was known to take out a book of poetry and calmly read from it. His own writings and those of his admiring disciple, Lyautey, showed him to be a passionate man of action, possessing admirable self-control, intense self-reliance, and a deep distrust of red tape and French bureaucracy.

Gallieni wrote that at all points the policy-makers of the hierarchy must seek information and advice from local administrators and give them maximum leeway. "The higher administration must depend upon the good sense and the initiative of territorial commanders who are in direct contact with the local population."[32] Disliking red tape, Gallieni declared in a famous dictum: "Our administrators and officials must defend, in the name of good sense, the interests with which they are charged, and must not fight them in the name of regulations."[33] In an equally celebrated passage, Lyautey recounted how as a young man in Indochina he had first met Gallieni. He had been assigned to Gallieni's headquarters, and on the first evening, Colonel Gallieni asked if Lyautey had brought with him the manual of regulations. When Lyautey said he had, the colonel asked for the manual, packed it up in gray paper and told his newly acquired disciple: "I shall send all of this to Hanoi. I do not want you to be tempted to look at it while you are with me; these breviaries would only confuse you; it is on the spot, while commanding men and things, that you will learn your profession."[34] While encouraging trusted subordinates such as Lyautey to be independent, Gallieni still supervised closely the men under his command. If in practice he did not always adhere to his own doctrine, that doctrine gained importance in its own right, since it was widely read and admired by colonial administrators.

Van Vollenhoven's message was similar to that of Gallieni. The son of Dutch parents living in Algeria who had become naturalized French citizens, Van Vollenhoven graduated at the top of his class at the *Ecole Coloniale* in 1903. The tall, blond, and quiet student won the admiration of his peers and teachers by his earnestness and brilliance. His law thesis on the Algerian peasantry was acclaimed by several colonial authorities. Rather than go overseas, Van Vollenhoven entered the central administration in Paris, where he impressed his superiors by his hard work. He received unusually rapid advancement and was made interim governor of Guinea and then Senegal in 1907, when he was only thirty years old. In 1914 he became France's youngest governor-general when he was appointed to administer Indochina, and three years later he took over the post of governor-general of AOF. However, he soon resigned that position to fight in the trenches,[35] where he died a hero's death for his adopted country. This premature end to his brilliant career gave Van Vollenhoven a kind of sacrosanct position in the minds of most French colonial administrators.[36] In brief and forceful circulars, which were cited by French governors until the very end of the colonial era, Van Vollenhoven

JOOST VAN VOLLENHOVEN

expressed the need for an administration freed from theory and adapted to the realities of the local situation. He mistrusted desk-bound administrators, and emphasized the importance of giving a free hand to the men in the field who had daily contact with the local realities. "To attempt to administer a colony by decrees from behind a desk," he wrote, "is really nonsense."[37] At another time he declared, "Only one's presence, personal contact, counts. The circular is zero."[38]

If the nature of the administrative structure itself and an influential strain of colonial doctrine tended to emphasize the importance of the man on the spot—that is, the *commandant*—then we must note the formal powers delegated to him. He was given wide powers, because in the end he was the man charged with transforming into reality on the local scene the schemes of his superiors either in the colonial capitals or in Paris.

The instructions issued by the governor of the Sudan in 1897 give a vivid idea of the multiple functions the administrators were required to fulfill. These instructions informed the administrators that they were the governor's representatives in all official business and were in charge of supervising tax collection in their *cercles* and of assuring "a wise growth in the revenue of the local budget." They were the sole civil officers and drew up all official acts. Each administrator was expected to take a census, map his region, and draw up an inventory of its soil, agriculture, mines, and forests. Construction of public works—roads, bridges, caravan routes, wells, and marketplaces—was an important function. So also was education, for the administrator must direct the French primary schools and survey the Islamic ones. He was expected to help the local population by offering advice for the improvement of agriculture, by encouraging the growth of rubber and cotton, and by helping to destroy locusts. In the Northern Sudan he was even expected to establish ostrich farms for the plumed hats of Europe.[39]

A manual issued in the Sudan in 1911 established further tasks for the administrators. It ordered them to visit every village in their *cercles* at least once a year and to act as propagandists for French colonization by informing the local populations of the benefits they enjoyed as a result of French rule: light taxes, complete safety of travel, and liberation from former tyrannical rule. The administrators were also to encourage local self-improvement in the villages, preaching the merits of hard work, advising as to suitable crops, and encouraging the villagers to produce for the commercial market.[40]

These multifarious functions made the administrators truly "jacks of all trades," as one governor called them. Delafosse drew up an imposing list of the many roles that the administrator was called upon to fill: "secretary, accountant, tax collector, judge, notary, bailiff, road surveyor, architect, mason, carpenter, gardener, postman, transportation agent, army supply sergeant, horse dealer, physician, meteorologist, male nurse, pharmacist, topographer, corporal, police commissioner, inspector of the *sûreté*. . . ."[41] Even the many-faceted Renaissance man, he remarked, would hardly have possessed enough talents for the French empire.

In addition to his administrative tasks, the *commandant* combined executive and judicial functions: after apprehending criminals, he had to try them as well. In civil cases he presided over the traditional courts. By a decree of September 30, 1887,[42] the *indigénat* code was established which gave colonial administrators disciplinary powers over all "natives" who were not French citizens. The *indigénat* code had already been in use in Algeria in the 1840s. In order to ensure their authority, the officers of the *bureaux arabes* had been given the right to impose fines or short prison terms without trial for actions that would not have been considered unlawful in France. The law of 1887 set the limit of punishment under the *indigénat* at fifteen days in jail or a 100-franc fine. The offenses punishable under the *indigénat* system were clearly defined. In time, the list increased; by 1888 it included sixteen different offenses.[43]

The *indigénat* was considered indispensable for the smooth functioning of the administration. Twenty-five years after its adoption, Governor-General Ponty described it as "a summary but indispensable means of repression in a country only recently occupied" whose population was "as yet primitive." In time, however, Ponty hoped that the *indigénat* code would be employed less frequently and rigorously "as the country becomes civilized, as the natives evolve, and as the regular courts are charged with the cases."[44]

The *indigénat* code has often been indicted for its harshness. By specifying the punishable offenses and their respective punishments, however, the code was intended, within an authoritarian framework, to set limits to the powers which the administrators could exercise over the people they ruled. But too frequently they failed to respect those limitations. The *indigénat* did not allow flogging as a punishment, but it was used with some frequency before World War I. Although imprisonment was limited to only fourteen days, administrators were known to give cumulative sentences of several fourteen-day periods. In order to ensure that the administrators would not impose unfair fines, they were required to keep a book where they inscribed all cases in which they had used their disciplinary powers. Some administrators, however, hid their own excesses by not registering them in their books. In 1904 Governor-General Roume of AOF sent a circular to the administrators in which he charged them with having failed to utilize the *indigénat* in the manner in which it had been intended, and he called on the administrators to be more careful and systematic in obeying the limitations of the law.[45]

The main fault of the authoritarian judicial system which the French had established was the lack of recourse against the whims of the administrators, for, as Roume noted, "the native has no way of appealing his punishment."[46] In 1912 Roume's successor Ponty also found it necessary to admonish the administrators for their misuse of the *indigénat*; there had been too many cases of excessive punishment, he wrote.[47] Two years later Ponty complained again about the same malpractices. He observed that there was no uniform application of the disciplinary punishments, but rather that they varied from *cercle* to *cercle*, depending on the whims of the individual administrators. The use of the *indigénat* in the Ivory Coast he singled out as being "incontestably too severe."[48]

If individual administrators may be blamed for acts of brutality the metropole also bears its fair share of responsibility. For Parliament, while proclaiming French ideals of colonization, provided only limited funds for the colonies.

In the 1820s the treasury of each colony paid its expenses from local tax and customs revenues; when these resources were not sufficient, the metropole paid the difference. After the middle of the nineteenth century the colonial treasuries were saddled with an increasing proportion of the expenses; the mother country paid only those that could strictly be considered "expenses of sovereignty," such as the salary of the administrative personnel. After the expansion of the empire in the late nineteenth century Parliament considered even those costs too burdensome and by a law of April 13, 1900, it established the principle that "all civil expenses including that of the gendarmerie should be supported by the budgets of the colonies."[49]

The French government financed a decreasing proportion of colonial expenditures. In 1896, the budget of the French colonies had totaled 175 million francs, of which 45 percent had been contributed by the metropole; in 1910 the total budgets of the colonies had doubled to 355.7 million francs. But in 1910, the metropole contributed nearly the same sum as fifteen years earlier—and now it represented only 25 percent of the colonial expenses.[50]

Only with the greatest reluctance did the metropole finance deficits. Since the governors were strongly encouraged to balance their budgets they minimized expenditures while heavily taxing local resources. As part of the tax burden, the French imposed forced labor on all colonies. In Madagascar during Gallieni's rule part of the tax burden amounted to fifty days of labor a year for every adult male; later it was reduced to thirty days. In AOF the heavy contingents of forced labor drafted to build the

Dakar-Niger railroad disrupted the lives of people in whole regions; in the words of the minister of colonies "villages have been partly deserted ... and harvests nearly abandoned."[51]

The railroad, to be sure, was built for the purpose of helping the French West African colonies develop, but in some cases forced labor was employed for totally useless projects. In one instance an administrator used thousands of labor days to construct an imposing but unnecessary plaza in the capital of his *cercle*; another built bridges which, because of his ignorance of architecture, soon collapsed.

Frequently the administrators, insensitive to the needs of the local populations, imposed excessive taxes upon them. This practice was blamed by an inspector for the series of violent uprisings that broke out in the Sudan during World War I. To varying degrees, wrote the inspector, the French administrators in the Sudan conceived of the Africans' duties

... to be boundless while their rights on the other hand are reduced to nothing. With what rigor taxes are levied in many cases! And in the *cercles*, the *prestations*, the *portages*, how often are they misapplied! It is so easy to impose them....[52]

In addition to a head tax, the administration taxed certain forms of property, such as cattle and rice fields, forcing the populations to enter a money economy. Colonial officials—French and others—made the necessity of raising taxes a virtue; they saw it as having economic, social, and educational value, since it forced the colonial populations to seek employment or to cultivate crops for a commercial market.[53]

In the French empire the taxation system was probably hardest on the Congolese—the poorest colonial people with the least means of providing goods or labor. Almost their only source of cash came from working for the private rubber plantations, which ruthlessly dictated prices for the rubber collected. Before the war, the head tax in the Congo was eight francs a year; it was estimated in 1919 that in order to collect enough rubber to yield this tax money, the inhabitants had to work between sixty and one hundred twenty days a year, depending on the area in which the rubber was collected.[54]

The dire needs of the budget in the Congo explain to a high degree some of the atrocities that occurred there. In 1903, Emil Gentil, the commissioner-general of the Congo, sent a circular to all administrators informing them that their promotions depended on their ability to raise taxes. Spurred by this incentive, officials resorted to harsh means. Often on their tax collection trips they found that all the males had abandoned the village at their approach and in reprisal they took children and women as hostages, releasing them only when the taxes had been paid. The system of hostages must have been sanctioned by the commissioner-general, for he had provided funds for the building of hostage camps in the colony's budget. These camps were inadequate for the number of hostages they held, and a large number died because of maltreatment. In one case, a village that did not pay its taxes was raided and sixty-eight hostages taken; through the intervention of a doctor they were released five weeks later, but only twenty-one were found alive. The rest had died of asphyxiation and starvation.[55] The administrator who was responsible for this camp was tried in court, but was found not guilty and was transferred to another post.[56] Such incidents, as Brazza noted, were not isolated phenomena.[57]

Thus it seems clear that both the metropole and the administrators in the field warrant a share of blame. The mother-country by its niggardly economic policy forced the administrators in the field to be dependent upon the limited financial capacity of the colonies; and it did not show sufficient concern for the methods employed in raising the needed funds. The administrators, in their concern to raise their quota of the budget, forgot Gallieni's dictum that their first obligation was to the people they ruled rather than to administrative regulations. The administrators often enough asserted their independence from superior rule, but they seem to have done so mainly to give themselves greater elbow room. Too few administrators used their independence for the benefit of the colonial populations.

This lack of concern reflected in part the absence of a clearly defined colonial doctrine which at most consisted of vague notions about the benefits that French rule bestowed on the colonial populations. Governor-General Ponty called the form of benevolent paternalism practiced by the French a policy of "taming."[58] But ideas like Ponty's did little more than stress the need for continued French control over its empire; the ideas were incapable of guiding or inspiring the administrators in their daily activities.

The Corps was recruited from too many sources to enable its members to share a common ideal. While many of the *Ecole Coloniale* graduates may have been filled with the mystique of humanitarianism which J. F. Reste described, too few recruits came from the school before World War I. Rather, most of the administrators were men who for one reason or another found themselves overseas; becoming an administrator provided but a convenient promotion rather than the opportunity for the exercise of a special vocation or mission.

A doctrine did evolve, however, regarding methods of "native rule": this was the doctrine of association. The colonial theory of assimilation which assumed that the overseas territories would be made over in the image of France, had been formed in the metropole, and had been advocated by the *Ecole Coloniale*; but in the early 1900s the theory of association was adopted—an indication of the ascendancy gained by the men in the field—the colonial military officers and civilian administrators. These men had discovered societies that were fundamentally different both in their political and social organization and in their level of economic development from those existing in Europe. Rather than make Frenchmen out of the colonial populations, French rule, the associationists urged, should tutor the colonial societies and help them evolve according to their own potentialities. France was to associate herself with the colonial societies. The doctrine of association, claiming the need for respect of the local societies, implied the need for instituting indirect rule—that is, rule through the indigenous political structures.

There were a few French officials in Africa who advocated a shift to indirect rule. Most of them had served in Indochina in the 1890s, where they had come under the influence of Governor-General Jean Marie de Lanessan. Echoing the thought of a long line of French officials in Indochina, de Lanessan had established the classical French argument for indirect rule:

Instead of dissolving the old group of rulers, one should use them; govern with the mandarin and not against him. Since we are and always shall be but an infinite minority, we cannot attempt to substitute ourselves [for them] but at the very most [we can] direct and control [them]. Thus, [we must] not injure any tradition nor change any habits, [but] remind ourselves that in all societies there is a ruling class born to rule, without which nothing can be done.[59]

There were, however, relatively few disciples of de Lanessan's doctrine, for although most administrators claimed to be advocates of the doctrine of association, only a few were willing to accept its logical correlate—indirect rule.

In stressing the uniqueness of the colonies, many administrators wanted only to ensure that the colonies would not, as in metropolitan France, be provided democratic controls over the administrative system. Thus, association was but the continuation of a policy of domination through the exercise of paternal authoritarianism.

Although a doctrine of indirect rule had developed, the men in the field often negated its basic assumptions. The French policy of association was similar to that of indirect rule advocated by the British, but it was less often practiced.

The differences in administrative practice of the two colonial services were due in part to different national traditions. In Britain the benefits of local rule in England were widely believed in—especially by the class of men who went overseas. This system, it was claimed, allowed local problems in Britain to be dealt with by men who were intimately acquainted with them. It saved the government from making excessive expenditures, and by limiting the central functions of the state, it limited its authority and thus presumably created the personal freedom which the British people valued. In France local rule was never seen in this light. In a continental country threatened by its neighbors, local rule was considered a centrifugal force undermining the unity of the nation. In its history the French people found ample evidence to show that local rights were upheld by feudal and retrogressive forces, while progressive forces were represented by central authority. In France, until recently, centralization has been considered a good system, and local rule a perilous one which gave the enemies of the state a base from which to challenge it. In effect, one can say that both colonial powers put into practice the policy of assimilation, for both powers attempted to establish overseas an administrative pattern similar to that existing in the homeland; the difference lay in the content of the policies, which was due to the differing traditions of the mother countries themselves.[60]

The original traditions of colonial rule for the two powers were also quite different. In British India and Nigeria—two areas which served as models for subsequent British rule—company rule had preceded government administration. Concerned with economical administration, companies in India and Nigeria established a minimal rule similar to that later labeled indirect rule. Government administration adopted company methods; in Nigeria, Lord Lugard drew heavily on administrative traditions established by George Goldie's Royal Niger Company. In the eighteenth century there had been company rule in French Senegal, but it had limited itself strictly to trade and had not been involved in ruling the local populations. If there had been French company rule, its administration, out of purely economic considerations, would probably have adopted methods similar to those of British or Dutch company rule—preserving the public peace with as little interference as possible in local political structures.

Much of British expansion overseas was pursued out of political and strategic necessity, but French expansion was to a larger extent actively motivated by a desire to affirm national vitality.[61] And for this to become a reality seemed to require widespread and firm control over the colonies. The traditions of the *ancien régime*, of Napoleon, and of the Republic required that administrative control be pervasive and absolute. Anything less would be an abdication of power and influence. In a parliamentary debate in 1888, Eugène Etienne made this point of view clear when he argued that officials in Indochina should exercise full authority, rather than serve as mere "advisers" to the local rulers. The latter, he declared, would be a *"politique d'effacement"* (abdication of authority; loss of face).[62]

The social backgrounds of the two colonial services also contributed to the differing manner in which they treated local authority. Although perhaps not sons of the most distinguished members of British society, nevertheless a very large number of British administrators could identify themselves with the gentry. And their education confirmed them in their aristocratic pretensions: a very large proportion were Oxbridge graduates.[63] Perhaps an even greater sign of their gentlemanly education was the large number who were graduates of the public schools.[64] Identified with the gentry and gentry values, the British administrators had a nostalgic sympathy for the local chiefs, while the French colonial administrators, most of whom came from the middle and lower middle classes, had a bourgeois disdain for everything that was reminiscent of feudalism or monarchism. The exigencies of colonial situations had their own ironies, sometimes requiring a French administrator of noble blood to crush a chief or unseat a king, and sometimes putting a commoner in the position of defending traditional rule. Delavignette described it best when he wrote:

Cavalry Sergeant de la Tour Saint-Ygest, who may have left France because he suffers from the equality brought by the revolution, goes to Upper Senegal-Niger to destroy the Tuaregs—that is, the feudality, the principles and feelings of which are dear to him. On the other hand, the representative of the powers of the Republic in Dakar, a member of French Masonry and the Radical Socialist party, will on the spot, in Africa, be an authoritarian governor, and he will use autocratic methods of rule to lead the natives toward progress.[65]

In general, however, the French administrators were ideologically hostile to the local chiefs. Even Delavignette stated:

Many administrators wanted to treat the feudal lords in the same way we had treated them during the French revolution. It was either break them or use them for our purposes. The British administrators had more sympathy for the feudal lords; it was aristocracy respecting aristocracy.[66]

Most French administrators were suspicious of the local chiefs and regarded them as backward, feudal elements of unreliable loyalty to France and exploitative of the local populations. The statement made by Louis Binger, the explorer and later governor of the Ivory Coast, about the desirability of suppressing the chiefs, was generally shared by the colonial administration:

When a chief is called *Damel, Brack, Bour, Massa, Almany,* or *Naba* [different royal titles in West Africa], once he commands a population of more than 25,000 people, he must be suppressed, for otherwise he will destroy instead of organize and regenerate.[67]

Republican officials going to the colonies had an inherent suspicion of feudal institutions. Many French officials overseas saw it as their mission to free the local populations from their feudal rulers. In Madagascar, where the Hovas had imposed their rule over the other ethnic groups, Gallieni instituted a policy known as *la politique de race*; he suppressed the Hova chiefs, replacing them with others chosen from among local ethnic groups. This policy was also carried out in West Africa; in the decade preceding World War I Governor-General William Ponty carried on an ambitious program to crush the chiefdoms. He advocated the need to

fight the influence of the local aristocracies in such a manner as to assure us of the sympathy of the multitudes, and suppress the great native chiefs who are nearly always a barrier between us and the administered masses.[68]

Ponty's attitude—as that of Gallieni and others—was formed in the Sudan. The struggle against El Hadj Omar in the 1860s and then against Samory in the 1880s and 1890s gave the French a unique view of the African chief. As Lombard writes, the Sudanese experience gave French officials the impression of the African chief as a "fanatic warrior, tyrannizing the populations around him and dominating them by force."[69] In a speech to Parliament in 1894, Delcassé declared the need to free the colonial masses "trembling under oppression." And he added, "We must substitute the beneficial unity of the French genius for the many violent tyrannies of kings . . . or chiefs."[70] Later Governor-General Ponty, who had served in the Sudan for several years, wrote his governors in a circular:

My long experience in West Africa among the black populations has permitted me to conclude in the clearest fashion, and you have certainly made the same observation, that the native intermediaries between the mass of the population and the administrators of the *cercles* or their subordinates are usually nothing but parasites living on the population and existing without profit to the treasury.[71]

Ponty's observation was reflected in the reduction of several important chiefdoms in AOF; in Guinea, for example, the prestigious chiefs of Labé and the Futa Djallon were removed. In some *cercles* his policy was so meticulously practiced that the chiefs were dismissed without being replaced; in one *cercle* an administrator abolished the *chefs de canton*, the intermediary chiefs between the village chiefs and the administrator, thus having to give direct orders to 1,085 village chiefs. He explained:

I am not in favor of creating a *chef de canton*. The more intermediaries there are between the taxpayers and the tax collector, the more chance there is that the money will be lost on the way. The notions of individualism, of personal obligations and rights, must be spread among the Africans.[72]

For practical purposes of administration, except for rare instances as the above, the office of *chef de canton* was generally retained. But the administrators determined the geographic limits of the canton, the powers of the chiefs, and the persons who should occupy the position. Former kingdoms like the Futa Djallon were carved up into several cantons; the purpose of this division, as an administrative report put it, was to "Divide in order to rule."[73]

Where the cantons were allowed to be coextensive with the former royal territory, the ruling house was dethroned or at least an amenable member of the family put in place of the former chief. In some cases, the administrator appointed his own houseboy or an interpreter as chief.[74] Village chiefs were usually not meddled with; they were allowed to stay on unless convicted of malfeasance.

It was obviously not only policy drawn up in the colonial capitals or the different appointments and dismissals of chiefs by the administrators that influenced the evolution of the French policy toward the chiefs. More important were the attitudes exhibited by the administrators themselves in their daily contacts with the chiefs. They felt a keen pride in French culture, and usually refused to show public respect or pay homage to the chiefs. Many of the administrators serving before World War I shared the feelings that Binger had expressed in 1892 after having made his exploratory trip in the lower Sudan region:

I feel that a white man travelling in this country, whoever he may be, should not prostrate himself before a black king, however powerful the latter may be. It is necessary that a white man should inspire respect and consideration wherever he goes; for if the Europeans should ever come here, they should come as masters, as the superior class of society, and not have to bow their heads before indigenous chiefs to whom they are definitely superior in all respects.[75]

And this kind of pride was not necessarily triggered by ignorance of local institutions or by an exaggerated dedication to assimilatory values. A man like Messimy, who could speak with feeling of the value of local institutions and traditions in the colonies and the need to help the indigenous populations evolve within their own civilizations,[76] announced in a flight of rhetoric in the very same book:

We must make countries out of these empty spaces, we must make nations out of these agglomerations of half-civilized or barbarian peoples, we must organize new states, give them traditions, morals, a political and social organization.[77]

There were few colonial officials who at heart did not consider the traditional political institutions undesirable. And they made no effort to show the chiefs any special mark of deference. Van Vollenhoven noted that chiefs were sometimes made to wait for hours outside the French administrator's office, only to be received brusquely by the latter's subordinate.[78] In a number of cases the administrators did not hesitate to slap the chiefs publicly.[79] When suspected of malfeasance, the chiefs were treated as common criminals; in Madagascar, former Hova chiefs who had been convicted of embezzlement were put into the same chain gangs as their subjects. An administrator who served in the 1920s attested to this general lack of respect for the indigenous chiefs:

We did not take the feudal lords very seriously; we found them rather ridiculous. After the French revolution we could not be expected to return to the middle ages.... We just used to slap them on the back and were rather familiar with them.[80]

Of course, this attitude was not always transformed into policy. In certain areas the French found it convenient to preserve the traditional authority and to try to rule through it. In Upper Volta the office of Mogo Naba (emperor of the Mossi) was preserved; in acephalous societies in the Congo, chiefs who had performed only religious functions were given a political authority which they had never previously possessed. A chief's power in the precolonial era was sometimes limited by local intrigues and the potential of popular revolt. The establishment of French rule automatically removed these former restraints and thus in a sense strengthened the chiefs.[81] Nevertheless, even when this occurred, the administrators hardly ever thought of the traditional structures as having intrinsic and lasting merit, as did the British proponents of indirect rule.

Whatever the French administrators' perception of power may have been, as Professor Brian Weinstein so brilliantly demonstrates, the local realities of power may have been quite different.[82] In Oubangui, for example, Félix Eboué, while serving as an administrator in the years immediately preceding World War I, thought he was exploiting local rivalries to consolidate French rule. At the same time, however, the local inhabitants were conveniently invoking French aid to liquidate traditional feuds. It would be hard to decide whether the local inhabitants, or the representative of the French republic, held the upper hand in this particular relationship. Administrators did not always manipulate local chiefs; sometimes it was the chiefs who manipulated the French officials. And administrators could not, because of limitation in their number and turnover of personnel, be as all-powerful as some of them desired.[83]

In several regions French rule led to the breakdown of the chief-system. In the precolonial era the chiefs had often been able to rule by means of consensus but under French pressure they were forced to squeeze taxes and labor dues from their subjects. Their traditional basis of rule was further undermined as they became little more than French functionaries, and the loss of the chief's traditional prestige and authority sometimes made it difficult for the French to use them to control the local populations effectively.[84] In 1912, after having reduced the chiefs, French administration in Labé, Guinea, "gave the impression of being completely powerless."[85]

If chiefly traditional authority broke down, it is worth repeating that the French presence often bolstered and strengthened the powers of chiefs in some regions, especially those in which chiefly power had been on the wane, or in which there had been no previous tradition of a larger political state. But in the face of the breakdown, or alleged breakdown, of the traditional chief-system, a number of colonial officials advised that the local hierarchies be preserved. But this advice was qualified in such a manner that it continued to limit the chiefs' authority; they were to be considered only as auxiliaries of the French administration. Gallieni, generally considered an advocate of indirect rule, wrote his administrators:

The native chief [is] to be closely watched, and to be controlled in all his acts, which sometimes are directed by insatiable greed and by personal interests. Whatever the inconvenience they may cause us, it is generally better to conserve this ghost of power to which the native is more accustomed and behind whom we can maneuver more conveniently. A little judgment in choosing him, a little ability in knowing how to incite his self-interest and ambition, will even sometimes make him a useful auxiliary.[86]

And Joost Van Vollenhoven, who as governor-general of French West Africa in 1917 did a great deal to encourage better treatment of the chiefs and a strengthening of the chieftain system, nevertheless concluded:

There are not two authorities in the *cercle*, the French authority and the native authority. There is only one; the *commandant de cercle* commands; only he is responsible. The native chief is only an instrument, an auxiliary.[87]

The adoption of the doctrine of association after 1900 had meant for the metropole the establishment of an administration more sensitive to the local needs of the colonial populations. The colonial administration, purposely decentralized, left nearly full powers to the local *commandants*. Often hostile to the local political structures they rejected indirect rule, although it was implicit in the doctrine of association. Using the full powers entrusted to them, many French administrators crushed the old political structures in the colonies and substituted their own autocratic rule.

While the metropole proclaimed vague goals about the French mission of civilization (for which, incidentally, it refused to make any serious financial contributions) the administrators were permitted to govern according to their whims and inclinations.

The decentralized administrative structure virtually gave a free hand to the man who wanted to build a bridge, establish a schoolhouse, or help increase local peanut production; it also gave the administrator in the bush nearly the same freedom to wreak destruction around him. Alone, living without supervision, and possessing nearly total powers, some of the officials serving in this early era were prone to strange impulses. Like Kurtz, the fictional character in Joseph Conrad's *Heart of Darkness*, some administrators, freed from the inhibitions of Europe, found a world of unlimited possibilities in which nothing was forbidden. Delafosse well described the process:

These [brutal men] are ... in our midst, we meet them constantly in the street, and also in the best frequented salons, but their instincts are not revealed, because they are repressed; therefore, these people while in Europe may live and die with an unblemished reputation for perfect honesty. Throw them into the bush without control, freed from the obligations which in France controlled every one of their acts, every one of their gestures; give them an authority which turns their heads, and beyond that demand results without specifying the normal means of attaining them, and these same men who had been honest in Europe, become criminals in Africa.[88]

Too seldom was the administration in Paris, or even the higher administration in the colonies, able to check acts of serious brutality. The investigations made after World War I of the events that led to the uprising in Dédougou, Sudan, in 1915-1916 read like a catalogue of horrors. The report found the *commandant* guilty of the following activities:

Serious maltreatment in several cases, followed by death. . . .
Young native girl raped. . . .
Villages partially burnt in 1914 . . .
Inhabitants imprisoned or transferred to Dédougou for forced labor. .
Natives beaten in December 1914. Arbitrary detention of one of these natives. False judgment of the court. . . . Fine irregularly levied. . . .
Native prisoner strangled in January 1916.
Two native prisoners strangled in February 1916.
Accounting irregular.
Expenditure of 11,995 francs supported by counterfeit receipts.[89]

In spite of the evidence, an administrative court of inquiry acquitted the *commandant*, putting the blame on his subordinates. Enough charges, however, remained for the administrator to be tried by a civil court for the murder of one of his prisoners and for the embezzlement of local funds. In reply to the murder charge, his defense cited as extenuating circumstances the administrator's overwork. As for the embezzlement, that evidently was common enough not to be noticed. The administrator was acquitted, later promoted, and upon his retirement in the late 1920s, was allowed to reach the top rank.[90]

Less serious offenses such as embezzlement, or at least false book accounting, seem to have been relatively common in the French colonies before the war. Some administrators apparently had two accounts, one official, and another secret, known as the *caisse noire*. Sometimes an administrator might have a pet project, a road, a bridge, or an agricultural project that did not receive sanction from the governor's office. In order to finance it, he would falsify his account, or raise illegal taxes. In a particular case the act might be useful, but such irregular bookkeeping meant that the administrators could also pocket *cercle* funds. The problem of the *caisses noires* was so serious that when Angoulvant became governor of the Ivory Coast in 1908 he questioned every administrator in the colony about his particular accounting. He was able to get "from several among them confessions of occult accounting," and he ordered them to surrender all their secret funds to the colony's treasury. Angoulvant promised the administrators immunity from prosecution, but he warned them of the consequences if they persisted in their activities. Seven years later Angoulvant noted that there had been little change; the administrators were still continuing the practice of double bookkeeping.[91]

The ministry in Paris and the governors in the colonies seem to have accepted with relative resignation the irresponsibility and brutality of many of the overseas functionaries. An administrator in the Congo in the

1890s had been certified by the colony's doctor as not being "in full possession of his mental faculties because of an overdose of certain drugs and alcohol"; he had burnt down two villages and his favorite sport seems to have been taking pot shots at people imprudent enough to walk past his residence. He was retained in the service, and he continued to spread terror.[92] An administrator in Senegal, noted as a chronic alcoholic in 1911, was allowed to serve fourteen more years until his death in 1925.[93]

Since most of the colonies were only recently conquered and "pacified," the administration did not seem to think they required better functionaries than they had. When in 1909 the governor of Dahomey was asked to describe the morality of one of his administrators serving in what was then a solitary post, he wrote, "Acceptable for Ouidah."[94]

Because so many of the administrators were of poor quality, a governor when dissatisfied with his subordinates found that his only option was to recommend transferral to another colony. When practiced by all colonies, this policy—baptized by one governor the *"politique de débarras"*—could lead to some ironic situations. The governor-general of AOF transferred an administrator accused of megalomania and rape to Madagascar;[95] in exchange he asked for an administrator from the island colony. The governor-general of Madagascar in turn used this opportunity to rid himself of one of his worst administrators, an embezzler with a former criminal record.[96] Thus neither governor-general had gained very much.

No matter how inefficient or brutal, most administrators were considered good enough for service in the Congo. That colony until 1914 was the receptacle for administrators unwanted in other French territories. When an administrator in Guinea was noted as having become "bizarre," he was transferred to the Congo[97]; another was sent there when his governor discovered that he was a neurotic[98]; and a drug addict and several alcoholics were banished to that colony.[99]

According to Corps regulations, an administrator suspected of malfeasance was to be investigated by a commission of inquiry consisting of fellow administrators within the colony. But as the governor of Dahomey angrily observed in 1915, these commissions nearly without exception were prejudiced in favor of the accused functionary, and mitigating circumstances were found for nearly every act of maladministration.[100] Because of the leniency of the commissions of inquiry, dismissal from the Corps was rarely recommended. Of 891 administrators joining the Corps between 1887 and 1910, only five were dismissed; twenty-two resigned but undoubtedly some of those did so under duress. In addition to its poor quality, the colonial administration also frequently suffered from a shortage in personnel. In 1898, for example, the commissioner-general of the Congo informed the minister of colonies that out of nineteen officials assigned to the Congo, six were in France, or preparing to go there; the four best were in Chad and Oubangui; three were occupied with special nonadministrative functions; of the six remaining, one had to be dropped from the service, one was being investigated for suspicious activities, two were in poor health, and one could not be trusted alone. "There remains," as the commissioner put it, "only one administrator capable of exercising a command."[101] A small number of administrators thus carried the burden of administering a colony. Their duties and the climate often took its toll. When Brazza visited Gabon in 1905 he found the administrators there to be "physically and mentally exhausted and incapable of serving."[102]

The deficiencies of the French administration before World War I were probably not peculiar to it. No study on a file-by-file basis has been made, for instance, of the entire British colonial service, but such an enterprise might yield unexpected results. Historians may have adopted too uncritically the self-image that British administrators had of themselves as being "plain, tolerant, gentlemanly men; they were on the whole just, and they were totally incorruptible."[103]

The rather negative picture presented here of the French administrators who served overseas before 1914 should not obscure the men of high quality and character who were members of the Corps. There was Henry d'Arboussier, a graduate of the *Ecole Coloniale* in 1898, who served most of his career in the Sudanic regions. He spoke fluent Arabic, Fulani, and Bambara. A good horseman, he frequently toured his *cercle* and knew it intimately. According to his superiors' reports, he was very popular in his region. While administering the area which later became known as Upper Volta he established friendly relations with the Mogo Naba—so cordial that during the war the Mossi emperor offered d'Arboussier a cavalry force of 500 men with which he won Togo from the Germans.[104]

Some administrators were deeply interested in encouraging local crop production. An official serving in Senegal who entered the Corps in 1910 had planted and developed fruit trees, peanuts, and manioc in several *cercles*. He and others like him helped develop the local economy.[105] An administrator in Guinea who entered the Corps after serving as an agent in the Sudan was described in 1918 as "loving the natives and exercising great authority over them. He desires to see them evolve rapidly, especially economically."[106] The top graduate of the *Ecole Coloniale* in 1904 served fourteen years in Madagascar before going to the Ivory Coast where he won his superior's praise as "the ideal of what an administrator can be: just, thoughtful, untiringly active, loyal, of superior intelligence."[107] Educated administrators were not the only ones of high quality. A judge's son with no secondary education served for nine years as an agent before entering the Corps in 1908; his governor-general characterized him as a "good administrator. Likes the natives and knows how to be liked by them."[108]

One can multiply the examples of hard-working, conscientious men who served as colonial administrators. Unfortunately, however, a large proportion of the administrators before World War I were men of relatively poor quality. Fortunately for the empire, the methods of recruitment and training that had been developed on the eve of the war produced after 1920 men who were better qualified and had a more abiding concern for the welfare of the colonial populations.

V The Colonial School and the New Generation

A decree promulgated in 1912 shaped the basic recruiting practices of the Corps of Colonial Administrators for over a quarter of a century. This decree, it will be remembered, had given the *Ecole Coloniale* a monopoly over the training of all administrators; it required that cadets attend the school for two years, and that lower colonial officials (the agents of civil affairs) take a one-year training program before becoming eligible for appointment into the Corps. Because of the monopoly of the *Ecole Coloniale*, it is important to study the school and the changes it underwent in the period between the two world wars. With the outbreak of the war in 1914, the school was temporarily closed, and its ninety students were mobilized. A measure of the cadets' brave "spirit of sacrifice," as a military citation was to put it,[1] may be seen in the fact that twenty-six, or nearly a third of the cadets who had been attending the school when war broke out, were killed. Thirty-eight graduates of the school, including four who had graduated at the head of their classes (among them Van Vollenhoven), were also killed.

During the war the Corps was short of manpower. A high proportion of administrators left the colonies to return to fight in Europe; and others needed to be relieved of their posts overseas where they had served as long as six consecutive years without furlough. German Togo and a part of the Cameroons were conquered by French troops, thus adding to the French administrative burden. Very few new recruits entered the Corps during the war.

Because of the lack of personnel, the officials of the ministry of colonies found it necessary to find new ways to fill the Corps. One method used was to waive temporarily the requirement that the agents attend the *Ecole Coloniale*, but even so, only a few were promoted into the Corps.

After 1912 Rue Oudinot was convinced of the virtues of the training given at the *Ecole Coloniale*. Furthermore, the record of the school's cadets and graduates during the war seemed additional proof of the school's success. As a result, the ministry of colonies continued to insist that all the men entering the Corps (except the agents) be trained by the *Ecole Coloniale*, although the period of study during the war was reduced. Cadets who had already attended the school for a year were appointed as administrators immediately after their release from the army, while cadets who had been admitted to the *Ecole Coloniale*, but had been drafted before entering it, were required to take only a one-year program before being appointed as administrators. A decree issued in 1917 provided that wounded soldiers with a baccalaureate degree or its equivalent and who were physically fit for colonial service could enter it after serving overseas as agents for a short period and undergoing a six-months' training program at the *Ecole Coloniale*. Approximately twenty-five wounded veterans entered the Corps under this option.

These were stopgap measures, but once the war was over, the administration returned to peacetime methods of recruitment. Beginning in 1921 the agents were again required to undergo a regular one-year training program at the *Ecole Coloniale* before being appointed as administrators, and the cadets returned to the regular two-year training program.

Immediately after the war there was a noticeable drop in the number of candidates applying for admission. In 1919 the school wanted to accept thirty-eight students, a record number, but only twenty-seven candidates took the entrance examinations. The number increased somewhat in 1920, but it still fell short of the pre-1914 figure.

Before the war there had been three candidates for every post, but in the early 1920s there were only two.[2] The professional association of colonial administrators found cause for worry in this state of affairs, and its president asserted that the major cause for the decline was economic:

Before 1914 a majority of the students belonged to the lower bourgeoisie, which consented to make the sacrifices represented by study in Paris to allow their sons to win a position with better pay than they could hope for in the metropole.

The war has hit a part of this class of the population. Today it is often unable to bear the considerable expenses of studying two or three years at the *Ecole Coloniale*. Young men who previously would have gone into a colonial career, now, by necessity, turn to professions requiring a less costly preparation.[3]

A few years later, when the number of candidates continued to lag, the blame was placed on the low salaries paid the colonial administrators.[4] Like most government services, the Corps was more poorly paid after the war than before it, but the administrators seem to have suffered more severely than other government officials—for example, military officers. A chief administrator earned more than an army colonel before 1914, but in the 1920s he had to serve eight years before he approximated the latter's salary. An assistant administrator before the war earned a salary equal to that of a captain in the army, but after 1920 it was hardly equal to that of a lieutenant.[5]

Still, the decline in candidates for the *Ecole Coloniale* did not simply reflect specific conditions within the colonial service. Generally speaking, after World War I there was a drop in the number of men seeking all government positions.[6] Jobs similar to those available in the civil service opened up in industry and commerce after 1918, and were generally better paid. An official in the ministry of colonies thought the drop in the number of candidates for civil service posts was owing to a process of "Americanization," which put sole emphasis on making money while neglecting the esteem granted before the war to people in government service.[7] The tragic loss of young men which France underwent as a result of the war certainly contributed to the decline in the number of candidates; 10 percent of France's active male population had been killed.

The sudden drop in the number of candidates made it necessary for the school to extend financial aid in order to continue attracting the needed students. The Indochinese administration felt the dearth of administrators most severely, and to attract future functionaries, it began to offer in 1923 a monthly stipend of 250 francs to all young men at the *Ecole Coloniale* preparing for service in Indochina. But in order not to lose all the young men to Indochina, the government-general in Dakar found it necessary to extend stipends to all men preparing for service in AOF also; shortly thereafter the administrations of the Cameroons, Togo, and Madagascar followed suit. (AEF, because of its lack of funds, was unable to offer stipends.) In 1923 the administration of the *Ecole Coloniale* provided free lodging for the students in greatest financial straits. The stipends given by the different colonial administrations and the free housing provided by the school helped to stimulate a new interest in the *Ecole Coloniale*. In 1923 there were forty-nine candidates, or nearly twice as many as in 1919.

Since the founding of the administrative section in 1889, the *Ecole Coloniale* had had as directors a number of men of varying abilities, who had seen their tasks primarily in terms of ensuring the daily administration of the school. A few courses had been added to the curriculum after 1900, but the main innovations had come indirectly. They had occurred less because of conscious planning than as a result of having superior teachers like Delafosse. The basic curriculum and the traditional methods of recruiting students, established in 1896, were retained for over a generation, until the middle of the 1920s.

The appointment of Georges Hardy as director in 1926 brought with it a profound change in the school's organization and curriculum. Before coming to the *Ecole Coloniale*, Hardy had been director of education in AOF (1912-1919) and then of Morocco (1919-1926). Overseas he had had the opportunity to think and to write at length about colonial problems. An academician both by training and by profession, Hardy was nevertheless aware of the limitations inherent in formal education; he introduced into the *Ecole Coloniale* a new curriculum which to a larger extent than previously avoided the traditional emphasis on legal studies, and thus gave the future administrators a training more applicable to the daily realities of colonial administration.

Having known Hardy in AOF, Gaston Joseph, *directeur du cabinet* to Léon Perier, minister of colonies, recommended that Hardy be appointed to head the *Ecole Coloniale*. After appointing him, Perier indicated to Hardy his desire to see the levels of both recruitment and training raised at the school and Hardy then worked out the details of the reforms which were immediately put into effect.[8]

One of Hardy's first innovations was to change the method of recruiting students; that method which had been initiated in 1896, no longer seemed capable of attracting a sufficiently large number of candidates. In France there were highly esteemed *grandes écoles*, such as the *Polytechnique*, *Saint-Cyr*, and the *Ecole normale*, which as a rule attracted better students than did the universities. Their success stemmed from the fact that they held competitive examinations, unlike the universities, and were considered more prestigious institutions because of the difficulty in entering them. In turn, the success of the graduates of these schools in French public life added lustre and prestige to the institutions.[9] Indeed, the success and tradition of the *grandes écoles* were so strong that Hardy saw no need to create a new pattern in recruiting young men and, using them as a model, he abolished the current preparatory section of the *Ecole Coloniale* and organized special preparatory classes in the same *lycées* in which the *grandes écoles* held their classes—a measure which put the *Ecole Coloniale* on a par with the noted *grandes écoles*. These preparatory classes were held in Paris at the *lycées* Louis-le-Grand, Henry IV, and Le Chaptal; and in the provinces at the *lycées* in Marseille, Bordeaux, Toulouse, Grenoble, and Montpellier, and were attended for a year by secondary school graduates wishing to take entrance examinations for the *Ecole Coloniale*. Attendance was not mandatory, but the overwhelming majority who passed the examinations after 1929 had attended these preparatory classes. Of the fifty-five admitted in 1934, for example, fifty-three had been enrolled in preparatory sections.[10]

By 1930 Hardy had completed the transformation of the *Ecole*

GEORGES HARDY

Coloniale into a *grande école*. In his efforts to give the *Ecole* cadets opportunities equal to those enjoyed by the students of the other *grandes écoles*, he introduced a further innovation in 1930—free tuition. This change in the school's status made its diploma highly desirable. For many young Frenchmen a diploma from the *Ecole Coloniale* became now as attractive as one from the *Ecole navale*. To those who had failed in their entrance examinations to the *Ecole normale* or the *Polytechnique*, the *Ecole Coloniale* now became an acceptable alternative. One result was a significant increase in the number of applicants seeking entrance to the school, partly because the students, since the establishment of preparatory classes in the *lycées*, could now prepare for entrance to the *Ecole* outside Paris. Another result was that the preparatory classes helped kindle a new national interest in overseas careers. The students of most of the major *lycées* in France, as a result of the preparatory classes in their schools, were aware from the beginning of their *lycée* careers of the possibility and attractions of the colonial service.

Under Hardy's leadership, the number of applicants to the *Ecole Coloniale* rose spectacularly. In 1927 there were seventy-two candidates for admission, 187 in 1930, 216 in 1931, and 410 in 1933.[11] After the mid-thirties, the school became increasingly selective, taking an ever smaller proportion of applicants, and finally became as difficult to enter as the best of its rivals. In the long run only the letters section of the *Ecole normale*, the most prestigious of all the *grandes écoles*, was as selective in its recruitment as was the colonial school.

Geographically, the school's recruitment tended to favor cadets coming from Paris; consequently, more than half of all the cadets came from preparatory sections in the capital—in 1935, of fifty-five students admitted, twenty-two came from the *lycées* Louis-le-Grand and eleven from Le Chaptal. This was partially owing to the concentration of sons of higher civil servants in Paris and to the heightened status of the *Ecole Coloniale*, which ensured the interest of the sons of an ambitious Parisian bourgeoisie. The tradition of intellectual concentration in Paris also meant that both the most gifted *lycée* students and the teachers most capable of preparing them for the entrance examination to the *Ecole Coloniale* were in the capital.

Of course, not all candidates coming from preparatory sections in Paris *lycées* had done their secondary school work in the capital. In 1938, for example, 60 percent of the students attending the preparatory sections in Paris had gone to secondary school in the provinces.[12]

Other administrative services recruited an even larger proportion of men from Paris. For example, 40 percent of the inspectors of finance came from Paris between 1870 and 1954.[13]

Table 6

Percentage of applicants admitted to seven grandes écoles*

Grandes écoles	1937	1938	1939	1940	1941	1942	1943
Ecole nationale de la France d'outre-mer (Ecole Coloniale)	12.0%	19.6%	33.0%	10.3%	9.5%	10.0%	11.1%
Institut national agronomique	34.0	35.0	30.5	28.5	17.0	15.0	15.3
Ecole normale (Lettres)	9.0	9.8	8.9	8.8	10.0	10.0	8.5
Ecole spéciale Saint-Cyr	22.5	24.5	31.0	4.3	6.8	17.0	–
Ecole navale	24.9	21.5	31.0	–	12.1	17.0	–
Ecole polytechnique	24.0	23.6	20.5	9.0	10.2	13.0	15.5
Ecole centrale	51.0	51.0	58.0	20.5	19.5	15.0	22.0

*Although the *Ecole nationale de la France d'outre-mer* (*Ecole Coloniale*) had the second largest number of candidates among the *grandes écoles,* the candidates for the different schools were not necessarily of the same quality. It is quite possible that for the most prestigious schools such as the *Ecole normale* and the *Polytechnique* a large number of candidates excluded themselves by hesitating to apply.

It might seem that Hardy's reforms would have had a democratizing effect on the recruitment of the school and that the financial aid given to the school's cadets would have led to a recruitment of men from more varied social backgrounds than before 1927. Also, the new measures which made it possible for candidates to prepare for entrance to the *Ecole Coloniale* outside Paris would presumably have permitted a greater geographic distribution of the recruitment. In reality, however, the Hardy reforms had the opposite effect, for they resulted not only in an elite recruitment but in an increase of students from the Paris area. Since some of the brightest secondary school pupils were attracted to the *Ecole Coloniale,* they made up an intellectual elite; and since secondary education was generally limited to the upper middle classes, the school also recruited a social elite.

The *Ecole Coloniale* began to keep statistics on the professions of the cadets' fathers in 1929, and these reveal (see Table 7) that the school remained basically upper middle class in its recruitment, and seems to have become even more socially selective in the 1930s than it had been before World War I.

Table 7

Percentage distribution of fathers' professions of students admitted to the Ecole Coloniale[14]

Fathers' profession	1929	1930	1931	1932	1934	1936
High administration	42%	30%	37%	42%	29%	34%
Industrial and business management	1.5	4	9	0	0	7
Liberal professions	30	25	20	28	16	17
Rentiers, small businessmen, *propriétaires*	14	2	16	24	9	10
White collar workers	8	18	12	3	34	16
Small farmers, artisans	3	15	5	3	5	2
Workers	1.5	6	1	1	7	14

The statistics in Table 8, of former administrators who attended the school, confirm the middle class recruitment of the *Ecole* in the interwar period and the proportion of cadets whose fathers had been in the higher civil service.

Rarely has any regret been expressed in France over the limited class origins of the administrators. It has been traditionally accepted that selectivity in quality be accompanied by a certain class restrictiveness. A high official in the interwar period (later governor-general of Indochina in the 1940s), who may be considered a representative of the high bourgeoisie, was asked if he regretted the socially circumscribed origins of the administrators. He answered that, on the contrary, the upper middle class recruitment was necessary for the very success of the Corps. "The middle classes," he added, "have certain virtues which are well known. They make honest, reliable, and generally impartial agents of the State."[15] The British deliberately recruited men belonging to the gentry, believing that this class possessed certain innate virtues,[16] but the French class-bound recruitment, limited to the bourgeoisie, was not a matter of policy. It was rather a result of the competitive examination system which emphasized formal learning. That the sons of the bourgeoisie tended to score best on the examinations and thus win access to the Corps was, of course, a reflection of the class-bound educational system of French society rather than of specific policies of the Corps itself.

Table 8

Fathers' professions of 138 former administrators who had attended the Ecole Coloniale *1920-1939*

Fathers' profession	Period attending Ecole Coloniale			
	1920-1929		1930-1939	
	Number	%	Number	%
High administration	8	25%	25	24%
Industrial and business management	1	3	4	4
Liberal professions*	9	27	32	31
Rentiers, small businessmen, propriétaires	4	13	13	12
White collar workers	8	25	15	14
Small farmers and artisans	1	3	14	13
Workers	—	—	—	—
No answer	1	4	3	2

*Nearly all the cadets' fathers who were in the liberal professions, according to the answers to the questionnaire of October 1965, were medical doctors or engineers.

With the change in methods of recruitment, Hardy also introduced innovations in the curriculum. Instead of two years, the students now were required to spend three years at the *Ecole Coloniale.* During the first year the students were to improve their general culture; during the second they were to do individual research under a professor in the area in which they intended to serve; and during the third they were to prepare themselves for their professional tasks in the colonies.[17]

Hardy was deeply concerned about the basic ignorance of the French relative to the colonial societies. In 1925 he observed that the French knew practically nothing about how and what the indigenous populations of the colonies thought.[18] Later he was to complain that "we lack almost completely any monographs on the psychology of tribes, of regions, of cities, of professions, or of social classes."[19] He argued for a greater understanding of the colonial populations, especially those that had been regarded as primitive or savage. "The most typical savage," Hardy argued, "is not a mere savage, he has a collective experience that should not be disdained; his good instincts are often but hidden behind a mask of barbarism. And one can guide him to lead a reasonable life without asking him to suddenly renounce all the habits of his race."[20]

By establishing new courses in geography, ethnology, traditional African law, African history, geology, botany, zoology, and agronomy Hardy hoped to reveal more of the colonial realities to the young men preparing for the service. In tune with the new emphasis on economic development in the colonies, the *Ecole Coloniale* also introduced a course entitled Economic Development.

The curriculum of the school, in spite of all these changes, retained the emphasis on legal studies as the backbone of the training program. It also retained much of its former encyclopedism, but now combined with new courses, it had the merit of being fused to a larger body of practical knowledge. Hardy quite consciously attempted to give his students practical training for the realities they were to face overseas. In his own words, his aim was "less to make men who knew everything, than to open minds and make men."[21] At least some of the former administrators seemed to think that he succeeded; a man who was a student at the *Ecole Coloniale* during the period of Hardy's directorship writes, "At the time, we had the impression that the multiple courses made us into superficial dabblers. But they opened up our minds and allowed us to mature."[22]

Through a series of practical programs Hardy attempted to give the future administrators not only theoretical knowledge but also practical experience in the study of societies. In 1932, for example, he had his students conduct a series of voter motivation research projects in France. And to prepare the cadets better for Africa, he began an informal program that encouraged them to spend their summers in North Africa. There they had the opportunity to observe not only the nature of a non-Western society, but also French administration in action. Two students additionally were given the rare opportunity to see Henri Labouret, the well-known French ethnologist, at work. In 1932 Hardy sent a student to Senegal to accompany the ethnologist, and two years later another student was sent with Labouret to the Cameroons.

As an educator he emphasized academic studies, but Hardy realized full well that the best students would not necessarily make the best overseas administrators. His evaluation of the students was important, for it helped the ministry decide where to place them. In considering a candidate's fitness for overseas service, Hardy, unlike most of his predecessors, not only evaluated his academic achievements but also considered the total person. He described a student graduating next to last in his class in the following terms:

[He looks like] Sancho Panza and appears to be greatly concerned with keeping himself in good condition and health. But under this somewhat amusing exterior there is an extraordinary sense of social service, a capacity to make friends immediately, and to obtain from them what he desires. Besides, he is very interested in ethnography and native languages. He will make a picturesque bush administrator, but he will prove brilliant, since basically he has a warm heart and an adventurous character.[23]

Hardy proved to be a good judge of human qualities. The following year the same young administrator was described by his governor as an "excellent recruit for the administration"; three years later as possessing "a high sense of duty."[24] Hardy was rarely wrong in his judgment of his students.

Hardy's reforms at the school, his enthusiasm for the colonial vocation, and his personal interest in his students gave him great influence over them. One-third indicated that of all the men at the school Hardy had had the greatest influence.[25] In both his writings and his courses, Hardy proclaimed his faith in the French empire and in its civilizing mission. In fact, one student of the *Ecole* during Hardy's directorship has described the school's task as "to instill in us a faith in our mission."[26] This role was aptly put in a speech by a former governor-general of AOF, later president of the *Ecole Coloniale,* who told the students:

Whom do we want to train in this institution? Good functionaries knowing their regulations well and ready to apply them with exactitude? Yes, undoubtedly, but that is the least of our tasks. We want them to have faith, the colonial faith; we want them to be suffused with the grandeur and the nobility of the mission which they have to fulfill.[27]

Hardy saw the French mission as being the protection of the colonial peoples and their gradual promotion toward French civilization. He saw colonization not as the right of conquest but as the responsibility of greater maturity (*devoir d'aînesse*).[28] He upheld the authoritarian and paternal system of rule existing in the colonies. If there were any deficiencies in the colonial administration, Hardy saw them as stemming mainly from a lack of understanding of the colonial societies by the administrators. Deep study of the social and political structures of these societies, Hardy believed, would remedy the defects existing in the colonial system.

Hardy's contribution to the school and his influence upon his graduates were certainly important, but his appointment of Henri Labouret in 1929 was of even greater significance in shaping the future administrators. Labouret, a military officer who participated in the conquest of the northern Ivory Coast, became a colonial administrator and published a number of studies on the peoples living under his rule. Upon Delafosse's death, he was appointed to the *Institut des langues orientales* where he occupied his predecessor's chair in ethnology. He also succeeded Delafosse at the *Ecole Coloniale*.

At the school, Labouret's students eagerly attended his classes. Those who had been at the school in the late 1920s and early 1930s almost unanimously called his course on African languages and history the most useful of all those given. His research methods in ethnology, stressing the importance of regional monographs, influenced a whole generation of French colonial administrators who were to make important ethnological contributions. Among these administrators were Gilbert Vieillard, who wrote on the Fulani of Futa-Djallon; Bernard Maupoil, who studied the Fons of Dahomey; Robert Cornevin, who authored a work on the Bassari of northern Togo; and Pierre Alexandre, who is one of the leading French experts on African linguistics. An eminent historian of Africa and a former student of Labouret said of him:

He marked several generations of students.... How can we signal the importance of Labouret for all students and the personal manner in which he was able to make us understand Africa? It was manifestly a magisterial course, but it was also and primarily a series of [personal] reflections.[29]

In fact, Labouret's influence and that of several of his students had an effect outside the walls of the *Ecole Coloniale* or the *Institut des langues orientales*. An African nationalist leader, Hamani Diori, in 1970 the head of state of Niger, has written about Labouret's works.

Like all my classmates at the *Ecole* William Ponty [primarily a teachers' training school in Dakar] I knew his works on black Africa which had made him the brilliant successor of the works of Delafosse. To us young students there was a feeling of joy and pride to discover that the African languages, the material civilizations of Africa ... were honestly studied, exposed, explained, and recognized as realities that were essentially different, but in no way inferior to those of the Western world. Thus this European, this "white man," revealed us to ourselves, liberated us from a certain complex and strengthened our feeling of dignity.[30]

Hardy's efforts had made it possible for future administrators to become more closely acquainted with the realities of the overseas societies. The program of studies he introduced was sound enough to win praise from the Australian critic of French colonialism, Stephen H. Roberts, who wrote:

The French educational system and the nature of French officialdom being what they are, the courses at the *Ecole Coloniale* represent a

HENRI LABOURET

conspicuous triumph—one of those touches of mystery that from time to time have transmuted the drabness of their colonial effort.[31]

Not all of the men who became administrators after World War I had been cadets at the *Ecole Coloniale*; of those appointed in the 1920s, nearly 70 percent were minor officials in the colonies, agents of civil affairs. Both before and after World War I, the colonial administration thought that the Corps needed not only men with academic training but also men with practical experience in serving overseas. Most of these minor officials had served between four and ten years in the colonies, often as aides to a *commandant*. To qualify for the post of administrator, an agent was required to undergo a one-year training program at the *Ecole Coloniale* before being appointed to the Corps.

In the 1920s most of the agents attending the school were not of very high academic quality. In 1928, although the *Ecole Coloniale* opened sixty-one places for agents, only forty-six were able to pass the entrance examinations. Once the agents were admitted, the school had to lower some of its standards to allow them to complete the course. In 1928, Hardy remarked that although all forty-four agents attending the *Ecole Coloniale* had been given their diplomas, the one who passed last in his class did so thanks only to the "encouragement and even indulgence" of the examining committee.[32] Two years later, four agents failed and others received their diplomas only because of the committee's leniency.[33]

The poor academic performance of the agents was doubtless traceable to the low average level of their formal education. Also, the pay received by the agents was hardly sufficient to attract the better educated young Frenchmen to the colonial posts. The American Raymond Buell remarked in 1929 that the agents were so poorly paid that their wives had to work to make ends meet.[34]

In the 1930s better salaries and more difficult examinations for the young men wishing to be appointed as agents meant that as a rule the agents applying for entrance to the Corps were better educated than those of a decade earlier. Since the entrance examinations to the *Ecole Coloniale* emphasized literary knowledge, only the most formally educated agents were able to pass. In 1939 the candidates with law degrees constituted 30 percent of the total admitted. Although 41 percent of the candidates had only a *baccalauréat*, they made up only 13 percent of the total admitted. As a result of the school's competitive entrance examinations, the agents were becoming similar in education and social background to the regular cadets of the *Ecole Coloniale*.

The French civil service has traditionally considered the quality of government functionaries to be determined by their degree of formal education. After World War I the ministry of colonies put greater stress than before on the *Ecole Coloniale,* but it still recognized the value of practical experience and therefore continued recruiting the agents. In the 1920s their continued recruitment was probably determined at least in part by the low number of applicants to the *Ecole Coloniale.* But in the 1930s, when there were several hundred candidates, it would have been quite simple to put an end to the appointment of agents as administrators. That this was not done may be partly because of the continued stress within the colonial bureaucracy on the value of practical experience.

A decree of 1920 had set the proportion of former agents in the Corps at three-sevenths; in the 1920s, however, two-thirds of those entering the Corps were former agents, and it was only in the 1930s that their recruitment was reduced to the proportion that had been set by the decree.

In 1938 Georges Mandel became minister of colonies. A man identified with the political right (a former aide and close friend of Clemenceau), he surprised the colonial bureaucracy by initiating a series of administrative reforms. He was disturbed by the irregular manner in which the agents continued to be recruited. The administrators since 1887 had been members of one Corps, subject to uniform methods of recruitment, hiring, and promotion, but the agents were still hired according to the whims of the individual governors-general in the colonial federations and of the governors in the mandated areas. This method of recruitment, Mandel observed, had "led in more than one instance to abuse. For many years efforts were made to stop certain practices of favoritism that damaged the public interest. . . . But they did not always succeed." In order to put a definite end to favoritism, Mandel established a corps of agents of civil services for all of French Black Africa and Madagascar, with uniform regulations for recruitment. All young men wishing to become agents from that time on took an entrance examination set by the ministry of colonies.[35]

In 1933 the Hardy era came to an end with his appointment as rector of the Academy of Algiers. His successor was Henri Gourdon, director of public instruction in Indochina and a respected scholar in the field of Far Eastern art. He had lost an arm and had only partial eyesight as a result of wounds in the first world war. This *grand mutilé* was regarded with considerable awe by his contemporaries, but his poor health led him to retire four years later, in 1937. One significant change occurred under Gourdon's directorship: in 1934, the school's name was altered from *Ecole Coloniale* to *Ecole nationale de la France d'outre-mer* (ENFOM).

Gourdon's successor, the man who was eventually to carry on Hardy's

ROBERT DELAVIGNETTE

innovations and bring about further distinguished change was Robert Delavignette. Delavignette was the first director of the ENFOM with previous experience as a colonial administrator in Africa. After serving in the war, Delavignette entered the colonial administration in 1919 as agent of civil affairs. As a veteran he was eligible to enlist in a six-months' training program at the *Ecole Coloniale,* and after serving for a brief period as an agent in Dakar, he returned to Paris where he received his training at the *Ecole Coloniale.* He was then appointed to the Corps of Colonial Administrators, in which he served for two years in Niger and four in Upper Volta.

Delavignette had preferred to leave for the unknown and seemingly unlimited horizons of the colonial world rather than remain in a France devastated by war. In the colonies he quickly showed an aptitude for territorial administration. His superiors found him a poor accountant but an excellent bush administrator. To a greater extent than most of his contemporaries, he was able to achieve the nearly impossible task of at the same time fulfilling the demands of the administration, which constantly clamored for increased crop production and higher taxation, and also of significantly improving the welfare of the local populations. Under his administration, his region increased its peanut production twentyfold within two years. Increases in production often profited only a handful of Africans, usually the local chiefs, but Delavignette saw to it that the profits were beneficial to the entire society. His method of administration was widely admired by his contemporaries, and Governor-General Jules Carde labeled him as the best administrator of his generation.[36]

In 1930 Delavignette returned to France, and though ill and fatigued, he not only occupied a post in the AOF economic bureau in Paris—a bureau which was a combination of an economic research group and a chamber of commerce—but also began his career as a journalist. In 1931, he wrote *Les Paysans noirs*; he also wrote for several colonial and Parisian journals and became an active contributor to the liberal Catholic review *Esprit,* writing on colonial questions. Delavignette was—and still is—an admirable stylist. He vividly portrayed the problems and needs of the colonial peoples, especially in *Les Paysans noirs,* which like nearly all his writings is semiautobiographic; undoubtedly it is his most important work. In it he has described the daily life of the African peasants and that of the young *commandant* charged with their welfare. The book was enormously influential in France and won the prize for the best colonial novel of 1931. In 1932 President Doumer, minutes before he was shot by a crazed Russian, personally handed the award to the winner.

Les Paysans noirs was an idealization of the life of the black peasants by a man who himself came from a rural area, Burgundy. Having studied in

Dijon, Delavignette was influenced by the historian Gaston Roupnel, who was both his teacher and his friend. Roupnel taught a mystique of the peasantry which he later expressed eloquently in his *Histoire de la campagne française*:

The rural soul is a complete richness. Filled by nature, it contains all of history and all of humanity. In it is reunited all the lives of the past, the whole ancestral existence.... Let us listen within us to this murmur!... you exist in us as the thousands and thousands of lives which still sigh in the spirit as if they still worked the earth!... Strong and pure lives, you are not memories of the tomb, a lost memory!... but you live in us, and we live but through you![37]

Les Paysans noirs was in many ways a transfer to the African scene of Roupnel's mystique of the peasantry, the toilers of the land in France. The title itself was important; it gave Africans an identity beyond the nebulous term *"indigène"* which was too often linked with African inferiority. By identifying Africans with their profession rather than with their color, Delavignette gave them universal significance. Both the title of the book and its contents—by emphasizing the similarities between the peasant existence of the Africans and that of the rural population of France—could have had an assimilationist implication. But the book did not, for Delavignette was thoroughly familiar with both the African and the French peasantry, and he carried these similarities to a point beyond superficial parallels. Did not the French peasants also have their own local customs, habits, and superstitions which had to be given consideration? The task of the administration, as Delavignette saw it, was to promote economic and social development, but to do so only if it were humane and in the short-term as well as long-term interest of the local populations.

All his writings, and especially *Les Paysans noirs,* of which a movie was also made, were influential in forming French opinion on colonial matters. Many young men were inspired to enter the colonial administration because of his book, and a large number of administrators have indicated that their methods of administration were directly influenced by it. If any one figure should be chosen in France as a shaper of public opinion on colonial matters after World War I, that person is Robert Delavignette.

In the late 1920s, while in the colonies, Delavignette had encouraged the work of the Dahomean Paul Hazoumé, who became an outstanding African researcher in ethnology. Later, in Paris Delavignette established important contacts with African intellectuals, many of which he still maintains. In the 1940s he became acquainted with and later indirectly launched Léopold Senghor on his political career. Senghor became one of the greatest twentieth-century poets writing in French, an eminent politician of the Fourth French Republic, and is now, in 1970, the president of the Republic of Senegal.

Delavignette also struck up a close friendship with the ethnologist Lucien Lévy-Bruhl, who introduced him to Marius Moutet, the Popular Front minister of colonies. Moutet, impressed by the young man so earnestly devoted to colonial change, appointed him as his *chef de cabinet.* When the vacancy at the ENFOM occurred in 1937, Delavignette was appointed as the school's director.

He had had no academic training beyond the *baccalauréat,* but Delavignette turned out to be an extraordinary teacher and an excellent director. He left his mark on a whole generation of ENFOM students. The students who attended the school during his directorate nearly unanimously claim him as the most important single influence at the school. Even after he resigned his post as director to become high commissioner of the French Cameroons in 1946 and later the highest permanent official of the ministry of overseas France, he retained a personal influence on the cadets at the school and the administrators overseas. In 1952 Delavignette left the ministry of overseas France and returned to the school as a teacher.

The curriculum changes that Hardy had instituted in the late 1920s were left virtually unchanged a decade later. He had done much to make the training more relevant to the tasks that the future administrators would be called upon to perform, but there still was too much useless encyclopedic knowledge and too much emphasis on the study of law. A student complained in 1938 that the school was making very little original contribution in training the administrators, for much of the curriculum still consisted of law, which could have been taught at any faculty of law, and most of the other courses were but "fragments of knowledge." He found the courses to be irrelevant to his future career and accused the school of being boring and devoted to producing sheep rather than men of action.[38] By coincidence, later in the same month reforms were instituted which attempted to solve exactly the problems the student had complained about.

Delavignette, before heading the *Ecole Coloniale,* had already expressed his opposition to the encyclopedic and basically sterile nature of the school's curriculum. In 1931 he had expressed the thought that it was vital to appoint as administrators young men capable of observing the realities of the colonial scene rather than those who were "strong in composition and could recite without error the membership of the *conseil de contentieux.*"[39]

Also, because of his personal administrative experience, Delavignette was probably more aware than were any of his predecessors that the school could perform only a limited function in preparing men for the colonial service, and that in fact the completed training could come only from experience of the job itself. As he stated in 1942:

The training of the administrator is not accomplished in . . . a specialized school; it is a training which lasts a whole lifetime and which is constantly put to the test; it is a training which demands the continuous enrichment of the character and the spirit. . . . The colonial administrator owes it to himself always to be—from the beginning until the end—a cultured and educated man.[40]

Education could be no substitute for experience, but Delavignette attempted to establish a program of studies that would help create a more realistic preparation for a colonial career. Previously, cadets preparing for overseas service in Black Africa or Madagascar were required to take courses on both regions. Delavignette split the African section into African and Malgache sections, thus freeing the administrators who were going to Black Africa from studying the Malgache language, history, and ethnology, and giving them more time to study the regions to which they would be assigned; also, of course, it freed the administrators destined to serve in Madagascar from needless study about Black Africa. To prepare the cadets better for local realities, Delavignette expanded the language offerings of the school: in 1938 Fulani, Mandingue, Djerma, and Hausa were added.

In spite of this emphasis on practical training freed from academic sterility, Delavignette, like all his predecessors, saw the study of law as an essential and necessary preparation for a colonial administrative career. He believed that the study of law would give the future administrators a sense of legality and a concept of what was right and what was wrong, and would inculcate in the cadets a sense of the importance of following regulations and their superiors' orders.[41]

But Delavignette was also well aware that in the past students had spent too much time studying law, and too little in studying courses dealing more directly with colonial problems. Therefore he required that all candidates for admission must have studied the equivalent of the first year of the law school curriculum. Thus, although the cadets upon graduation were required to obtain a *licence en droit,* they were not required to take as many law courses while they were attending the ENFOM. The academic training, Delavignette believed, had a double role:

. . . on the one hand to teach what is legal, on the other hand what is humanly possible in the native society. If the first notion can be taught by the study of administrative sciences, the second is no more than a sensibility, which can no more than be awakened at the school by the study of native countries and peoples.[42]

Delavignette emphasized on-the-job training and in January 1939 a decree was issued requiring all cadets to serve overseas in the middle of their studies. The outbreak of the war, however, temporarily prevented this reform from being instituted.

The full impact of the changes and the reforms in the ENFOM were to be felt only after World War II, when a preponderant majority of the Corps consisted of men who had graduated from the school. In the interwar period, just as before 1914, only a minority were former cadets of the *Ecole Coloniale*. In 1938 only 28 percent of the Corps consisted of former cadets of the ENFOM;[43] the remainder were former agents who had studied at the school.

As a result both of the greater selectivity of the *Ecole Coloniale* during the interwar period and the special training given the agents at the school, a much more highly educated Corps was being formed. The heightened prestige of the school and its change into one of the *grandes écoles* of France meant that it now attracted young Frenchmen of the highest quality.

In education and social background the Corps began in the 1930s to consist of men very similar to those in the higher civil service within France. But in addition, the young men entering the *Ecole Coloniale* were as a rule motivated by a desire for adventure and a high sense of social service to the colonial populations. A career guide of 1931 described the colonial service as providing an outdoor life which included hunting, fishing, long trips by horse or boat, palavers, and native feasts.[44] It was this idyll of government service under conditions resembling the life of a boy scout rather than that of a bureaucrat that attracted many young men. The colonial vocation was generally born of an urge to flee the more repressive aspects of French society. When in the 1930s Delavignette asked his students why they had chosen their careers, he found that "all the answers throb with desire for freedom."[45] Many administrators came from small provincial towns, places that were often stifling for the young. "I wished to get out of the limited horizons of the French hexagon," one administrator wrote.[46] The petty-bourgeois environment of the provinces offered few exciting career possibilities for young men, and among the provincial bourgeoisie it was usually expected that the sons would take on their fathers' careers. The son of a pharmacist in a small provincial town wrote that he became an administrator because "I wished to do something other than pharmacy, law, or medicine, and live somewhere other than in

Riom [Puy de Dôme]."

Exoticism was of course deeply connected with a desire to escape French life. An entrant to the school in 1924 wrote that he had chosen his career because of a "desire to travel and to know other modes of life, other peoples, other civilizations, other climates than those prevailing in France, a desire and curiosity that had been awakened as a result of exoticism in art and literature." One administrator mentions Rimbaud and Robert Louis Stevenson as influencing him in his "wish to escape the bourgeois life of the provinces, love of the ocean, curiosity about other countries and peoples."

There were many influences extolling the colonial opportunity to command and to serve. There was the religious influence. A number of young men became interested in the colonies after attending schools run by religious orders carrying on missionary activities overseas. Some even regarded their profession as the lay version of missionary activity.

There was also a rich historical tradition which influenced many young men. There were the heroes of the past such as Cartier or Champlain. There were contemporaries or near-contemporaries, men especially like Gallieni and Lyautey who indeed had a most important influence in determining the administrators' choice of career. In their writings, especially their published collections of letters, Gallieni and Lyautey glorified the life of action in the colonies. Other French colonial figures influencing young aspirants were Savorgnan de Brazza, the explorer of the Congo, and Auguste Pavie, the explorer of Laos. Individual acquaintances or relatives who were in the colonial service also, of course, inspired colonial vocations.

Public glorification of the territories overseas, such as the international colonial exposition held in Vincennes in 1931, strongly affected many young men. Almost all of the imperial powers had been invited to the exposition. In the Park of Vincennes, the French had reproduced colonial villages, mosques, temples, and other structures; every colony within the French empire was represented. The most impressive and widely admired exhibit was a full-sized replica of the Khmer temple of Angkor Vat. Lyautey lent the exposition the prestige of his name by presiding over it. He also provided it with its slogan: "Colonization is essentially constructive and beneficial. Native policy is primarily a policy of concern."

The architectural wonders, the exhibits of colonial products, the presence of famous colonial figures and of people coming from all corners of the French empire made the exposition immensely popular. An average of 150,000 people a day visited it; within one month of its opening three and a half million people had seen it. For the six months of its duration the exposition continued drawing visitors, especially school children. It inspired a large number of them to aim at overseas service. Many of the men who entered the colonial school in the 1930s mention the Vincennes exposition as having had an important influence on their choice of a career.

By the 1920s a number of families had lived in the colonies, and a relatively large number of the young men entering the *Ecole* had either been born and raised in the colonies or had parents employed overseas. Twenty percent of the administrators in 1939 had been born in the colonies, and roughly 30 percent were connected with the colonies in one way or another—born or raised in the colonies, or having parents in a colonial career. By 1938, 35 percent of the students in one preparatory class for the ENFOM were from a general colonial background.[47] Many young men who were raised overseas had little desire to live in France; they could not easily adjust to what they considered to be a humdrum life, and many felt emotionally attached to the areas they had known as children. One administrator born in the colonies wrote that he chose the career because of his affection for "the colonial environment I knew as a child in Sudan. The great beauty of the sky, the earth, the rivers, and the African steppe."

The colonial career opened opportunities for exercising nearly unlimited authority and responsibility. An entrant to the school in 1928 wrote that his choice of career was shaped by a desire "to change the world. To assume real responsibilities, to dispose of real powers of tutelage and protection. In sum, to be a chief."

In republican France the feudal order was long abolished, but the colonies represented a world in which the sons of the bourgeoisie could exercise an authority which not even their forefathers had possessed in France: namely, to belong to a ruling caste. A colonial administrator who was an active member of the Socialist party was to write in 1931:

We leave [France] to become kings. And soon because of the development of revolutions, we shall be the only kings on earth. And not do-nothing kings, but sovereign artists, enlightened despots, who organize their kingdoms according to maturely reflected plans.[48]

The kind of satisfaction that young men experienced from their positions overseas was demonstrated by Gilbert Vieillard, a graduate of the *Ecole* in the 1930s. He wrote his family that his service overseas made him happy because it was physically invigorating and because it made him proud to be a white man. He wrote his mother:

In the country to be "white" means to be surrounded by a certain respect.

When I cross a market, a village, I receive the welcome of the women, the grave and cordial greetings of the men, the skipping and laughter of the children; to create happiness with small things, instead of being evil, makes me feel good and makes me proud.[49]

The colonies also had a patriotic appeal; they would be the means through which France would be strengthened. A pamphlet on colonial careers published in 1937 spoke of a beleaguered France needing the material power of the colonies. The tract evoked the ideal "of a hundred million men conforming to the same laws, working for each other, exchanging freely their products."[50]

In general, there was a whole set of motives that attracted young men to enter the ENFOM and then to go overseas. If their motives were not much different from those of some of the men who had entered the school before World War I, there now were a greater number of such men in the Corps and they gave it its imprint.

Albert Bernard, a young administrator who was killed in 1935 while defending the people he administered in Somali against a raiding nomadic tribe, was quite typical of a breed of young men entering the colonial service in the interwar period. Shortly before his death Bernard wrote to his family about his vocation:

Our profession is not difficult; it consists of doing good around onself. One must do that; one must give some of one's salary to good works, to schools and clinics. There is a need for justice and humanity.[51]

And of the indigenous populations, he wrote: "They are good people. They are poor. They deserve pity and our friendship."[52]

The American Raymond Buell, by no means a friendly critic of French colonialism, remarked in 1929 that the graduate of the *Ecole Coloniale* was "usually a high type man, having both character and intelligence."[53] One French writer observed that the image of the colonial service as the refuge of men who had failed at home was receding, as a new elite, trained at the *Ecole Coloniale,* was growing in number in the Corps.[54]

VI The Era of Lost Opportunities

The men entering the Corps of Colonial Administrators in the interwar period were generally speaking men of high ability, possessing personal integrity and a sense of dedication. Many of them were worthy of the praise given a graduate of the *Ecole Coloniale* in the 1920s: he is "impassioned by his vocation, to which he brings the enthusiasm and real faith of an apostle."[1] The governors claimed that only superlatives could be used to describe some of the administrators.[2] It could be said of many more administrators than before the war that they were "good and gentle with the natives."[3]

The quality of the Corps was to a large measure shaped by the increased selectivity in recruitment, by the fact that all the administrators were required to receive their training at the *Ecole Coloniale,* and by the improvements in curriculum which the school itself had undergone. The young men entering the colonial service in the interwar period were then a new breed of men.

In spite of this renovation of the Corps, the colonial service nevertheless was rigid, and in fact crystallized the status quo in the interwar period. Hubert Deschamps, one of the keenest observers of the French colonial scene and himself a member of the Corps of Colonial Administrators between the two world wars, observed that French colonial rule, characterized at times in the early period by the innovative spirit of men like Faidherbe, Gallieni, and Lyautey, seemed to deteriorate into rigidity after World War I. Deschamps described the years 1919-1939 as decisive, but "lost years." Of this period, he wrote: "We fell asleep somewhat from a political point of view . . . , when it would have been wise slowly and resolutely to lead an evolution."[4] It was because the French failed to take any initiative during the interwar years, Deschamps declared, that "from then on we could do nothing more than follow developments without being able to guide them."[5]

Gallieni had advocated the establishment of a supple administration, sensitive to the ever-changing needs of the colonial societies.

The administrative procedure which is excellent today should be rejected a few months from now if events modify the situation. . . . There is nothing that needs to be more supple, more elastic, than the organization of a [colony]. To all political and economic evolution must correspond an administrative evolution.[6]

The colonial administration in the interwar period, Deschamps wrote, betrayed Gallieni's thought by preserving unchanged the administrative system that he had established, while admitting no innovation.[7]

In the aftermath of World War I there was some interest in establishing a reform of the colonial system—an interest triggered by the wartime sacrifices of the colonial populations to French victory. During the war 818,000 men were recruited overseas for military service; 636,000 were sent to France, of whom 187,000 served in the French labor force and 449,000 as combatants. The losses of the colonial troops were heavy, amounting to almost 70,000 men. The material contribution of the colonies was also impressive: 2.5 million tons of produce were shipped to the mother country.[8] The French clung to the image of the loyal colonial subjects, ignoring a series of rebellions which had broken out in the colonies because of excessive French efforts to force local production and to recruit men for the army. The noble "Senegalese," as all black troops were called, became part of popular legend. The wartime contribution of the colonies apparently demonstrated the dependence of the French on their colonies; the welfare and prosperity of Frenchmen, it seemed were intimately connected with the welfare and prosperity of the colonial populations.

Albert Sarraut, who was minister of colonies for four years (1920-1924), became the official spokesman for this doctrine. He was a Radical Socialist politician who had served as governor-general of Indochina before World War I. In 1921, he proposed that the French Parliament establish a program of economic aid to the French overseas possessions, amounting to 3.5 billion francs, to be invested over a ten-year period.[9] Sarraut argued that until World War I the French had to concentrate on consolidating their empire and establishing a regular administration over it. Since the period of territorial aggrandizement was now ended, Sarraut claimed, the time had come for considering an overall plan for the *mise en valeur,* for the utilization of the colonial resources through economic development.[10]

In a world in which the French would presumably be facing stiff international economic competition and in which there might again be a serious need to bolster up their defense forces, Sarraut said, the French would become increasingly dependent upon their colonies. It was essential therefore to have easy access to raw materials, and to ensure that the indigenous populations of the empire were healthy and well educated.[11] Conversely, he also stressed the moral debt that the French owed the colonies as a result of their aid and loyalty during the war. His arguments were generally utilitarian, however, stressing the advantages to France of the program of economic aid to the colonies. This line of argument was probably not merely a tactic to convince a reluctant Parliament; it also represented Sarraut's personal convictions. Outside the Palais Bourbon, Sarraut, mapping colonial policy in the more intimate surroundings of the offices of Rue Oudinot, again advocated that "all our efforts must be employed so that the colonies render the maximum ... [in] the interest of the metropole."[12]

Whatever the motives of the Sarraut proposal, it did have the merit of attempting planned economic development of the colonies. In spite of the accomplishments of individual administrators in developing their districts, there was little overall effect in changing the economic and social conditions of the overseas populations. Georges Barthelemy, who had served as a colonial official in 1908-1909, went overseas in 1922 in his role as deputy and parliamentary reporter on the colonial budget. On his return to France he declared that in his twelve years' absence from the colonies, "little has been accomplished over there."[13] Henri Cosnier, another parliamentarian on an inspection trip, blamed the economic backwardness of French West Africa on the lack of economic planning. Only railroads had been built as part of a coherent economic plan.[14]

The French Parliament, however, was unwilling to make a major sacrifice for the colonies. Even Sarraut had hoped that the aid would be financed in part by the massive German reparation payments, which most French politicians expected the defeated enemy to pay. The significant reduction in the amount that the Germans finally did pay, and the financial difficulties that the French encountered after the war, put a serious strain on the budget. In 1922 Sarraut himself felt that it was impossible to realize his plan of the previous year,[15] and as for Parliament, it never acted on his proposal.

The French did not give grants-in-aid as Sarraut had proposed, but in the early 1930s Parliament permitted the colonies to float loans. They borrowed over 5 billion francs, but the interest on the loans used up an excessive proportion of their budgets; in 1937, it was 29.7 percent of the year's budget of AOF, 40.6 percent for AEF, and 17.1 percent for Madagascar.[16]

The colonial treasuries continued to pay the major share of their budgets for administrative costs. In the Congo in 1930, for example, 70 percent of the budget was spent on such expenses.[17] In addition, the colonies shared the expenses of certain services they shared in common with France—such as the French national defense costs. In 1927 the AOF treasury contributed the not insignificant sum of 19.4 million francs to the French budget. In a speech to the colonial council, Governor-General Carde noted that this was indeed an important part of the French West African budget, but he added that the charges were little in comparison with the charges weighing on the mother country. "Well then, messieurs, our duty is plain; France calls, we respond."[18]

The lack of funds meant that the colonies could contribute only a very meagre portion of their budgets to the improvement of the lives of the African population. In 1930 the Middle Congo, the wealthiest colony in French Equatorial Africa, spent only 2 percent of the budget on public works; medical care and hygiene for the areas outside the two urban regions of Pointe Noire and Brazzaville accounted for only 1.5 percent of the budget. A medical post serving 80,000 people in the area of Stanley Pool had a yearly budget of 200 francs.[19] When André Gide traveled in the Congo in 1927 he was told that "when the medical service is asked for medicines it generally sends, after an immense delay, nothing but iodine, sulphate of soda, and—boric acid!" He himself saw that "everywhere people suffer from the lamentable penury by which diseases that might easily be checked are allowed to hold their own and even to gain ground."[20]

Sarraut's doctrine of the necessity of concentrating on economic development was adopted, although the necessary correlate, serious investment by France, was rejected. This meant that most of the cost of economic development devolved upon the colonies themselves. The first effect of this policy was to impose heavier tax burdens on the colonial population than were levied before the war. In 1926 in the Sudan the taxes increased 618 percent over those of a decade earlier; in 1926 alone the increase was 65 percent over the previous year. In the Ivory Coast taxes were raised from 11 million francs in 1925 to 14.7 million francs in 1926.[21]

The entire administrative machinery tended to concentrate its efforts on developing local production. The administrators spent an ever increasing amount of their time in spurring the production of crops; in Senegal it was peanuts, in the Ivory Coast cocoa and coffee, and in AEF cotton and rubber. The growing concern with economic development can be seen in the changed emphasis of the administrative reports being sent from the administrators to the governors. Before 1914 their reports were largely concerned with problems connected with establishing or maintaining French rule; in the 1920s, however, the reports stressed developments in local crop production, and informed the governors at the same time of local improvements such as the building of roads or the erection of bridges. The stress on production became so strong in the administration that governors were accustomed to saying in praise of a subordinate, "He is a man of quantity."[22]

In spurring production a number of administrators forced their population beyond its capacity. In the Ivory Coast, for example, an administrator in the 1930s imposed on the people he ruled impossible quotas of production of cotton. To avoid punishment for failure to comply with the administrator's orders, the Africans went across the border to the Gold Coast where they bought the cotton at excessively high prices. The administrator also dictated the prices at which the inhabitants were forced to sell the cotton to French dealers; the prices were lower than those the people themselves had paid for the same cotton in the British colony. The administrator also exacted honey from the people in his *cercle*. Since there was none in the region, the local young men had to make a three-week journey by foot to the Sudan to collect it. There was so much suffering that, according to the report of a French inspector, the people wished for the times of Samory, the African empire builder whose methods of conquest in the 1890s had laid waste vast regions of West Africa.[23]

And this example was not untypical. Marcel Olivier, who had served as governor-general, wrote in 1931 that the administrators too often ordered the people in their districts to grow certain quantities of produce without discovering whether such demands were realistic. Olivier claimed that the administrators, trained in the general skills of administration, were ignorant of the technical aspects of agriculture. There were few technicians overseas to direct or even to advise on colonial agricultural policy;[24] the first expert on cotton production, for example, was sent to AOF only in 1924.[25] The development of agriculture, the very foundation of the colonial economies, "lacked method, logic, and efficacy" because of lack of expertise.[26] This lack was one reason for the gap between the administrators' economic expectations and the true potential of their regions, but the authoritarianism of the system and the lack of participation of the population in decision-making also contributed to the situation. The French, like the other colonial powers, placed primary emphasis on coercion as a means of bringing about technological change.[27]

Some French officials, however, were openly opposed to the system; in the Ivory Coast a *commandant* declared that the administration had no legal right to coerce the population into crop production. He also refused to aid the white settlers in the recruitment of local labor, because the local French plantation owners were not paying their laborers enough. The colonial administration seemed at times closely connected to the white plantation owners and traders, but in this particular instance the administrator's independent stand does not seem to have hurt him; he received a rapid promotion, reaching the top rank of the Corps within a short time.[28]

In numerous writings administrators and former colonial officials attacked the emphasis on production. Delavignette, for one, was a spokesman for the younger men in the service when he emphasized that the policy of *mise en valeur* must be aimed not at increasing export production, but rather at increasing the standard of living of the local populations. "I worry when people speak of the land without taking account of the men living on the land," he wrote in the liberal Catholic review *Esprit*.[29]

Labouret, a member of the generation that had served overseas before World War I, also complained that there was far too much talk in the metropole about economic exploitation of the colonies, and too little concern for their human resources, the colonial populations.[30] Many administrators identified profoundly with their *cercles*. Nearly all the administrators, Deschamps wrote, had "a passion for their profession and pride in the progress that their command achieved." This attitude had its ridiculous side, Deschamps added, for many administrators

had the feeling that the country was their possession, their work, and this feeling gave to some of them an extraordinarily possessive language; we all used to say "my *cercle*," "my roads," "my buildings." Some even said "my natives," "my river," "my rain."[31]

Nevertheless, the possessiveness of the administrators meant that a very large proportion of them were genuinely concerned for the welfare of "their people." Many administrators were deeply embittered by the governmental failure to provide sufficient funds to enable them to help those they administered. A fairly large number of the administrators complained of the metropolitan financial neglect of the colonies.

The British also emphasized economic development of the colonies, but the British Parliament showed a greater willingness than did the French to make financial contributions to its overseas empire; in addition to guaranteeing loans it voted in 1929 to establish the Colonial Development Fund, which made available a modest but annual aid of one million pounds.

World War I led to a quickened pace in the evolution of the colonized peoples. For the French colonies the war had meant that half a million of their populations had participated in a white man's war. The experience of seeing white men killed and even defeated in battle probably destroyed any image there might have been of the white man's invincibility. The French army practiced segregation of its fighting forces, but many of the colonial troops, because of their wartime experience, began to assimilate European mannerisms and even values. A report of the governor of Dahomey in 1919 revealed changes undergone by some Africans who had participated in the war, and the kinds of problems that the colonial authorities had to face as a result. The governor reported that the *commandant* of one of the Dahomean *cercles*

remains preoccupied ... by the attitudes of former *tirailleurs* having returned to their homes, whose state of spirit is far from satisfactory. Several times he had to intervene to reestablish order ... upset by some troublemakers presuming to have the right to interfere in the life of the *cercle,* to pursue the witch doctors, and to free themselves from the authority of their native chiefs.[32]

In fact, administrative reports for AOF from 1920 to 1930 are filled with complaints about *tirailleurs* giving villagers examples of insubordination against the traditional chiefs.[33]

Contact with European values was undermining the allegiance of segments of the colonial populations to traditionalism. The limited yet rising tempo in establishing communications within the colonies and bringing them increasingly into a money economy led to the partial disintegration of the old social fabric within the colonial societies. Faced with the possibility of the disintegration of entire indigenous societies, Van Vollenhoven had addressed himself to that problem even during the war. Van Vollenhoven saw the populations of AOF as comprising "a mass of natives" and an elite group. The masses, he wrote in 1917, needed to evolve within their own environment. In order to assure them of security "in their families, their villages and their traditions," the indigenous society had to be consolidated. "A collapse" of the traditional society had to be prevented.[34] Van Vollenhoven saw the elite as a small group of individuals who stood apart from the masses because of their greater aptitudes and ambition:

This elite was ostracized from the native society because it no longer lived in the native manner and would not return to it. Proud of their effort, presumptuous and sometimes unbearable in their vanity, this category represents the young, the *avant garde,* the example.

While the masses were to develop within their own traditions, the elites, Van Vollenhoven stated, "must evolve more and more in our environment."[35]

After the war many officials deplored the degree to which the chief-system had been destroyed. In a written report to the minister of colonies in 1921, the governor-general of AOF regretted the "inevitable errors which accompanied the beginnings of European occupation." The first generation of administrators had misunderstood the nature of the indigenous societies. Experience, the governor-general stated, had shown the value of respecting the traditional cohesion of these societies.[36]

Henri Labouret warned that the destruction of tribal organizations was producing a crisis of authority. He called for a more careful study of the evolution of the colonies in order to stem the crisis.[37]

Concern was also expressed in the highest official circles. The minister of colonies, André Maginot, in a circular of 1929 to the governors-general, expressed his misgivings about the disappearing authority of the indigenous chiefs. The administrators alone, Maginot warned, would be unable to keep order; the chiefs were an important element in making it possible for the administration to maintain its authority over the masses.[38]

Governor-General Jules Brévié of AOF, who had served as governor of Niger and had experience in dealing with the great Hausa emirs of that colony, stressed the need to preserve and strengthen the chiefs. In the past, Brévié indicated, French officials had been too impatient with the chiefs. They had been unrealistic:

> To want to transform from one day to the next the *amenokal* of Ouillimède into a perfect collaborator of our administration would be equivalent to trying instantaneously to change the Sire de Coucy into a Prefect of the Third Republic.[39]

Brévié advised his subordinates to make a special effort to choose as chiefs men who by tradition were entitled to their positions. He specifically warned the *commandants* against the habit that had been relatively widespread before World War I of appointing former NCOs or other close collaborators of the French as chiefs. Brévié, like the British, wanted to modernize and strengthen the chief-system. Men having a traditional right to succeed as chiefs should be appointed, Brévié wrote, but they would be required to go through at least a four-year French education. In 1931 Brévié predicted that within a few years every chief would have an education equivalent to that of a primary school graduate.[40]

Brévié—like the British—wanted the advantage of traditional chiefs without the bureaucratic inefficiency that accompanied reliance on generally illiterate men. Ironically, Brévié's modernization of chiefs would not, as he imagined, strengthen traditional society, but rather would undermine it; after several years of French schooling, the chiefs no longer wholly belonged to the traditional world.

In the interwar period the French generally found the British policy of indirect rule attractive. Lord Lugard, the great organizer of Nigeria, had made the clearest and most systematic presentation of the British doctrine of indirect rule, and was now admired and read by French officials. "Lugardisme" became popular.

Before World War I, French administrators had thought that they would eventually use educated Africans as intermediaries between themselves and the large mass of the population. But the Africans who gained an education were by no means unconditionally enthusiastic about French rule. A number of young Africans as early as the 1920s smuggled, dispersed, and read publications from Paris that were critical of French rule. The governor-general of AOF noted in 1927 that "subversive ideas propagated by certain newspapers" could be found among "town dwellers, artisans, government employees, [and] *tirailleurs*."[41]

The French faith in assimilation was somewhat blunted by the experience of seeing men, dressed in European clothes and speaking French, denouncing the very country that had brought them the supposed benefits of civilization. The group most affected by French rule, contrary to expectations, could not, it seemed, be counted on as reliable intermediaries. There was a turning away from the elites and instead a concentration on the more simple rural population; the local elites were not used, the chiefs being retained instead.

Accompanying this development was an increasing understanding and tolerance for the traditional aspects of the colonial societies. Delavignette, writing of a French official, observed:

Often he would go so far as to admit that his own civilization was not universal, that it was not the only one, that he was dealing with different civilizations which it was his job to understand and protect.[42]

Robert Arnaud, a superb administrator and one of the finest writers of colonial fiction in the interwar period, described in his semiautobiographical novel *Les Meneurs d'hommes* how an administrator attempted to bridge French values with those of local tradition in the colony. Faced with traditional law requiring the death sentence of an adulteress, he wrote:

I admit with the assessors of a native court that the adulteress must die. I thus proclaim the force of tradition. Then by subtle arguments . . . I reduce the punishment to short imprisonment. I thus establish a suave compromise between the unchanged tradition of the ancestors and the doctrine of modern philosophy based on love.[43]

Increasingly, responsibility and duties were transferred to the chiefs. Yet in the final analysis, there still could be no doubt that all authority remained in French hands. Brévié quoted Van Vollenhoven's phrase, "Only the *commandant de cercle* commands; the native chief is only his instrument," and added, "This principle remains."[44] To allow the colonial populations to rule themselves without external control would imply, Brévié stated, the "existence of a well-policed society, a well-organized social structure, a native elite interested in public affairs.... Now, that is not the case in Black Africa."[45]

If the aim of French policy had really been to strengthen the chiefs, then, as a former French administrator asks, "Why were they not given the power to levy taxes and to have their own budgets?" The real reason for the granting of greater authority to the chiefs, Pierre Hugot suggests, was the desire "to simplify the administration." The administrators, unable to handle the severely increased work load, turned to the chiefs, whom they transformed into something "like a police chief."[46] French administrators intervened less zealously than they had before 1914 when the chiefs were guilty of malfeasance. A chief whom an administrator had described as a "sinister rogue ... [a] former trader living from monstrous exactions, [who] carries on a real reign of terror in his canton," was retained because he was useful to the administration.[47] As the governor of Guinea remarked in 1956, "We have for several years out of administrative convenience closed our eyes on the behavior of chiefs ... who were useful to us. Let us recognize the hypocrisy of our lack of interest in the means used by the chiefs, as long as they followed our orders."[48]

In spite of the strengthening of the chiefs that went on in the interwar years, the French never surrendered the goal of eventual assimilation of the colonies. Association practiced in the interwar years, with its respect for local institutions, was mostly thought of as a tactic to achieve more conveniently and thoroughly the same end—assimilation. Governor-General Olivier declared in 1931 that "a good native policy is one which, without upsetting anything, permits the sane and normal evolution of native societies toward a civilization that will be as close to *Western* civilization as possible."[49] The reason Olivier favored the values of Western civilization was that they had "best succeeded in conciliating respect for individual liberties with the needs of society and progress."[50] Thus the new emphasis on local institutions was motivated either by the need for administrative efficacy or by the persistent desire to achieve eventual assimilation. It did not connote any fundamental belief in the inherent virtues of traditional structures, such as that displayed by the most enthusiastic British proponents of indirect rule.

The French leaned so heavily on the chiefs that they transformed them into mere tools of the administration. As the governor of Senegal observed in 1931:

> The chiefs are auxiliaries of our authority.... Increasingly they have the tendency, under heavy pressure of daily obligations, to reserve all their activity for the execution of orders emanating from the local authority, [thus] abandoning gradually their role as born protectors in the traditional framework of the populations that under our administration, our tutelage, they command.[51]

In two ways the chiefs ceased to be genuine spokesmen of their populations. First, they remained too traditional for the parts of the population that had come into contact with modernizing influences, such as, for example, the war veterans. Over these men the chiefs could no longer pretend to rule. Second, because the administration had reduced the chiefs to auxiliaries of the regular administration, the chiefs also ceased to be full members of the traditional society. The chiefs were forced to do the bidding of the local French *commandant*; they had ceased to be the "protectors," as the governor of Senegal put it, of their own societies.

French rule had emptied the traditional structures of their meaning, but it did not replace them. The French had destroyed the old structures in the name of liberty, equality, and fraternity, but once the societies were in the process of disintegration, they hesitated to transform their ideals into reality. The colonial system was in dire need of change, for it no longer corresponded to the needs of the African societies. These had undergone profound change, but the colonial system was virtually the same as it had been at its inception in the 1880s. Yet no basic reforms were introduced in the interwar period.

The only reforms were palliatives, making colonial rule somewhat less harsh than it had been before World War I. For example, although forced labor was to exist in the French colonies until 1945, its use was increasingly controlled. In AOF all labor service was limited in 1930 to a maximum of ten days per year, and a decree provided that no labor could be proscripted during the harvest season. Also, in the 1930s provisions for exemption from labor service were made for all those paying the equivalent of the price of labor from which they were being exempted. In 1937 the Popular Front governor-general of AOF, Marcel de Coppet, ordered his governors to abolish forced labor in the developed regions of their colonies and to institute instead an additional tax which would finance the public works. Four colonies adopted this suggestion: Senegal, Guinea, the Ivory Coast, and Dahomey. Forced labor was thus abolished in twenty-five out of 109 *cercles* in AOF. In the regions where it was kept, it was somewhat milder in form; in the Ivory Coast in the nonexempt areas, the maximum age of those required to perform labor was reduced from sixty to fifty years.[52]

The *indigénat*, which had been a major hallmark of the colonial system, continued in force, although in the interwar period its use was limited in application. The first limitation on the exercise of repressive justice was established in 1917 in AOF when *chefs de canton* were exempted from the *indigénat*; further immunities were granted in 1918 to veterans and their families. In 1924 a decree promulgated for all the colonies suspended the *indigénat* for government employees, members of local assemblies, assessors in indigenous courts, recipients of French medals, owners of elementary school diplomas or their equivalents, and merchants with trade patents.

Individuals could also be exempted "because of their participation either in the commercial or agricultural development of the country or in general work of public interest, or in service to the French cause."[53] In 1925 in AOF the total number of acts punishable by the *indigénat* code was reduced from forty-six to twenty-five; in Madagascar the categories of acts punishable were reduced in 1937 from seventeen to five. Women were exempted from the *indigénat* in AOF after 1934. The maximum fine was still 100 francs, but because of inflation it no longer represented as severe a penalty as it had before the war.

The governors-general and the governors reminded the administrators to employ the *indigénat* sparingly, and its use was gradually reduced in the 1930s. The following table for the Sudan demonstrates the general decrease in the number of disciplinary punishments.

Table 9

Application of the indigénat *code in the Sudan in the 1930s*[54]

Year	Number of punishments	Total indigenous population	Number of population punished per thousand
1931	5,165	2,853,621	1.8
1932	5,023	2,884,000	1.7
1933	5,505	3,532,935	1.2
1934	5,138	3,546,645	1.4
1935	3,023	3,565,513	0.8

The colonial system had become more humane, but it underwent no basic transformation. Most administrators continued to believe in the necessity of the authoritarian system with which the *indigénat* was associated. In 1934 the governor of Senegal reported that all the administrators in his colony agreed with him in his estimation:

The *indigénat*, in spite of the generally good spirit of the populations, remains an indispensable institution. We must for a long time to come maintain the disciplinary punishment that will allow us to punish in a quick and striking manner acts incompatible with the public order and acts that do not justify referral to a court.[55]

The authoritarian system remained intact, basically unchanged. The *commandants* were still the "real chiefs of the empire." Men who served in the colonies in the interwar period, even authoritarian ones, were to express later on a feeling of surprise that they had been entrusted with so much power. And one of them was to quote and concur with Lord Acton's dictum that all power tends to corrupt, and absolute power corrupts absolutely.[56]

The totality of powers that the administrators had arrogated to themselves meant that any change in the colonial system could occur only through their activities. The Corps in the interwar period, however, maintained a form of stability overseas that easily led to stagnation, as Deschamps observed.[57]

This stagnation was due in part to the influence of the older administrators, recruited before World War I, who had reached the upper ranks of the Corps in the 1920s. Accustomed to old routines, they were not aware of the changes that had occurred in the colonies. Since promotion was to a large extent by seniority, many mediocre administrators had reached the top echelons of the administration. A commission of the ministry of colonies suggested in 1928 that one way of improving the top ranks of the Corps would be to require officials to take examinations and to write monographs before being appointed as chief administrators. Governor-General Carde was opposed to these strictly literary prerequisites, suggesting that some administrators who were brilliant essayists made poor administrators, and vice versa.[58] Promotion would have to be granted men possessing administrative rather than literary abilities. The commission recommendations were dropped.

Eventually the older administrators who had clogged the top ranks of the Corps were there no longer; by the end of the 1920s nearly a fifth were either pensioned or retired; sixty were pensioned because of infirmities acquired in service and 156 were retired because of age. The Doumergue government's economy laws of 1934, which required the premature retirement of the top ranks of the various French bureaucratic organizations, led to the withdrawal of 120 additional administrators, or 10 percent of the Corps.[59]

As a result of the Doumergue decrees, a growing proportion of the older generation, that is, men who had entered the service before World War I, left the Corps. This process continued so rapidly that by 1939 only 14 percent of the men serving in the Corps had received their appointments before 1919; 34 percent had entered in the 1920s, and a majority—52 percent, or 602 men—had been appointed after 1930. Thus on the eve of World War II the French colonial administration consisted overwhelmingly of young men. These young men were cadets of the *Ecole Coloniale* or agents who had had a one-year training program at the school. That training, as has been shown in Chapter V, emphasized the need for careful observation of the colonial societies and the need for flexibility in administration. But in their methods of administration, the colonial functionaries seem to have been relatively unaffected by the *Ecole Coloniale*.

In the field, the young, newly arrived administrators were most influenced by senior officials in the field, and turned instinctively for inspiration and guidance to their elders. This was as it should be, for the older administrators were superb masters in teaching their young colleagues the complexities of local administration. The system of apprenticeship prepared the colonial officials well for the day-to-day practical problems of ruling a *cercle*. It had its disadvantages, however, in that it permitted the older generation of officials to pass on many of their attitudes to the younger men. The writings of both Van Vollenhoven and Lyautey, which a number of former administrators claimed as having inspired them in their administration, again tended to reinforce traditional attitudes.

The authoritarian system in the colonies provided an ideal opportunity for effective and conscientious administrators to form a new and better society. Delavignette described the situation thus: "The colony becomes a sort of totalitarian party and the colonials compulsory members, working overtime to draw towards themselves the territory's whole native life."[60] The system, Delavignette wrote, is "the only humane form of government in Africa, Europe, or anywhere else, because it is the only one where those who govern see those who are governed as living men." The dangers inherent in the system, he recognized, would emerge if the officials lost this contact with those they administered.[61] As the quality of the men going overseas improved, the system became more bureaucratic. The administrators were men with higher education and character; they were reliable officials. But these very qualities made them prone to routinization: content with the establishment of an administration which seemed a near-perfect form of benevolent paternalism, most administrators failed to bring any real change to the system. One of the main reasons for the failure, as Delavignette had warned, was precisely the fact that the administrators lost contact with the populations under their rule. In a 1931 letter to the minister of colonies, the governor-general of AOF wrote:

> We have lost contact with the native. We are poorly informed of his sentiments, of his complaints, of his aspirations, of his eventual reactions; and we may one day have a cruel surprise.[62]

The administrators serving in the bush before the war seem to have lived closer to the local populations than had their successors. A large number of administrators in the early period of colonization had arrived at their posts without their wives. As a result, they generally traveled widely within their *cercles*. The local girls, with whom the administrators often lived, tended to serve as useful guides to the language and other mysteries of the local societies. But as living conditions improved, administrators began to bring their European wives with them. This development meant that the administrators were less inclined to leave their residences and to go on tours of their *cercles,* a situation which led to a somewhat less effective administration. Even before the war, Governor-General William Ponty observed that the administrators who brought families with them lost approximately 50 percent of their efficiency; the comfort of the hearth, he had said, was detrimental to good colonial administration.[63] In 1932, Brévié remarked that administrators on tours often took their families with them, and were more preoccupied with assuring the comfort of their wives and children than with observing the realities around them.[64]

The arrival of white women in the colonies after World War I put an end to the relatively unrestrained social intermingling that had been prevalent in earlier years. And the introduction of the automobile further tended to make it more difficult for the administrators to keep in close contact with the local populations. A governor of the Sudan correctly warned his subordinates that "the seat of a car can become nothing more than a bureaucrat's chair (*rond de cuir*)."[65] The car allowed the administrators to travel faster and farther in their *cercles,* but it also meant that they could only go where there were roads; villages off the beaten track became relatively less accessible.

But probably the main factor preventing the administrators from maintaining close contact with their people was the chronic shortage of personnel. During the interwar period the duties of the administrators had significantly increased. They were required to spend an ever larger proportion of their time in interminable office work, filling out reports and sending statistics to the colonial capitals. The governor of Dahomey estimated in 1933 that since the time of the French occupation in the 1890s the workload of the administrators had quadrupled.[66] But although the duties increased, the personnel did not, largely because the administrations, pinched for funds, had to limit their main expenditure—personnel costs. Thus, there were scarcely more administrators than there had been before the war. In 1912 AOF had had 341 administrators; in 1937 there were 385. In AEF there were even fewer administrators in the 1920s than there had been before the war; in 1913 there had been 398 administrators; in 1928 there were only 366 (of whom only 250 were actually in AEF exercising their functions).[67]

After the war an increasing number of administrators was used for bureaucratic tasks in the colonial capitals, and as a result there were fewer men available for work in the bush than there had been before and a number of administrative posts had to be closed. Many *cercles,* because of their size and importance, required assistant administrators in addition to the *commandants de cercles,* but fifty-one such *cercles* lacked assistants. The governor-general of AOF pointed out in 1931 that his administration would require 200 more administrators to perform adequately.[68] Yet eight years later only thirty-three additional administrators had been added to the administration of AOF. Because of the shortage in personnel, men known to be unfit were entrusted with important posts; by the governor-general's admission, nineteen out of 118 *cercles* in AOF in 1930 had been given to administrators who were manifestly incompetent, and of the 130 subdivisions twelve were in the hands of unsatisfactory administrators.[69]

Another factor that prevented colonial officials from establishing contact with the people was their constant turnover. Governors remained in many cases less than a year: between 1928 and 1933 Dahomey had six governors; between 1929 and 1933 the Ivory Coast had five and Guinea four. The impermanence also of the administrators was well known. In one *cercle* in Chad, a former administrator noted that there were thirty-three different administrators between 1910 and 1952. Only seven of them remained for two years or longer, and some as briefly as four to six months.[70] In an extreme case in Senegal in 1937, there were four different *commandants* of one *cercle* within five months. The displacement of administrators was so frequent that Cosnier declared that the instability of personnel was "the most obvious characteristic of our colonial administration."[71]

Of course some administrators served many years in the same region; Félix Eboué served for twenty-one years in Oubangui-Chari, René Isambert for fourteen years in the same colony.[72] But these were notable exceptions; in Senegal, for example, the average period of service between 1887 and 1940 was about six years.[73] Some writers on French rule, such as Suret-Canale, claim that after World War I administrators were rotated more often than before the war, but the statistics reveal that the practice of short assignments and frequent rotation existed from the outset. (See Appendix III.)

British administrators, on the other hand, often stayed in the same colony for their entire career, since they were in the employ of a specific colony's service. Even if they transferred from one colony to another, their stay was usually a long one. But within districts there are examples in the British colonies of rapid turnover; in one district in Southeast Tanganyika (now part of Tanzania) twenty-six men served between 1919 and 1962, and in another district there were twenty-eight men during the same forty-three year period.[74]

The French tended to rotate their governors, and even more their administrators, for fear that they might become too independent of superior authority or too partial to any one party in their administrative regions. (Because of the intense complexity of administering nomads, the French administration usually made an exception to this practice and permitted administrators in nomadic regions to remain in the same area for several consecutive assignments.) The furlough system also made it difficult for administrators to serve consecutively in the same *cercle*. After serving two years in the colonies, they were sent to France for a six months' leave. In the meantime their places were taken by other administrators and upon their return they were assigned to other regions. One administrator bemoaned the bewildering variety of regions to which the administrators successively had to adjust. He wrote:

When we got to know the forest, they sent us to make our apprenticeship in the jungle, and then to the borders of the desert. We pass successively from fetishist people to Islamic tribes, from disorganized tribes to hierarchical kingdoms.[75]

After twenty-three administrators in five years had passed through the *cercle* of Tougah, the governor of Sudan remarked, "The *cercle* resembles a building to which everyone has contributed a brick, without having considered the shape of the building."[76] In the same vein, an administrator remarked shortly after World War II:

As a result of frequent changes there is a lamentable lack of continuity, a number of praiseworthy initiatives without a future, and as a result after twenty years the country has not progressed more than in two, the efforts of some having reversed those of others, or at least not having continued them.[77]

A Cameroonese clerk who served the French administration during the interwar period and, after his country achieved independence, served as its ambassador to the United States, wrote a fascinating portrayal of the variety of successive administrators in the *cercle* in which he was employed:

The first [French administrator] was in 1916, a military officer.... [He was] impetuous, authoritarian, rowdy, and severe, but not spiteful. [He was] more of a passing horseman than a stationary administrator.... He did not remain a long time. He celebrated the event of November 1918, danced with the villagers on the public place, and left....
M. le Commandant B. [was] silent, timorous, afraid of everything, intimidated by everything, exaggerated everything. Of a wisp of hay, he would make a haystack....
Then there was Commandant C., a small old twisted man who rarely came to the office, or came rather when the clerk was gone, searched in the latter's writing pad and read the scraps of paper in the wastepaper basket....
The writer still remembers Commandant E., a very conscientious, humane, honest, just, understanding, and Christian man. When he returned to France, he wrote the clerk a friendly postcard....
The clerk also got to know M. le Commandant F. Alas, this one was mad.... The very day of his arrival he had asked the clerk what the "going rate" was for the local wenches. When the clerk answered him, ... he pulled out his wallet and exclaimed, "I only have enough for six sessions." His whole stay was marked by this weakness. He had a deficit in his treasury.... He also left and was subject to public ridicule....
The clerk had known M. le Commandant H., a hard worker and a married man. His wife had small get-togethers with the wives of the functionaries in the region. Both learned the local language. The population was very happy, they had a child during their stay to whom they gave a name from the country. They were well liked in the region....[78]

From this sketch it should be apparent that no clear and persistent policy could be carried out, for given the authoritarian framework during the interwar period, the style of administration in each *cercle* changed each time the region had a new administrator. The administrators would have had to be retained for longer periods of time within each *cercle* to allow the development of any really constructive policies.

A number of sporadic efforts were made to keep the administrators for longer periods within the same *cercle*. Sarraut in 1921 and one of his many successors in 1932 proposed the adoption of measures that would have remedied the situation. Both, however, failed in their efforts. In 1938 Mandel finally issued a decree requiring administrators to remain for five consecutive years in the same region.[79] But this decree was hardly put into effect when it was abrogated by the Vichy regime.

The frequent change in assignments generally meant that there was little incentive for the administrators to learn the local languages and very few bothered to learn them; no sooner might they have mastered the language than they were assigned to another region where they had no use for it. There was really no language that could serve as a *lingua franca* in either AOF or AEF. In the Ivory Coast alone, for example, there were over eighty different languages.

From 1887 until 1939 only a little over 12 percent of the administrators spoke an African language, which meant, of course, that relatively few were able to converse with the people living in their regions. In 1933, fewer than one out of every ten administrators spoke the local language.[80] Further, since the officials were so frequently moved about, their language abilities were of minimal use. Administrators knowing Wolof, which is spoken in Senegal, could find no use for this language in Niger or Guinea, nor for that matter could they use it in the southern part of Senegal itself.

In general, the colonial administration did little to encourage the study of the local languages. Gallieni founded a school of interpreters and encouraged his subordinates to learn the local languages in Madagascar, yet he thought of this as an interim solution. He impatiently awaited the time when the Malgache population would have learned French, thus easing the administrative burdens of the French officials.[81] A colonial official in 1934 expressed the concern of many of his contemporaries when he wrote that it was admirable for some administrators to learn the local languages in the colonies, but

Under the guise of advancing the natives within their traditions will we go through their school? ... are we going to renounce the essential and fundamental principle of the access of the natives to the French language?[82]

The administrators were largely dependent on their interpreters. Traveling through AOF in the early 1930s, a young Englishman, Geoffrey Gorer, observed of the administrators that he had "never met one who was independent of an interpreter."[83] This situation often led to abuse. The complaint voiced by a Dahomean in 1909 certainly does not describe a unique situation; he declared that the interpreter in his *cercle* has established a court in which he regulates all matters before submitting them to the administrator; this is not done for nothing, chicken, sheep, money ... have to be paid.... [He] has said that the white man will believe anything he says.[84]

As Delavignette showed in his *Les Paysans noirs,* the indigenous interpreters continued, in the interwar period, to be a barrier between the administrators and the local populations; often through bribes they misled and misinformed inexperienced young administrators. The undesirability of having interpreters was recognized by the colonial administration, but they were generally considered a necessary evil. As Governor-General Brévié wrote in 1935, "It would be desirable to suppress all the native interpreters, but it is impossible."[85]

The administrators, as Delavignette noted in a critical article in 1931, had lost contact with the indigenous populations and had failed to carry on research about the societies in which they were working. Delavignette remarked that missionaries and occasional travelers were contributing far more to an understanding of the local societies while "the administrators live on the fruits of old works."[86]

In general, the colonial administration did little to encourage the administrators to study the societies in which they were serving. An official who served in the interwar period was carrying on ethnological research when his superior called him in and told him:

I have observed that you are not very serious; you carry on completely superfluous ethnographic studies, and during your tours in the bush you take many photographs.

Only in secret was he able to continue his research.[87] This obstructive attitude toward ethnological research, Delavignette suggested, was quite common.[88] Ethnological reports were "considered taboo and buried away among the administrative files."[89]

In 1938 Mandel issued a decree that encouraged the learning of African languages in the colonies; all administrators having a knowledge of the language spoken in their region were to be paid an additional annual allowance of 5,000 francs. This provision meant for the intermediate ranks of the administration approximately a 10 percent raise in their salaries. Again, however, this provision was introduced too late to have any effect in the interwar period.[90]

In the end the administrators themselves—rather than the administrative system—must be blamed for the general lack of research on the colonial societies, for they had remarkably little interest in the indigenous societies. Gorer, during his tour of West Africa in the 1930s, found that

I was practically never able to get any information about the habits or customs of the Negroes they were ruling; they were almost all convinced that there was nothing of interest to be found.[91]

A former British administrator who had frequent contacts with his French counterparts wrote in 1947:

French administration has slight interest in and gives little time to native customs and ideas and languages. The ignorance of French officials is in fact astounding.[92]

It is something of a mystery how a Corps that after 1930 consisted of such a large proportion of graduates from the *Ecole Coloniale* (many of whom had also studied at the *Institut des langues orientales*) could be so little concerned with the study of the customs and languages of the colonial societies. Of course, the administrators were heavily burdened with administrative tasks which left them very little time for research. But Governor-General de Coppet was undoubtedly right when he accused the administrators, especially the younger ones, of having fallen into "a certain inertia" which prevented them from studying the colonial societies.[93] Because the administrators had become seriously estranged from the local surroundings, they were unable to appreciate fully the evolution going on around them and therefore had few, if any, proposals for a change in the colonial system. As Delavignette observed in his article of 1931, as a result of the failure of the administrators to keep in close touch with the developments of the colonial societies,

It follows that the natives are evolving faster than the administrators or the administration. It follows that the natives are very far beyond the goals we have assigned for them from the official observatories in which the administrators are confined.[94]

The establishment of representative institutions would, to a great degree, have helped keep the French abreast of the developments of the colonial societies. Furthermore, such institutions, by giving the African populations a greater role in the process of governing their own societies, would have taken into account the new demands that were being raised by the local elites within the colonies. One of the striking aspects of the French empire, as Cosnier noted, was that "the governed people are not represented by anybody."[95]

Toward the end of World War I Governor-General Angoulvant noted that new political institutions would have to be adopted in view of the effect that the war was having on the colonial populations. "The indigenous populations must inevitably develop toward a more advanced political and social situation.... The war unquestionably accelerated the speed [of change] and has set aside all our previous plans.... There is no doubt but that one could have wished a less speedy evolution."[96]

In 1920 Sarraut proposed the establishment of representative assemblies in the colonies. Their existence would have constituted a French recognition of the extent to which the colonies had evolved and would also have helped lead the social and political evolution overseas. The representative bodies should first have a restricted electorate, Sarraut argued, and it should be gradually enlarged to become finally fully representative of the colonial populations.[97] The prerogatives of these assemblies were left somewhat vague, but Sarraut evidently envisaged that they would play an important role in voting the local budgets and in controlling the administration of each colony. In spite of the modesty of his proposal, Sarraut found it necessary to deny in advance, before any objections might be raised against it, that his plan, which would give the colonial populations experience in local rule, would lead to a demand for independence.[98] Rather than weaken the bonds of empire, this system would strengthen them, Sarraut claimed. Besides, he assured his readers, the colonial populations did not desire independence; too many of them were presumably aware of their own incapacity to rule themselves and recognized the blessings of French rule.[99]

Inspired by Sarraut's proposals a group of parliamentarians presented a project in 1922 which would have created assemblies in AOF, AEF, Madagascar, and Indochina that would have permitted them to possess real financial powers, and deliberative powers in administrative matters. At most a third of the assembly members were to be indigenous; the remainder would be colonial officials, and the governors-general would have veto powers over the councils.[100]

This rather limited project for self-government was not accepted by the Parliament nor by colonial officials. Even Delafosse, who had advocated that greater responsibilities be given the Africans, found this plan too bold; he opposed the election of the African council members, instead advising that they be appointed.[101] A decade later Marcel Olivier, a member of the colonial service who had been governor-general of Madagascar, showed the same reluctance to allow the colonial people active participation in public affairs. "There is not a single Frenchman concerned with the interests of the Fatherland and its empire," he wrote, who could favor such a proposal.[102]

In 1919-1920, strictly advisory councils were created at various administrative levels of AOF and Madagascar. (AEF, considered more backward, was given such institutions only in 1938.) During the interwar era, they remained advisory bodies and were not permitted to develop into genuine legislative bodies. At the government-general level an AOF council—an advisory body consisting of the top functionaries within the federation—was instituted. When the council met in plenary session, one appointed African chief from each colony was allowed to participate in the deliberations. When the council was in working session, only one chief, appointed by the governor-general, was permitted to participate. At the level of the governors' councils in each colony, two chiefs, appointed by the administration, participated in the deliberations. At the *cercle* level local notables formed a council, the object of which was to advise the *commandant* on taxes, labor dues, and public works. The powers of these councils remained strictly advisory. It is doubtful that the councils of notables were genuinely expressive of popular feelings, for the members were easily cowed by the administrators.

In a number of urban areas *communes mixtes* were established in which city councils were set up, the members of which were elected by a limited suffrage; the office of city mayor was occupied by the French administrator.

The failure to found further representative political bodies, especially one that might have had some effective control over the administration, can be attributed to the tendency of the administration to favor the preservation of a system that would continue to be untroubled and unhindered. Concerned mainly with administrative efficiency, the administrators could only regard with hostility the establishment of bodies that might question their acts. As an administrator who served in the interwar period noted:

It would really be unnatural for functionaries holding in their hands the totality of power to work for the establishment of local representative institutions which would have the effect of troubling the good harmony and the satisfactory serenity of their services.[103]

Most officials were basically wedded to a policy that would preserve the status quo. If any kind of criticism of the French was voiced in the advisory councils, then the entire council system became suspect. In 1931, Governor-General Carde noted that in the colonial councils the chiefs were appearing to be the representatives of the colonial peoples, for they were defending their interests by arguing for a tax cut. This situation, Carde wrote, showed that "one cannot be too prudent in the granting of political liberties to the natives."[104]

When the more liberal Brévié, Carde's successor, suggested in 1934 a slight increase in the prerogatives of the colonial councils, he had to defend himself against a vehement charge by the ministry of colonies that he was advocating autonomy for the colonies and the liquidation of the French empire.[105]

The resistance to representative institutions was not, however, peculiar to the French. The British had established a system in India in which considerable power was entrusted to representatives of the local populations, but British governors by no means looked always with favor at the establishment of representative institutions. Governor Cameron of Tanganyika in 1925 specifically cited India as a warning example of setting up "European" institutions in the colonies.[106]

To the administrators, popular participation in decision-making would have interfered with the efficiency of the administrative process. It would also have given a disproportionate voice to the small educated elite that was emerging. As events were to show after World War II, the introduction of parliamentarism did mean a nearly complete capture of political power by the elite group.

French colonization, by encouraging economic development, had created centers containing sizable urban populations. The spread of education also contributed to the emergence of a restricted but educated elite. The administrators, used to serving in the bush, were ill equipped to handle these new developments. In the bush benevolent paternalism was still applicable, but in the urban centers this method of rule was becoming quickly outdated. Many administrators felt that the elites developing in the cities were unrepresentative of the colonial societies in general; therefore only a few officials recognized the need to give an outlet to the African elite in political and administrative responsibilities within their own societies. Brévié, in a circular to his subordinates in 1932, could only suggest that the administrators in their dealings with the new elite be just, kind, and patient.[107]

A few officials, like the liberal Governor de Coppet of Dahomey, sensed the occurrence of these political changes. When the governor-general of AOF suggested some minor reforms in 1934, de Coppet observed that they would not be sufficient to satisfy "the aspirations of Dahomean public opinion." The Dahomean, de Coppet wrote, "aspires for neither more nor less than the status of a citizen and to enjoy the civic rights given the natives of Senegal in the four communes."[108]

Jules Reste, the governor-general of AOF, quoted de Coppet in a report to the ministry of colonies, and added:

The same tendencies are beginning to appear among the intellectuals in Sudan, Guinea, the Ivory Coast. They refuse to accept that even the lowest-born of their fellow Africans of the *communes de pleins exercices* of Senegal, solely because of their place of birth, with no regard to their personal merit, can enjoy privileges from which they are excluded.[109]

These comments were unusually perceptive, but in general the colonial administration repressed all demonstrations of protest and remained unaware of a developing nationalist sentiment in a number of colonies.

When a serious nationalist uprising, the famous Yen Bay revolt, broke out in Indochina in 1930, the ministry of colonies blamed the uprising on the lack of communication between the administrators and the colonial populations. Rather than recognizing that the entire colonial system needed to be changed in order to give an outlet to the newly developed elites and to take into account, at least to some extent, the developing forces of nationalism, the minister of colonies recommended that the administrators both in Indochina and in Africa keep in more intimate contact with their populations, that they multiply their tours of the countryside, and that they take a more personal interest in those they administered.[110]

In AOF Boisson was aware of the development overseas of an elite that was not necessarily sympathetic to the French. If contacts with the elites were not strengthened, Boisson feared that they would fall under anti-French influence. Boisson therefore expressed in a circular the wish for the development

of a number of athletic and cultural associations, guided by us, receiving their means from us, dependent on us for their prosperity and expressing themselves in festivities attended by the European population.[111]

Implicit in his statement was the notion that the elite could be guided by the French, and that it would accept such tutelage. While perceptive in recognizing the development of an elite hostile to the French administration, Boisson nevertheless still shared the belief of most officials that the disaffection could be remedied by increased social contacts between the administrators and the people in their districts.

Some officials vaguely sensed a crisis, but few envisioned the emergence of a fully developed nationalism, or the breakup of the empire into nation-states. Camille Guy, a long-time member of the colonial service, who had been governor of Senegal at the turn of the century, declared that independence was impossible since the colonies were inhabited by backward people. The Africans, he declared, also recognized their own inferiority. "It will take several generations before they catch up with our civilization and are able to rule themselves."[112]

Hand in hand with administrative stagnation overseas went an immobility in colonial doctrine in France. The paucity of new ideas and approaches in the interwar years is reflected in school textbooks in this period. There was no change in the concepts about the empire in the period from 1919 to 1939. In fact the school manuals insisted even more on the twin themes that had already evolved before World War I: the French need for empire and the blessings that French rule brought to the overseas populations.[113]

One of the most persistent intellectual legacies of the pre-1914 era inherited by overseas officials in the 1920s and 1930s, was the notion that the only solution to the colonial problem lay in the application of either the doctrine of association or that of assimilation. Each doctrine was considered an indissoluble entity. The advocates of association who spoke of the uniqueness of colonial societies and their need to have different institutions from those in France found it difficult to argue at the same time that these institutions should be more democratic and less authoritarian. But when they did so, they were accused of favoring the autonomy of the colonies, which would lead to independence. Generally, French colonial theorists considered the maintenance of the empire as incompatible with the granting to the colonial populations of human and political rights similar to those enjoyed by French citizens. This point of view was reflected in the warning issued by the Superior Council of Colonies, an advisory board of colonial experts which met at infrequent intervals to advise the minister of colonies. In 1925, the council warned:

One must above all avoid the error the British made in India of recognizing the same rights for the natives as for the conquerors; to do so is clearly to prepare the eviction of the colonizing element.[114]

Those arguing for a revision of the authoritarian colonial system found only in the doctrine of assimilation a system which gave democratic rights to the colonial populations while ensuring the maintenance of tight bonds forever connecting the overseas possessions to the mother country. Few colonial officials were willing to see assimilation carried out immediately, although many claimed that they favored the eventual assimilation of the colonial populations at some unspecified time. Hubert Deschamps, a young administrator, a Socialist who served as Léon Blum's *chef de cabinet,* was one of the few calling for immediate assimilation. In an article in 1930 he had fought against "Lugardisme," arguing that its effect would be only to perpetuate the rule of the most backward elements of the overseas societies, the traditional chiefs, thereby preventing assimilation.

The ancient societies were disintegrating and the only solution was to Westernize the elites and to assimilate the colonies to France. In 1938, Deschamps ended his thesis on Madagascar with the plea, "Let us be good educators and let us prepare good Europeans."[115]

To Labouret and Delavignette the solution lay beyond the two categories of assimilation and association. Nearly alone these two men were able to break loose from those traditional doctrines. They fused some of the better elements from both doctrines. Labouret, while wishing to see the authoritarian colonial structure ended, opposed assimilation. Assimilation, he predicted, would mean that France would share a common parliament with her colonies; thus as a result of the demographic advantage of the colonies, "the newly civilized" would take political control over the mother country itself. Since such an eventuality was unacceptable to the metropole, the solution, Labouret wrote, was gradually to give the colonial populations full political and legal rights within their own countries. The colonies themselves would be connected to the mother country in the form of a federation,[116] In a general way, Labouret indicated the direction that France was to take after 1945.

Delavignette in all his writings argued the necessity of freeing the colonial system from all formulas, since formulas were divorced from reality. In essence, there was to be no doctrine, only a system corresponding to the needs of the colonial populations. In the interwar period, Delavignette saw those needs as consisting of some form of internal autonomy, at the same time maintaining close ties with France. After World War II, Delavignette became one of the most impassioned advocates of a Franco-African community based on equality between France and its overseas possessions.

Labouret and Delavignette were speaking only for themselves; although they were influential publicists, they were not at the levers of power. What the colonies really needed was an overall plan emanating from the central administration in Paris. Yet the very organization of the ministry at Rue Oudinot prevented such a development. It was seriously understaffed; in 1896 it had 133 employees, but forty years later, in spite of the ministry's increased responsibilities, it had only 129.

Because of parliamentary instability, no minister headed Rue Oudinot long enough to impose his views on the colonial administration. Formulation of policy remained in the hands of the top officials, the directors-general. These men had risen through the ranks within the ministry; by the time they arrived at the top of the hierarchy, Deschamps observed, they "were formed by tradition and they worked to preserve it. We arrive thus at a kind of fossilization and a nearly total lack of vision for the future." In addition, Deschamps suggested, the legal education of these officials prevented them from conceiving of the need for dynamic change; they lacked what Deschamps called a "historical sense."[117]

The ministry itself was not in close touch with developments overseas. There was very little interchange of personnel between the offices of Rue Oudinot and the administrations in the colonies. The work in the central administration was considered dull, and few able administrators chose to serve in its offices.[118] Usually only older and ailing administrators who could not return to the colonies served in the central administration. There were so many of them that one official facetiously suggested that the ministry, a stone's throw from the Invalides, the home for the aged and wounded war veterans, was itself the "Invalides" of the French colonial service.[119]

A conference of governors-general meeting in Paris in 1936 proposed a regular interchange of officials between the colonies and the central administration. Rather than assigning the older and more inefficient members of the Corps to the ministry, the conference advocated that the brightest of the younger men serving overseas be brought to Rue Oudinot for short periods of time. These men would bring to the central administration current practical knowledge acquired from recent active service overseas. From their experience at Rue Oudinot, it was also hoped, the young men would acquire a broad understanding of the French colonial system and would thus become capable of assuming in their later years positions of high responsibility within the service overseas.[120]

Minister of Colonies Marius Moutet issued a decree in 1937 by which administrators were limited to a three-year period in the central administration. In the past, some members of the Corps, once they had arrived at Rue Oudinot, remained there for prolonged periods. When Mandel became minister in 1938, he declared that "because of an unfortunate tolerance [by the ministry], which has slowly transformed itself into a real tradition, certain functionaries have practically ceased residing in the colonies."[121] This habit, Mandel declared, meant that officials serving in the ministry lost contact with the realities of the colonial societies. Strengthening the Moutet decree, Mandel announced that administrators failing to return to the colonies after serving a maximum of three years in the central administration would automatically be considered to have resigned. If the Moutet and Mandel decrees had been adopted earlier, they might have had an impact on the formulation of policy in the central administration during the interwar period, but they were hardly in effect before the war broke out.

Thus, during the interwar period, no satisfactory system was established which brought the offices of Rue Oudinot in close touch with

MARIUS MOUTET

developments overseas. As Delavignette suggested, "a time lag" developed "between the highest level of the colonial administration and the fragmentary but valuable experience of the men on the spot."[122]

The first real initiative for a reorganization of the colonial system occurred during the Popular Front government, when Marius Moutet became the first Socialist to head Rue Oudinot. As a deputy Moutet had been a vigorous critic of the French colonial system, particularly of its repressive aspects. Moutet replaced the governors-general: in AOF, de Coppet, a Socialist and a liberal governor of Dahomey, was promoted to governor-general of the entire federation; in AEF and Madagascar equally liberal officials were appointed. Men like de Coppet gave the administration a different style; he was the first governor-general ever to invite African students to an official luncheon at his palace. In spite of such signs of change, however, the men below the level of governor-general in the administration nevertheless remained. And they retained the paternalist-authoritarian spirit.

Moutet attempted to establish a comprehensive Popular Front plan for colonial reforms, and in 1936 called a conference of the governors-general. A similar conference had convened in 1935 to deal with imperial economic problems, but its results had been disappointing. Except for announcing a hope for some plan "to coordinate and develop the economies of all the colonies making up the empire," the conference had achieved nothing.[123]

Moutet's conference was intended to help the minister of colonies draw up an all-inclusive program of reform. But once it met, the governors-general limited their discussions strictly to economic and administrative matters.

In the economic field the conference proposed the establishment of a capital investment program in the colonies amounting to between 200 and 300 million francs annually. A massive program of public works was also suggested. The conference went on record as favoring the use of paid, rather than forced, labor for the program of modernization. The governors-general attempted to improve the financial position of the colonies by asking that all the costs of maintaining French sovereignty overseas, such as the salaries of overseas officials and military officers, be paid by the mother country. For the colonial populations, the conference favored a reduction in taxes.

The conference also made specific recommendations regarding the use of French overseas personnel. The governors-general recommended that the agents of civil affairs cease being used as aides to the administrators and be retrained for technical positions in agriculture and public works. As a result, the technical services would be significantly increased in size

(AOF and AEF each had approximately 400 agents) and would be able to launch a massive program of economic development. The conference suggested that the positions vacated by the agents be filled by qualified members of the local elite. By using Africans as agents, the administration intended to make sizable financial savings, for Africans serving as agents would be paid only about half the amount French officials received.[124] Another advantage of using Africans as agents, the conference perceived, would be to make available more outlets for the local elites.

The conference recommended that only cadets of the *Ecole Coloniale* be appointed as administrators. This measure was intended to ensure that only highly trained men be appointed to the Corps, but by making the Corps inaccessible to the agents, the conference in fact was further limiting the possibility that Africans enter the Corps.[125]

The governors-general had concentrated on the need for administrative efficiency and on economic matters. But they had made no effort to draw up a political program. This failure mirrored the general attitude of the colonial service that gave priority to economic and social change over political reform. Olivier, former governor-general of Madagascar, demonstrated that attitude when he declared that the colonial populations could be given political rights only when they had bridged the cultural gap between the metropole and themselves. For this reason, he declared, he was more interested in *"politique sociale"* than in *"politique tout court"* (social policy rather than simply politics).[126] The latter he relegated to a very distant future, since he thought it would "take several generations of patient effort to transform a primitive people into a civilized one."[127]

The Popular Front government in 1937 presented a proposal for the establishment of a Colonial Fund for Economic Development to Parliament; it was defeated. Since all the other proposals were dependent upon increased expenditures for the colonies, virtually all the recommendations became unrealizable.

Parliament blocked the possibility of reform in the colonies, but in an exercise of good will, it recommended in January 1937 the appointment of a commission to study colonial problems. The commission was charged with reporting back to Parliament on the needs and aspirations of the colonial peoples. The task, as Moutet outlined to the commission, was "to consider the application to the overseas countries of the great principles of the Declaration of the Rights of Man and of the Citizen."[128] After this call for reform, Moutet added, in words which clearly demonstrated his caution and his unwillingness to introduce fundamental transformations into the colonial system, that he trusted the commission would "be solely concerned with the general interest [of all parties in the colonies] and take care not to create certain exaggerated hopes which might lead to painful disillusionment."[129]

A subcommittee of twelve was appointed to deal with Black Africa, five of whom were members of Parliament and three former colonial administrators known for their interest in reform (Delavignette, Deschamps, and Labouret); there were four other public figures, of whom the best known were the famous ethnologist Lévy-Bruhl and the writer André Gide. The administrators were assigned to study technical questions such as economic development, while Gide and Lévy-Bruhl, who had little preparation for that kind of task, were asked to draw up a report on the "aspirations" of the colonial peoples.

The commission was wholly ineffective. It held its first meeting six months after Parliament called for its establishment. The subcommittee, rather than going on its own fact-finding mission to Africa, drew up a questionnaire regarding the living conditions of the colonial populations, and sent it to all administrators. This took another six months. In the end, the commission never carried out its assignment. Lévy-Bruhl was one of the few members of the commission to make a final report—and his report was an investigation of the causes for continued cannibalism in certain remote areas of the French possessions. Thinking back on the work of the commission, thirty years later, Delavignette claimed that the commission never made any specific recommendations. After the Blum government fell in July 1937, the commission lost any real interest in proposing colonial reforms, for such reforms had little chance of being adopted.[130] In 1938 the Senate Finance Committee refused to make the small appropriation necessary to allow the commission to continue its work, and thus it was disbanded.

That the Popular Front government had achieved only limited results in the colonial field was admitted even by Deschamps, one of its most active supporters.[131] Thereafter, in the face of mounting internal crisis and external threats from across the French frontiers, successive French governments found it impossible to give any serious thought to implementing colonial reforms.

World War II transformed the colonies to an even greater degree than had the war of 1914. The colonial administration was poorly prepared to deal with the vast transformation that the colonies were undergoing. A report written by an inspector of colonies after his tour of AOF in 1940-1941 sheds some light on the extent to which the colonial officials had lost contact with the local populations and with the changes occurring. The administrators hardly ever used the archives of the *cercle*, and as a result they ignored the activities of their predecessors. Because of such practices there was no progress, and often even retrogression, in the administration of a *cercle*, for the administrators often unknowingly canceled out the efforts of their predecessors. For many administrators, the inspector observed, "statistics, inquiries, monographs, classified archives seem... to be superfluous and useless." The inspector found that in some areas a census had not been taken for several years, although it was required annually. And the number of tours made by the administrators had declined. The inspector did not consider these failings a reflection on the personal value and character of the administrators; he blamed them rather on the constantly increased tasks of the administrators. But the colonial officials themselves, the inspector observed, had undergone a certain "sclerosis." They were not always able to keep up with the rapid evolution of the colonial societies, and had therefore lost contact with the colonial realities.[132]

The virtual immobility of the French administration disillusioned a number of educated young Africans. In the late nineteenth century most of the French-educated Africans had identified colonial rule as a harbinger of progress. That attitude essentially remained in the interwar period, but a small minority became impatient with the slowness of change. In the end the colonial powers did not transform the African continent as dramatically as they had announced they would. Lack of funds, fear of social and economic disruption, and the essentially conservative outlook of the colonial administrators led to stagnation. The *Race nègre,* the organ of a small impatient group of African intellectuals in Paris, argued, "It is not that Negroes cannot modernize themselves within our own organizations, but Europeans stand in the way."[133]

The caution of the administration led it in the interwar years to bolster the power of the chiefs, at the cost of the rising elites. In Dahomey a newspaper denounced French rule and the chiefs in Porto Novo, arguing that "the reactionary politics of placing these imbeciles over educated men is offensive to the native and the native elites."[134] Another Dahomean newspaper, impatient with the slow and hesitant realization of the French commitment to the spread of universal education, described the French presence as an impediment: "The French came to civilize us, but they prevent us from learning to read, to write, and to speak.... The government itself betrays its principles of civilization."[135]

The young wanted immediate assimilation; failing that, an end to French rule. The Dahomean Kojo Tovalou-Houenou wrote that the choice was *"L'assimilation intégrale ou le home rule."*[136] At this point the local elites, with less ambiguity than that evinced by the colonial administrators, embraced a program of modernization. Ironically, the French administrators at the same time were cast in the role of preservers of the traditional society, the very society they had originally set out to destroy, or at least transform.

Too many administrators in the interwar years had become increasingly bureaucratized and attached to routine, and they shunned innovation. Governor-General Boisson complained in 1941 that the administrators had become engulfed in an "ever increasing formalism" and at the same time their sense of personal responsibility had diminished.[137]

The shortcomings of the French colonial system were part of the larger failure of the European powers to keep in step with the evolution of their empires. For the British, there were peculiar doctrinal and administrative problems that prevented them also from keeping up with changes among their overseas subjects. Prosser Gifford has convincingly argued that the enshrinement of the policy of indirect rule was largely responsible for focusing British attention on the traditional aspects of African society, and blinding them to the rise of the urban, educated elites.[138] There was also a breakdown in administrative vitality, at least in some areas. Writing of Tanganyika, Lord Hailey noted that "the progress of the Territory as far as native affairs are concerned seems to have come to a standstill. Improvements continue to be made in the machinery, but as a whole, the machine does not seem to move forward."[139]

One wonders whether this loss of contact with the nature of the changing societies might have been avoided if the colonial services of the imperial powers had functioned differently, or held another ideology. By the very nature of the colonial situation, the men who made the important decisions were born and formed in a culture different from that of the colonies, and this made contact very difficult indeed. The very reasons impelling men to join a colonial service prevented them from seeing the evolution around them. It was the exoticism of the colonies and the apparent helplessness of the colonial populations that first attracted the men overseas. The more the local populations resembled Frenchmen at home the less interesting they became; and indeed the very existence of the elite seemed to betray the young administrator's original image of the African. The search for the lost world of his ancestors, J. C. Froelich wrote, gave him his original interest in ethnology and the colonial vocation.[140]

It has been argued that the Western interest in exoticism stems from the attempt to seek and recreate the perfect society, which our ancestors are presumed to have enjoyed in primeval times.[141] In nearly all cases, the interest in the exotic was linked with an unhappiness with the metropole; the colonial vocation seemed to offer an opportunity to leave the cramped atmosphere of the homeland. Paradoxically, once abroad, the administrators were committed to spreading the very culture that they had—at least partially—rejected. Nevertheless, many administrators could only view with alarm the spread of institutions similar to those existing in

France. And thus, in spite of the French devotion to eventual assimilation, there was an ambiguity toward modernization. Few were the men who with Delavignette could sing the praises of the traditional African peasant and at the same time welcome the emergence of the new elite represented by Léopold Senghor, the first African *agrégé*.[142]

Administrators encouraging modernization tended to follow a Saint-Simonian tradition; although sympathetic to social and economic change, they were highly authoritarian. P. O. Lapie, who had served several years in Africa, wrote of the thrill of overseas service in the following terms:

There is no question here, as in civilized countries, of having to fight against opposing views, public opinion, the press, committees, or councils; you just grasp bodily the mass of sand, clay, and human beings and mould it into roads, towns, and men. . . . What regions in our cramped European countries offer such opportunities for modelling both soil and men?[143]

The technocratic vision which Lapie and many of his colleagues held did not permit the sharing of power with members of the colonial societies.

The men who entered and dominated the colonial service in the interwar period were with some exceptions conscientious, hard-working men who ensured for the colonies a humane and efficient administration. But the bureaucratization of the Corps—in terms both of its structure and of the attitudes of its members—together with the persistence of an authoritarian tradition, prevented the Corps from being as innovative a force as it might have been, particularly in the political field. Some might, with Deschamps, argue even more strongly that the interwar years constituted an era of lost opportunities, and that if the Corps had introduced reforms, it would have made unnecessary, or even impossible, the kind of nationalism that swept the French Black African colonies after World War II.

VII The ENFOM, 1940-1959

The *Ecole Coloniale* had been closed during World War I, but it continued to operate during the second world war. In fact, at no time in its history had there been as many graduates during a five-year period as between 1940 and 1945—approximately 350. The war confronted the school with a whole set of unusual circumstances. From 1939 on, in the face of vast changes overseas, the school's directors found a continuous need to readjust both the curriculum and the methods of recruitment. This chapter studies the efforts of the ENFOM to cope with a changing world from 1940 until it was transformed in 1959 into the *Institut des hautes etudes d'outre-mer* (IHEOM).

During the war, Delavignette who was the director at the time, persuaded the Vichy regime to continue recruiting a large number of students for the ENFOM in order to replace retiring officials and to enlarge the overseas personnel. Those measures were necessary, he argued, because the empire would play a central role after the war. In advocating the expansion of the student body, Delavignette was also motivated by a desire to spare as many young men as possible from labor service in Germany, for all the cadets of the school were exempted.

Considering its location in German-occupied Paris, the ENFOM enjoyed surprising liberty during the war. The school was virtually free of supervision from Vichy. The Pétain government appointed a new council of administration, but, significantly, it retained the director and most of the faculty. The full weight of Vichy control made itself felt, however, in regard to the recruitment of students. Since the cadets were civil servants, the Vichy civil service statute excluding Jews and other specified groups was enforced. By law the students were also required before entrance to have served a tour in the army or in the Vichy youth organization, the *Chantiers de jeunesse*.[1] Although it was located directly across from the German *Kommandatura* in the Luxemburg Palace and next to a German casern at Lycée Montaigne, the school was left relatively free of German intervention. Since the Germans had promised to respect the integrity of the French empire, the occupying authorities evidently decided that intervention in the institution that was training colonial officials might seem to indicate Nazi designs on the French possessions; and such a move would needlessly alarm the Vichy regime.

Because of the war, Delavignette was unable to carry out some of his far-reaching plans for curriculum reform. In 1941 he suggested that the program of studies be extended to four years. His plan was as follows: during the first year the cadets would complete their general education; in the second, they would choose the section they wished to enter (Indochinese, African, or Malgache) and would begin following specialized courses pertinent to those regions. At the end of the second year the cadets would be appointed as student administrators to the colonies. For a year they would serve in subordinate administrative positions overseas before returning to the ENFOM for their last year of studies. Delavignette saw this probationary period in the colonies as "a physical and moral test." He placed it in the middle of the cadets' studies in order to "illuminate the studies, to give a concrete sense to education by giving our students contact with the men of the country in which they will practice their profession."[2] During their probationary period the students were to be paid a salary of 24,000 francs per year. This would inculcate in them "professional morality" and a *pride in earning their own living.*[3] After a year in the colonies, the cadets would return to the school where in light of their experience they would complete their studies.

Delavignette's suggestions were embodied in a decree,[4] but it was soon rescinded. The plan survived in a somewhat emasculated form in which the curriculum was limited to two years. During the summer between the first and second year of studies, the cadets were sent overseas for a study trip, after which they returned for their last year at the ENFOM. Upon graduation, they served for a year as probationers, either overseas or in the central administration of the undersecretariat of colonies, before being appointed to the Corps.[5]

The reduction of the period of study and the emphasis on practical training overseas "served as a means of getting the students away from the Germans."[6] Members of the school took an active part in opposing the German occupation. When war broke out, 135 students were mobilized, of whom fifteen were killed and sixty were taken prisoner. Especially toward the end of the war a number took part in resistance activities; seven of these were executed by the Germans.[7]

Delavignette was an official of the Vichy regime, but he refused to report on the resistance activities of his students. In fact, he and his family provided help to the resistance.[8] When called to Vichy and asked the whereabouts of a number of students, Delavignette answered that he could not be made responsible for his students' whereabouts. He told Admiral Henri Bléhaut, the undersecretary of colonies, that "these were difficult times when even parents could not be expected to control their own children." This was an allusion to the admiral's own son, who had joined de Gaulle in London, and thenceforth Delavignette was not asked to account for his students.[9] Perhaps because attendance at the school gave immunity from labor service in Germany and was a way of eventually getting away from war-torn France, the school's popularity increased during the war. Between 1940 and 1944 there was a yearly average of 360 candidates for seventy-three posts. This large number permitted the school to be very selective, and during those years only 20 percent of the candidates were admitted. Immediately after the war the school became even more popular; 618 candidates applied for eighty-five posts in 1945, 900 students competed for ninety-five posts in 1946.

In wartime France, the colonies looked attractive to young men who wanted to escape the stifling atmosphere of German-occupied or Vichy ruled France; but overseas duty also represented a patriotic activity. An entrant to the ENFOM in 1942 wrote that it was "the humiliation of defeat" that caused him to go to the colonies, and "if I had been strong in mathematics I would have become a naval officer." A young man who entered the school three years later recalled that he chose the colonial career because "I wanted to participate in the reestablishment and the spread of influence of my country following the humiliating war, and I also wanted to leave this humiliated country." Another young man who entered the school during the war wrote that he prepared for a colonial career because of his "desire to share in the tasks which France has taken upon herself to carry out in her colonial empire; namely, to bring civilization to people still submerged in the night of mankind's primeval age."[10]

A pamphlet published by an agency of the colonial ministry listed reasons why a young man should be interested in a colonial career:

The colonies attract you because of your reading and exotic movies, because you are tired of the pettiness of metropolitan existence, [and] because you have had disappointments.
You want to leave! You hope to find in these distant possessions a better life, which will be unrestricted and more attractive.
The colonial functionary ... participates in the great task of French expansion, he is in contact with the native environment on which he acts every day. He is in every post and at all times the representative of the civilizing nation.[11]

A striking aspect of this pamphlet, and also of the statements by the former students of the ENFOM, is the persistence of certain ideas about the colonial vocation. In no way had they really changed during half a century. And perhaps those ideas which combined a desire to serve other peoples with a heavy interest in exoticism were the only ones capable of attracting Europeans overseas. But the very prejudice in the ideas toward modern society in France created an ambiguity toward modernization and made the administrators into less effective instruments of change than they otherwise might have been.

In addition to young students in France, there were others who gained admission to the ENFOM after the war; among them were men who had participated in the Free French movement. During the war the Free French developed a certain hostility toward the career civil servants. Had not most of the regular military officers and civilian officials collaborated with Vichy? The French bureaucracy should be reinvigorated by appointing the men who had participated in the arduous task of liberating France. René Pleven, the Gaullist commissioner of colonies, originally planned to appoint 400 men from the Free French forces to the colonial service, but eventually he appointed only about 150. And after receiving six months' training at the ENFOM and a year's probationary service overseas, they were named to the Corps.

Veterans of the Free French forces, former war deportees and prisoners, and regular veterans of World War II were favored in entering the normal training program of the ENFOM. While other candidates required the equivalent of one year's law study before applying to the school, the men belonging to the above-mentioned categories were only required to have the *baccalauréat*. They also received bonus points in their entrance examinations. By 1946, however, the special recruitment of resistance fighters and veterans came to an end.[12] These men had a lower educational level than the average entrant,[13] although many had had practical experience overseas and several, as colonial troop officers, had administered desert nomads.

After the war Delavignette continued to emphasize the need for practical experience, and in March 1945 he declared:

The school must form administrators, that is, men involved in our present world, accustomed to social contacts and not rigidified in a world apart. And these administrators must understand very different men.... Finally, our school is worth less through the sum of knowledge that it dispenses than by the ideas it suggests, and by the personal reflection it favors.[14]

The men appointed to the staff of the school also reflected Delavignette's interest in bringing to the students the latest and best information available on the overseas territories. Immediately before the war he had appointed the brilliant young ethnologist Jacques Soustelle as a teacher. When war broke out, the latter was succeeded by Marcel Griaule, famed for his research on the Dogons in the Sudan. After the war, Hubert Deschamps, an authority on Malgache society and an experienced administrator, joined the school. It was Delavignette, too, who appointed the first African ever to teach at the school. This was Léopold Senghor, a deputy from Senegal, who was given the responsibility of teaching a course on African civilization and one on African linguistics.

After World War II a limited program, separate from the ENFOM, was instituted to give additional academic training to some of the most outstanding administrators. In 1936 the Popular Front government had established the *Centre de hautes etudes d'administration musulmane* (CHEAM) to provide additional training for some of the government functionaries serving in French North Africa and in the French mandates in the Middle East. The aim of the Center was to give the functionaries gathered from those different areas an opportunity to compare their experiences and mutual concerns, and thus gain a better understanding of the social, political, and economic problems of Moslem areas. Originally, no administrators serving in Black Africa were included; but in 1946 the Center enlarged its interests to include the study of Islam in Black Africa and Asia. While the Center remained strong in Islamic studies, it gradually enlarged its scope to include general problems of overseas territories and the underdeveloped world. In 1958 the name of the Center was changed to *Centre de hautes etudes administratives sur l'Afrique et l'Asie modernes* which was a belated recognition of the change in emphasis.

Government officials who had been in public service for six years or more, at least four of them in Islamic areas overseas, were eligible to compete for entrance to the Center. The competition consisted of two stages: first, the writing of an essay on some political, social, or economic aspect of the area in which they had served and second, an oral examination in an African or Asian language. At the Center a series of seminars was offered dealing with contemporary problems, fundamentals of sociology, ethnology, economics, applied psychology, and the civilizations, religions, and ideologies of Africa and Asia. After attending the Center for three months its members had to present another *mémoire*, again dealing with some aspect of the area in which they had served, and had to pass examinations in the following fields: general problems of the Islamic world, the French colonies in general, the foreign empires, and an African or Asian language. Upon finishing those requirements, the students were awarded a *brevet*. Between 1946 and 1959, seventy-six overseas administrators received that degree from the Center. Although the Center accepted only officials who were already intellectually alert, its training helped update their information.[15]

In 1946 Delavignette was appointed high commissioner of the French Cameroons, and was succeeded as director of the ENFOM by Paul Mus. The latter was a Far Eastern expert; in fact, he was one of the best-known French scholars on Far Eastern languages, religions, and archaeology. During World War II he played a leading role in the resistance movement in Indochina. His appointment to the ENFOM was in line with the traditional alternation of directors between men associated with Africa and those of Indochina. The war in Indochina also seemed to make it imperative that the administrators destined for service in that area be trained by a man who knew it intimately.

Delavignette had been director of the school in an era in which there was relatively little change in the methods of French rule. Within the authoritarian framework that existed until 1946, the teachings of the ENFOM seemed relatively progressive. The school was almost alone in offering courses dealing with overseas France. It advocated understanding of the overseas peoples, and taught the future administrators "how to command in order to serve better."[16]

Mus, on the other hand, became director of the school in a period of vast change. The ENFOM no longer retained the monopoly in giving advanced instruction on the overseas territories; universities and other institutions such as the *Institut d'etudes politiques* had also established their courses on the territories. And overseas vast social, political, and economic changes were going on at an unprecedented speed which not even the most sensitive observers could always appreciate.

Much of the spirit of the school after the war seemed somewhat atavistic. The emotion-laden "baptismal" of the class of 1944, named "Eboué" after the governor-general who had just died, seemed to have little to do with the new challenges developing overseas. Kneeling on the ground in the ENFOM courtyard, the neophytes vowed to consecrate their lives "to the service of Empire, for the grandeur of France, and the development of our civilization."[17]

Mus, a man of liberal views, was never able to transform the school to fit the image he conceived for it.[18] He shared responsibilities with the administrative council of the school, and as its director he could have influenced the council, but he left his powers largely unused. Some of Mus's personal friends, who still claim to be his warm admirers, have intimated that although a first-rate scholar and thinker, he lacked administrative skills.[19]

In fact at no time in the history of the school was there such a discrepancy between the ideals of its director and the curriculum and spirit of the school as existed during this period. Most of the faculty at the ENFOM consisted of prewar colonial administrators or of university men, many of whom had not been overseas for a long time. For many teachers at the ENFOM the reforms of 1946 were not the beginning of an evolution in the overseas territories, but the last step in that evolution. Before the war many of the teachers at the ENFOM had advocated a change in the institutions of the overseas territories, but after 1946 the school became, instead, an upholder of the status quo.

Mus himself, however, was a vigorous proponent of change overseas. The colonial populations, he stated, did not want administrators who knew colonial customs; what they desired was the introduction of "social and political institutions, certainly adapted to the colony, but inspired by those existing in France and in the white man's world."[20]

Beginning in 1946 the students at the ENFOM tended to be less impressed with the curriculum of the school than their predecessors had been. Before the war colonial questions had been debated only among a small number of specialists, but after 1946 overseas problems increasingly became the topic of discussion among the educated classes. Thus the students coming to the school often had definite ideas on overseas policy. The summer months that they spent in the training program overseas also gave the cadets valuable insights into the changes occurring in the territories. Comparing their experiences and the knowledge acquired from associating with African students on the Left Bank, many cadets found themselves in conflict with their teachers.

The cadets who spent their summers overseas were required to write essays expressing their opinions on some of the problems connected with the territories. One of the cadets returned to Paris in 1948 after serving in Brazzaville, and chose as his topic "Some Reflections on the New French Colonial Policy." It was an attack on French policy, arguing that the evolution overseas was so rapid that the provisions of the Brazzaville Conference of 1944 and of the French constitution of 1946 had become irrelevant. The essay pointed out the eventual need of granting the territories independence; but typically, it still insisted on the desirability of establishing a genuine liberal federation between France and her possessions. The teacher grading the essay thought the student a traitor to the French cause, and gave him the failing grade of nine out of a possible twenty points.[21] These differences between students and the institution were to become even more apparent a few years later.

The curriculum of the ENFOM, compared with that of the pre-World War II period, no longer seemed impressive. Many of the postwar graduates felt that the curriculum of the ENFOM was in no way as challenging as the feat of gaining admission to the school. As one former administrator put it, the "school gave one a well-deserved two years' rest."[22] An important effort to make the school more relevant was made by decree in October 1950, when a series of reforms was introduced. The bachelor of law degree, requiring two years of study, became the diploma required for entrance to the school. Once they had gained admission, the students would thus have to spend only one additional year to acquire their *licence* in law and therefore could devote more time to studying strictly overseas subjects. The school also permitted an alternative to a legal degree; that was the possession of two certificates in the study of overseas peoples, a *licence d'études des populations d'outre-mer* (a new degree offered at the University of Paris) of which one certificate would be in *droits et coutumes d'outre-mer* (overseas laws and customs). But since candidates for entrance to the ENFOM were required to study for either a *bachelier en droit* or a *licence d'études des populations d'outre-mer* before they knew whether they could gain admission to the school, most of them preferred the study of law. If they failed to enter the ENFOM, they could then complete their law studies and enter the metropolitan civil service, in which case the certificates in *licence d'études des populations d'outre-mer* would, of course, be practically useless.

The decree of October 1950 set the apprenticeship—the on-the-job training program overseas—at eight months, following four months of orientation in Paris.[23] The experience overseas was intended to acquaint the cadets with problems of overseas administration and to test their aptitude for that service. While those were the ultimate aims of the apprenticeship, the officials of the school also saw its effects in more modest, immediate terms; they described the eight months overseas not as a "period of apprenticeship, but [as an] introductory experience intended to prepare the student for the instruction which is to follow."[24]

After their orientation program in Paris, the cadets went out in pairs to rural areas in AOF, AEF, or Madagascar for four or five months. They served the rest of their assignment in the territorial capital, learning about the administrative services. They worked in different departments and were graded by their supervisors. Unfavorable grades could eliminate a student, but this rarely occurred. At the conclusion of their apprenticeship, the cadets were required to write an essay on an overseas problem—for example, peanut commercialization in Senegal, the process of urbanization in a particular region, or some particular ethnic grouping.[25] After their overseas experience the cadets returned for two more years of study in Paris. During the third year they spent five weeks in on-the-job training in the ministry of overseas France, or in private industry.[26]

The decree of 1950 lengthened the period of training required of lower civil servants wishing to become overseas administrators. Instead of one year, they now had to spend two years at the ENFOM, following the same curriculum as the other students returning from their overseas apprenticeship. Until World War II the majority of administrators were lower officials who had received supplementary training at the ENFOM, but after the war the overwhelming majority entering the Corps were cadets of the school. Only a small number of lower civil servants chose to go to the ENFOM for additional training.

Significantly, the reforms of 1950 made no changes regarding the learning of languages, and the traditional disregard for indigenous languages remained, except for a token bow toward the teaching of the most rudimentary and theoretical elements of African languages. Even during the overseas apprenticeship, no special provision was made for learning the local language. In fact, even the *licence d'études des populations d'outre-mer* did not require the knowledge of any language spoken overseas. A very weak incentive, the granting of a yearly supplement of 15,000 francs ($43.00), was made to the administrators who knew the local language.[27]

While the reforms of 1950 attempted to bring about change, Paul Bouteille, the new director appointed in that year, was ill-suited to infuse the institution with a new and innovative spirit. Before becoming director, he had served as Mus's administrative assistant; earlier he had been an overseas administrator. While Delavignette and Mus were known for their liberal attitudes, Bouteille was more closely identified with the conservative wing of the overseas bureaucracy. He had occupied a high position in Madagascar during the brutal repression of the Malgache revolt in 1946-1947.

The school underwent a certain decline beginning in the 1950s, and by the mid-1950s, enrollment had dropped dramatically. The decline was due almost entirely to external forces rather than to any fault of the management, for the Corps was restricted in size by law, and therefore replacements were allowed only for those leaving the service. Further, by 1954, the French had lost control over Indochina and thus no longer recruited any functionaries for that region. In 1945 the ENFOM had had 367 students, but in 1947, only 240, and in 1953, 120.[28]

In spite of the fact that entry into the school was highly selective, it did not enjoy the status of the *Ecole nationale d'administration* (ENA) which was founded in 1945. The two schools recruited students from similar social and educational background, but the ENA, which was training men for higher civil service positions within France, was more respected than was the ENFOM. To combat the situation Paul Mus had vainly suggested in 1948 that the ENFOM be incorporated as part of the ENA. The opposition to Mus's plan came from the ENA, which did not wish to expand its facilities, and from the alumni of the ENFOM, who were sentimentally committed to the continuation of their alma mater.[29]

Thus the two institutions continued to exist side by side, with the ENA enjoying a higher status. Roy Jumper in his dissertation on the ENFOM has suggested several reasons for this disparity. The ENA, he argues, was connected with the metropolitan civil service, which traditionally has enjoyed higher prestige. Second, the curriculum and administration of the ENFOM lacked the stability of those of the ENA, for they were subject to changes deriving from varying overseas policy. Third, the positions for which the ENA trained tended to be better remunerated than those given the graduates of the ENFOM. Fourth, the entrance requirements to the ENA were stiffer than those of the ENFOM. Fifth, the staff and facilities at the ENA were of higher caliber than those of the ENFOM.[30]

In spite of the differences between the two institutions, the students were similar since they came from the same social background (See Table 10). Probably the only difference in the type of men attracted to the two institutions was that the cadets of the ENFOM tended to be more adventurous and had a greater urge to live in a world of large horizons than did the ENA students destined for the metropolitan civil service.

Table 10

Percentage distribution of fathers' occupations of students admitted to the ENFOM and the ENA[31]

Occupation of fathers of student entrants	ENFOM 1950	ENFOM 1953	ENA 1952
High administration	33%	40%	34%
Industrial and business management	6	3	6
Liberal professions	3	5	13
Rentiers, small businessmen, *propriétaires*	3	16	29
White collar workers and other employees; low rank civil servants	23	14	29
Small farmers and artisans	13	14	3
Workers	3	3	2
Unknown occupations	16	5	0

As to the ENFOM students themselves, there was little difference in social background between those of 1950 and of twenty years earlier, except for a decline in recruitment from families in the liberal professions (Table 7). Families belonging to the upper middle classes, especially to the higher civil service, continued to be the main source for the recruitment of the Corps.

This remarkable continuity in social background was due to the persistence of certain patterns of recruitment. In spite of the many reforms the school underwent after 1927, the method of the *concours,* with its heavy emphasis on general literary knowledge, continued. In 1936 the question in French composition had been to discuss "The pessimism of Leconte de Lisle in the *Poèmes barbares*; its nature, its limits." In 1942 the assignment had been to comment on a long section chosen from Montaigne; in 1946, from Michelet's works. The *concours* of 1948 required a discussion of "Solitude in Rousseau's and Pascal's thought."[32] Other topics included in the *concours* were the history of French colonization, economic and human geography, *morale* and sociology, and living languages. In the first field, i.e., French colonization, in 1952 the examination called for a description of "desirable constitutional changes in the French Union." In the field of economic and human geography the question was about migration patterns within the empire, and in the last field, *morale* and sociology, the candidates were asked to discuss whether *engagé* literature was desirable.[33] Living languages were tested, as in the late 1920s, orally. Only candidates with superior education, such as that received by the sons of the bourgeoisie at the better *lycées,* could usually pass the examinations.

In spite of the relatively homogeneous background of the cadets, they were as a rule alert and intelligent young men. Their apprenticeship overseas and their contacts in France made them increasingly aware of the gap between the realities overseas and the picture presented at the ENFOM. In 1952 some students formed a secret discussion group known as the *Groupe d'études politiques de l'Afrique et Madagascar,* also known by its acronym as GEPAM. With increasing anxiety this group saw that while the world was rapidly changing, the curriculum at the ENFOM and the institutions overseas were in no way taking account of those changes. The curriculum of the school still was aimed at forming "generalists," men having a broad training, who knew how to command. Thus the curriculum, as in the late 1920s, included a smattering of subjects, such as tropical medicine, cattle raising, ethnology, and administrative law, but it did little to prepare the students for the changing world overseas. There were no serious courses on economic development, sociology, and contemporary events. In 1956 the student newspaper estimated that the three-year curriculum consisted of 872 hours of courses, of which only eighty-five were devoted to the study of economics, and even less (thirty-two hours) to the study of politics.[34] No course, the student newspaper charged, mentioned the recent Bandung Conference of African and Asian peoples or the charges regarding Algeria brought against France in the United Nations. The issues that were really crucial to the evolution of the French Union, the paper charged, were being ignored.[35]

In February 1956 three-fourths of the students issued a manifesto denouncing the overseas political institutions and the curriculum of the ENFOM as being irrelevant to the changes taking place overseas. They declared it desirable that the overseas territories achieve internal autonomy, that political power be "returned to the Africans and the Malagasy." The role of the French administrator, they suggested, should be limited to that of economic adviser or to temporary administrative tasks. The signers of the statement, seventy-one of the ninety-seven students attending the school,[36] asked that "a radical change be instituted both in the entrance examinations and in the training, by transforming the school into a section of the ENA." Or, alternatively, they suggested "the complete transformation of the spirit, the recruitment, and the training" of the ENFOM students. Furthermore, the manifesto demanded progressive Africanization of the Corps of Overseas Administrators, the introduction into the curriculum of specialized technical education and "of serious economic and sociological training."[37]

Most of the signatories, according to one of the sponsors of the manifesto, were Socialists. They reflected the ideas of the Socialist student movement which was ahead of the Socialist government in its demand for the establishment of territorial autonomy overseas. By spring the National Assembly was to pass a *loi-cadre* that made possible overseas autonomy. Yet there was a subtle difference: the Socialist government of Prime Minister Guy Mollet was to present autonomy as a generous reform, while the student manifesto had spoken of it as a measure which "returned" political power to the overseas populations. Though the published reports make no mention of it, witnesses claim that the declaration accompanying the publication of the manifesto also spoke of the need to "end the era of *commandants mitrailleurs* (machine-gun-toting *commandants*)."[38] This was an unnecessarily violent and patently unfair attack by the future administrators on the overseas service, but it guaranteed public attention.[39]

Among the twenty-six who did not sign the manifesto were sixteen cadets in their last year of studies. They were undoubtedly more concerned than were their younger colleagues about the effect that participation in the manifesto might have on their careers. One of those not signing was an African student who found the wording too extreme. Ironically, he is now a cabinet minister in his independent country. In spite of the attention given the manifesto when it was published and the general perturbation it caused in the administration of the ENFOM, none of the signers (according to one of the instigators) suffered in his subsequent administrative career.[40]

The manifesto caused no change in the curriculum of the ENFOM, but it was a measure of the degree to which the cadets were aware of overseas developments and favored a general shift in French policy.[41] Clearly it was not as radical as both its opponents and its proponents had thought. But in any case, the *loi-cadre* adopted in the summer of 1956 paved the way for increased political autonomy overseas and the Africanization of the Corps.

There had never been many Africans in the Corps; nearly all of its members with black skin had come from the French Antilles. A small but steady stream of *métis* had entered the service, the majority of them born in Senegal. At most a half-dozen Africans entered the Corps from the time of its founding until 1945, but after 1951 Africans were eligible for entrance to the ENFOM on an equal basis with the inhabitants of metropolitan France. Africans, however, clearly had less opportunity to become successful candidates. Fewer educational facilities were available overseas than in France; until the late 1950s there was no preparatory class for the ENFOM overseas, and in addition the social and cultural milieu of African candidates prepared them poorly for the *concours*. Many Africans who were potentially qualified to enter the administration preferred to enter the liberal professions and local politics. In the early 1950s an average of two African students a year entered the school.

Hubert Deschamps noted in 1954 that as a teacher in the school he found fewer black students than he had thirty years earlier when he was a student. Most of the black students then had been Antilleans, but even they had declined in number. The failure of the school to attract black students, Deschamps claimed, was due to the unpopularity of the French administration overseas.[42] An article in the student newspaper of the ENFOM in 1956 suggested that the odiousness of the ENFOM as a "colonialist institution" made it unattractive to Africans; it was not the educational and cultural disabilities of Africans that kept them away from the school, for a large proportion of those taking the entrance examination passed it; the real trouble lay in the fact that few Africans wished to apply. The solution, the paper suggested, was to end the affiliation of the school with such a patently colonial establishment as the ministry of overseas France. It suggested that an overseas training division be set up at the ENA, or that an *Institut d'outre-mer* be established as part of the

University of Paris.[43]

In 1957, the school began a program of Africanization.[44] Alongside the regular competition for entrance, known as *concours A,* and the competition for entrance for lower government officials wishing to enter the Corps after a preliminary two years of training at the school, known as *concours B,* it established a new examination for entrance, known as *concours C.* This new competitive examination was open only to higher overseas officials who were indigenous to the overseas territories. The entrance requirements were relatively stiff; in addition to passing the entrance examinations, the candidates had to have the equivalent of two years of law studies or general university education and to have spent two years at the ENFOM receiving further training, before being appointed to the Corps.

The changes in 1957 also stipulated that 66 percent of all new appointees to the Corps of Overseas Administrators were to originate in the territories. Under these circumstances, the process of Africanizing the Corps would have been a long and painful one. The Corps in 1958 had approximately 1,700 administrators. With twenty-five new administrators being appointed yearly, of whom sixteen would have been Africans, it would have been long indeed before the majority of the Corps would be Africans.[45] To speed up the process the school shut its doors in 1958 to all but Africans. In the following year, the ENFOM discontinued operation. A new institution, the *Institut des hautes etudes d'outre-mer* (IHEOM), administered by the office of the prime minister, took over the old quarters. Its role was to train young Africans for positions of responsibility in their countries, which were rapidly achieving independence.

At first the *Institut* had to give low-level courses to prepare lower civil servants, some of whom had only an elementary education, for higher administrative posts. Some of the former teachers of the ENFOM, who had been retained, resigned on the grounds that the students lacked proper academic preparation. Others, like Delavignette, noted that there were difficulties in teaching the African students because of their uneven educational background ("inégalité de la culture des élèves"), but he also found that some of the best and most enthusiastic students had only an elementary education.[46]

With the establishment of national schools of administration in each of the successor states, only the better educated students, or higher civil servants, continued to be sent to the IHEOM in Paris for more advanced, or additional, training. Other French-speaking states such as the former Belgian colonies also found it profitable to send their young men to the

IHEOM. The enrollment of the school grew markedly: in 1959 it numbered 107 students; by 1963 there were 646.[47]

Like the ENFOM, the IHEOM prepared young men for regional administration, for the magistracy, and for a number of other state services. Like the ENFOM, it gave the same training to all its students regardless of where they would serve. The training also combined course work with practical experience. But rather than being sent overseas, the Africans were sent for on-the-job training to a prefecture or an industrial plant in France.

Some of the general courses, such as African ethnology and administrative law, were still taught in much the same way as they had been before, and indeed by the same teachers from the ENFOM. In that way some continuity in administration overseas was assured. Furthermore, by training so many Africans in France the IHEOM created an administrative elite which continued to look to France for inspiration.

A visitor to the IHEOM in 1965 might have noticed two wooden Buddhas once located in the stairways of the old *Ecole Coloniale.* And it might have occurred to him that in times long past they must have gazed at the sons of the mandarins and the young prince of Porto Novo, and later on at the generations of young Frenchmen who studied to become "the real chiefs of the empire." And now they gazed upon Africans who read many of the same books, attended similar lectures, and listened to some of the same professors, as they in their turn prepared to become the masters of a new Africa. As the halls continued to buzz with animated discussions about administrative law, about ethnology, about the differences between penal and customary law, about dreams and hopes for the future, the visitor might have imagined that he could hear through the din the Buddhas murmuring something about the immutability of time.[48]

In 1966 a decree renamed the IHEOM and it became known as the *Institut international d'administration publique* (IIAP). While the IHEOM had been specifically intended to train men originating from the former colonies, the IIAP is a school for all foreigners wanting to prepare for an administrative career. A number of students come from Latin America, Asia, and English-speaking Africa, but most of the students still come from former colonies.

Much of the curriculum and the student body has changed since the *Ecole Coloniale* was first founded, but the school at the Rue Observatoire, as in bygone days, continues to ensure the spread of French influence overseas.

VIII The Corps in an Era of Change

"When Africa becomes independent, we will have to raise a statue in memory of a cursed person in history, Hitler," Albert Tevoedjre, an African writer, stated in 1958.[1] Hitler's war, he said, prepared Africans for independence by making them conscious of the outside world and like the French desirous of an end to alien rule. Also, the war had weakened French power and made it difficult for France to maintain domination over the overseas possessions against the will of the inhabitants. Seen in perspective, World War II must be considered as marking the beginning of the end of the colonial empires, including that of the French. This chapter will consider the reactions of the Corps to the immense changes that began with the war and culminated in independence.

The war had important effects on the Corps. Like all French civil servants, the administrators were faced in June 1940 with the dilemma of either recognizing the Vichy regime and with it the armistice it had signed with the Germans, or of heeding de Gaulle's call to continue fighting the Germans.

In AOF some administrators gave early support to de Gaulle. The chief administrator of Upper Volta,[2] Emile Louveau, sent a telegram of adherence to de Gaulle on June 22, 1940. He gave public speeches in favor of continued resistance, and encouraged the military officers in his region to go to the Gold Coast, and from there to London to join de Gaulle. But Governor-General Pierre Boisson in Dakar, who was loyal to the Vichy regime, punished those administrators who had too hastily made known their sympathies for de Gaulle. Louveau, for example, was lured to Dakar and then imprisoned in France.[3]

Governor-General Boisson faithfully enforced the Vichy decrees that eliminated from the civil service all foreign-born, Communist, Freemason, and Jewish officials. Of the 400 administrators serving in AOF, twenty-one were dismissed for "political reasons" and ten because they were Freemasons. After this purge the Corps in AOF remained loyal to Vichy; only five administrators fled into neighboring British territories and

Liberia to join the Allied forces, and four officials took a public position for de Gaulle. The administration in Madagascar also remained loyal to the Vichy regime, and since the country did not border on any British territories, fewer administrators were able to flee and join the Free French than was the case with AOF.

In AEF, the story was quite different. Almost immediately after General de Gaulle's famous call of June 18 to continue resisting the Germans, Félix Eboué, a black man and the governor of Chad, had rallied his colony to the side of the general. Shortly thereafter the entire federation was brought under Gaullist control by a coup, and Eboué was made governor-general of AEF. He was born in French Guiana, had studied at the *Ecole Coloniale* before World War I, and in Oubangui, where he had been sent, he proved himself to be a remarkable administrator and ethnologist. A Socialist, Eboué was appointed governor of Guadeloupe during the Popular Front period, and in 1938 was appointed governor of Chad, by Mandel, minister of colonies.

This man, ruling in the name of France over other black men, was the perfect symbol of French assimilation. Because of his services in the liberation of France, he was signally honored after his premature death; he was buried in the Panthéon—the only black man and the only former colonial administrator so honored.

Most administrators in AEF remained loyal to the Eboué regime. Of approximately 400 administrators only forty refused to serve the pro-Gaullist regime, and they were duly repatriated to France, or allowed to go to AOF. While it is certain that many administrators felt sympathetic to the Vichy regime,[4] the prime responsibility for that adherence in AOF must be seen as being due to the individual influence of Governor-General Boisson. Both in AOF and in AEF the members of the Corps proved loyal to their administrative superiors, adopting their political attitudes.

The war brought vast changes in the methods of colonial administration. In AOF the program of liberalization introduced in the 1930s came to an abrupt end. Forced labor service was increased, greater production quotas were imposed on the local populations to meet the needs of the motherland, and the code of the *indigénat* system was more harshly used. The few representative organs that existed, such as the colonial council in Senegal and the elected city councils of the four communes in that colony, were dissolved. Africans in AOF who joined the Free French or were sympathetic to them were dealt with more harshly than were pro-Gaullist Europeans. Some cases of extreme brutality occurred. When the king of Abron and 1,500 of his followers left the Ivory Coast for the Gold Coast in January 1942, the French administration took reprisals against the indigenous notables who had remained behind.

According to Soustelle, they were subjected to "almost unbelievable sadistic cruelties: torture by fire, beatings, mutilations."[5]

Governor-General Boisson, because of his loyalty to the Vichy regime, is usually considered a reactionary. But most of his policies were very much within the colonial tradition of the Third Republic. His native policy was articulated in his *Trois directives de colonisation africaine*: "To colonize is essentially to make the native societies advance along the roads chosen by us. ... The elites and the masses must follow us simultaneously."[6] In his circulars on education, agricultural development, and industrialization, Boisson even made new and constructive suggestions.

The tension produced by the war and the establishment in France of a government with definite racist overtones (witness the laws against Jews and the foreign-born) encouraged racism in the Vichy-controlled colonies. It was the "golden age" of the "true" colonialists.[7] But Boisson, in the face of this situation, vigorously attempted to combat racist attitudes among both the French settlers and the officials.[8]

The Vichy regime abrogated the traditional civil service codes, and could thus dismiss without regular procedures any of its civil servants. Those powers, of course, led to abuse, but also made it much easier for the central administration to dismiss administrators of poor quality. In several cases the Vichy regime rid itself of some of the older administrators who were brutal or lazy. Many of these men had been considered poor administrators in the 1930s, but because of the civil service code the ministry of colonies had found it difficult to dismiss them. The ministry also had been reluctant to dismiss some because of their political connections or because of their remarkable war records. As Boisson said, a tradition "had become deeply established" of rotating unsatisfactory officials, rather than ousting them from the service. As a result, "deplorable functionaries have during their entire career with impunity been guilty of maladministration." Some officials have had "very honorable careers, while their services were less than honorable."[9] By using arbitrary power, the Vichy regime dismissed at various levels 140 unsatisfactory officials in AOF, and thus to some degree contributed to an improvement in the quality of the colonial personnel. Among those dismissed were a veteran wounded in World War I who suffered severe psychic disturbances, an extremely brutal official, and another administrator suffering from a persecution complex.[10]

Since the defeat of France in 1940 was basically a defeat of the ground forces, the navy gained in prestige; consequently, naval personnel were put in charge of the colonies, as they had been half a century earlier, and the ministry of colonies was reduced to a secretariat, headed by an admiral. None of the admirals who served between 1940 and 1942 was well prepared for the task. In 1942 the undersecretary of colonies, Admiral Platon, was replaced by Jules Brévié, the former governor-general of AOF. Brévié was one of the few former colonial officials ever to head the offices of Rue Oudinot. Brévié brought to the undersecretariat the experience of several decades as an administrator in Africa, and he knew what it was to deal with Parisian officials who were ill-acquainted with the colonial scene. Applying his knowledge to the situation, he issued at the very outset of his regime a decree which merged officials of the higher administration of Rue Oudinot with those of the Corps of Colonial Administrators. Henceforth, there would be a constant interchange between the men serving overseas and those in the offices of Rue Oudinot. With the exception of this reform, the Vichy regime brought no changes of any consequence to the colonial administration.

At one point, however, the Vichy regime did consider in some detail the possibility of establishing a new relationship between France and the colonies. It studied the idea of drawing up a new French constitution; special provisions concerning the colonies were to be proposed by the *Académie des sciences d'outre-mer,* a scientific body composed of experts in all fields connected with the colonies, from distinguished colonial administrators to overseas meteorologists.

In discussing the constitutional draft, the *Académie* decided to concentrate primarily on the complex problem of whether French citizenship should be granted to the colonial populations. The overwhelming majority of the subcommittee studying this problem, which numbered among its membership such well-known figures as the colonial sociologist René Maunier and Jules Brévié himself, was against granting citizenship to the overseas populations in one broad sweep. French citizenship, they stated, must never be considered a right, but rather a privilege to be extended to those few who either by their actions or by their education deserved it. Furthermore, French citizenship could be extended only to those who would give up their personal legal status.

Paul Azan, a general who had served in Algeria and who represented a distinctly minority position, attempted to convince his colleagues that a Moslem with four wives (thus enjoying a personal legal status) should, if he reached a certain educational level, be given the chance to become a French citizen. "Surely," he said, "we can ask that one broaden French laws sufficiently so that one can be both Moslem and citizen at the same time." Speaking for the rest of the committee, a member answered: "No, no, I refuse absolutely."[11] Somewhat cynically Maunier suggested that if the Moslem "really has a great desire to be able to say that he is a French citizen, let us call him 'honorary citizen.' "[12] This was the germ for an idea to declare all the colonial people citizens, but at the same time to establish degrees of privileges that the different types of citizen would enjoy. The committee recommended three grades of citizenship: "Frenchmen enjoying all civil and political rights, those with partial rights, those who will have none." Frenchmen living in France would be in the first category; the second would include the educated indigenous elites in the colonies; and the third would comprise the noneducated overseas populations. In the constitutional draft, the committee of the *Académie* indirectly provided for those categories by stating that the populations of the French motherland and of the colonies enjoyed, or could enjoy, the rights of citizenship. With amazing candor the committee demonstrated the artifice lying behind its proposal:

> *M. Sambuc*: Do you think that among the 38 million citizens there will be one who will make the distinction between "to enjoy the rights of citizenship" and "can receive those rights"?
>
> *M. Maspéro*: Exactly. He will not know. That is what we want. We want to give confidence.
>
> *M. Sambuc*: Then, what we wish to put in the constitution is something that nobody will understand.
>
> *M. Maunier*: In the constitution it is a question of proclaiming a principle, and not to give a solution.
>
> *Admiral Lacaze*: But then what will be done to leave the door open to them for citizenship?
>
> *M. le Près*: That lies in the future.
>
> *Admiral Lacaze*: But the future, you are leaving that out of the constitution.
>
> *M. Maunier*: We shall be unable to avoid saying that among these 100 million Frenchmen there are some who are more French than others.[13]

The formula recommended by the *Académie* was a compromise between the generous and egalitarian principles of assimilation and the authoritarian principles of the associationist doctrine. Superficially, the constitutional draft regarding the overseas territories seemed to embody the most generous of principles: all the overseas populations were to be made into French citizens. But a closer study reveals that the intention of the *Académie* was to continue French domination over the colonies. The *Académie*'s recommendations are not of isolated interest.

The Vichy regime never did proclaim the constitution, but as later events were to show, many colonial experts continued to announce generous principles of full equality, while in reality wanting to keep the colonies subjugated. Neither the provisional government of General de Gaulle nor, later, most of the cabinets of the Fourth Republic were to be entirely free of such attitudes. In spite of the dramatic rhetoric on colonial affairs, successive French regimes ever since the Revolution have attempted to preserve their dominance over their overseas possessions. As Robert W. July so aptly put it, French colonialism was always a "unique blend of theoretical democracy and practical autocracy."[14]

While the *Académie* was debating possible Vichy reforms, some innovation and change did occur in that part of the empire controlled by the Free French. To coordinate his rule over the Free French colonies, de Gaulle in October 1940 appointed a Council for the Defense of the Empire. Eboué was a member of that council, and since the wartime situation did not allow close supervision, Eboué was left in full command of AEF. Through circulars drawn up in November 1941, which were issued collectively under the title *La Nouvelle politique indigène pour l'Afrique équatoriale française,* Eboué attempted to establish a new colonial doctrine for the Free French.

Eboué was primarily concerned with the erosion of traditional society which he blamed on the policies of assimilation and direct rule. What was needed, he wrote, was respect for the local societies. In his denunciation of the methods of direct rule and his advocacy of the traditional structures, Eboué echoed preceding generations of colonial officials, men like Governors-General Van Vollenhoven and Brévié.

He stated his doctrine in the following famous passage:

Who should be chief? I shall not answer with the Athenians, "the best man." There is no best chief, there is only one chief, and we do not have a choice. The chief is not interchangeable; when we depose him public opinion does not depose him. The chief pre-exists.... Having distinguished the legitimate chiefs, we shall bring them all our effort, and it is through them ... that we shall get to the masses and shall be able to develop them.[15]

What was new in Eboué's doctrine was his genuine support of the indigenous institutions. For men like Van Vollenhoven and Brévié the stress on the respect for local institutions had primarily been dictated by the exigencies of their administration. But there was something new in Eboué's words:

Instead of vague and inadaptable conceptions which seem to associate certain natives with the Government of all of France or all of the Empire, we advocate ... transforming them first into excellent citizens of their own country.[16]

FELIX EBOUE

In 1942 Eboué created the status of *notable évolué* for the educated chiefs. These men within their own colony were to have legal rights similar to those that Frenchmen enjoyed in the metropole. They would become the leaders of their own colony. Compared with British colonial developments, Eboué's doctrines were a generation behind their time,[17] but within the French colonial tradition they were an important new achievement. It was the realization of some of the concepts propagated a decade earlier by men like Labouret and Delavignette. Like them, Eboué evidently had in mind the development of autonomous colonial governments which would be linked with the French motherland into a federation.

Eboué drew up his suggestion to meet what he recognized to be the growing discontent among the educated African elites. The French defeat in the second world war and the rival claims of Pétain and de Gaulle did much to erode French authority overseas. In addition, the Free French felt they owed the overseas populations a threefold debt of gratitude. First, at one time more than half their military forces had consisted of indigenous recruits; second, the overseas populations had labored to produce foodstuffs; and third, de Gaulle's control of part of the French empire had been for a time his only claim to legitimacy.

De Gaulle recognized that after the war the contributions of the colonial populations would have to be rewarded and reforms would have to be instituted to take into account the vast changes that had occurred. In 1943 when his provisional government moved to Algiers from London, it took important steps to satisfy the demands of the educated Algerians—reforms which foreshadowed later ones. In Algeria there had been two electoral colleges, one consisting of French citizens, the other of Moslems. The first college elected a large majority of the municipal and regional councillors and was qualified to vote for deputies to the French Parliament. De Gaulle decreed that several tens of thousands of educated Algerians should become members of the first college without having to abandon their personal legal status—that is, without having to renounce their traditional laws, such as the Moslem laws on marriage and inheritance. In addition, the prerogatives of the second college were made coequal with those of the first.[18]

Thus, in Algeria and in AEF, the two major areas controlled by the Free French in 1943, some reforms had been made. And when toward the end of that year the Free French had seized control of all the French possessions in Africa, the moment seemed to have arrived to consider a comprehensive plan for the future development of the African empire. The time for change, de Gaulle's commissioner of colonies René Pleven noted, was long overdue. While the colonies had undergone profound evolution since their conquest, the administrative system established then had been preserved with only a few minor changes. In January 1944 Pleven called a meeting in Brazzaville of all top colonial officials; its purpose was

> to clarify, to organize, and to render French colonization more efficacious. We shall fight racial prejudice, excessive economic subordination of the colonies to the metropole, bureaucracy, fear of responsibility, laziness of spirit, respect for the letter [of the law].[19]

But if the imperial structures were to be reformed, Pleven made it clear that no parcel of French authority should be sacrificed. Before the conference met, Pleven instructed the delegates:

> It may be convenient to remind ourselves that the political power of France must be retained so that it will continue to be able to control the empire. Whatever the local liberties or the attributes of a federal institution, the French government reserves to itself, or to its representatives, the right to choose the higher representatives of authority: governors-general, governors, prefects, residents-general, magistrates.... Thus, local initiative and a federal representative institution will not endanger or diminish the influence of France on its empire.[20]

De Gaulle, to show the importance that he placed in the conference, flew to Brazzaville and opened its first session on January 30, 1944. In his speech he asserted that even at the outbreak of the war "the necessity appeared to create a new basis for the conditions of economic development of our African territories, to ensure the progress of the men who live there, and that of the exercise of French sovereignty." The mission of France was "to elevate men step by step toward the peaks of dignity and fraternity." France, de Gaulle said, was determined "to choose nobly and generously" the new and practical roads toward the future.[21] Both Pleven, in his instructions issued to the delegates in late 1943 and in his speech, and de Gaulle, in his address to the conference, laid down the general framework for the members of the Brazzaville Conference.[22]

The conference was attended by eighteen governors and governors-general, by administrative advisers from Algeria, Tunisia, and Morocco, by officials from the commisariat of colonies, and by members of the French Consultative Assembly sitting in Algiers. One striking feature of the conference was that although it had been called to decide the future of French Africa, no Africans actively participated in its deliberations.

At Brazzaville the Free French had a twofold task to perform: they had to draw up plans for the future evolution of the colonies, and to respond to the expectations of broadened liberty that had developed in Africa. Ever since the promulgation of the Atlantic Charter in 1941, an Allied victory had been identified with the end of all forms of suppression. The third principle of the Charter had been "respect [for] the right of all peoples to choose the form of government under which they live...." Also, it had promised the restoration of "sovereign rights and self-government ... to those who have been forcibly deprived of them."[23] Pleven in his opening speech attempted to answer those who urged that France divest herself of her empire. In the presence of the American consul in Brazzaville, Pleven told the conference:

We read from time to time that this war must end by what is called the liberation of the colonial populations. In the great French empire there are neither people to liberate nor racial discrimination to abolish. There are peoples who feel French, who wish, and to whom France wishes to give, an ever greater part in the life and in the democratic institutions of the French community. There are peoples whom we are going to lead step by step toward realizing their personality; the more mature will be granted suffrage, but they know of no other independence than the independence of France.[24]

The conference echoed Pleven's speech when it declared that France "refuses all idea of autonomy, all possibility of an evolution outside the French bloc of the empire; the eventual, even distant establishment of self-government is to be rejected."[25]

Having decided that the colonial populations should remain closely tied to the French motherland while enjoying greater liberties, the conference opted for the policy of assimilation. Although Eboué played an important role in the conference, many of his recommendations regarding the need to respect indigenous institutions were not accepted. Thus, the conference recommended a change in the lowly position of the woman, the abolition of polygamy, and the introduction of a uniform criminal code for all of Africa. French education was to spread, and through economic development the colonial populations were to be brought ever closer to the French level of civilization. The aim of French colonization, the conference declared, was "to make this native mass evolve in the direction of an ever increasing assimilation with the principles which constitute the common basis of French civilization."[26]

It is not surprising that a conference made up of French colonial officials would, while making such grandiose statements, remain very conservative in recommending the granting of political rights to the colonial populations. Representative assemblies were to be established in each colony, but they were to have deliberative powers only in voting the local budget. In all other matters, the assemblies were to be given only

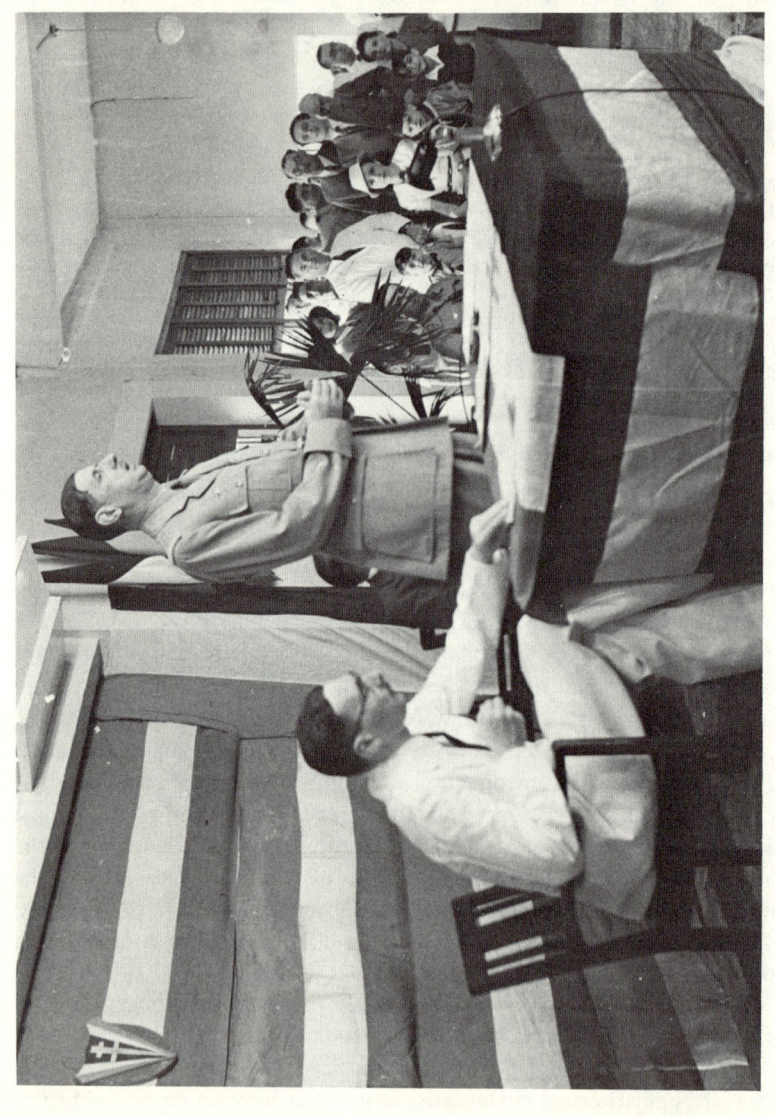

CHARLES DE GAULLE OPENING BRAZZAVILLE CONFERENCE

consultative powers. According to the recommendations of the conference, the local assemblies were not to have any powers of control over the administration; as before the war, the colonial bureaucracy was to be appointed from Paris and in the last analysis was to be responsible only to the minister of colonies. The conference declared, "It is desirable that the political power of France be exercised with precision and rigor in all areas of her empire."[27] The colonial populations were to elect members to the French Parliament, but their exact numbers and their powers were left undefined, to be decided by the future constituent assembly.

In the administrative field, the conference made several recommendations: it advocated administrative decentralization, an improvement in the recruitment of overseas personnel, and a greater access of the indigenous populations to administrative posts. But the conference declared at the same time that "the positions of command and direction cannot admit any but French citizens."[28] The conference echoed the recommendations that had been made by the Governors-General Conference of 1936 to abolish the agents of civil services, and to replace them by technicians or by indigenous personnel;[29] it had been defeated then, but this time, the recommendation was followed, and the Corps of Agents of Civil Services was abolished.

Often considered notable as a new departure in French colonial policy, the Brazzaville Conference was more remarkable for its basic conservatism and its advocacy of the continuation of traditional policies. Many of the declarations of principle sounded generous, but the specific suggestions proved to be of minor importance, or were rendered inoperative by contradictory statements. Nevertheless the conference was a dramatic focusing on the empire and its problems. More strongly than ever before, members of the colonial administration had declared the need for a reform of the empire. As such it was an important step.

When the Free French took control of the empire, very few members of the Corps of Colonial Administrators were eliminated. At the most, about twenty were dismissed from the AOF administration after it passed under Gaullist control in late 1942, and these had either been members of an extremist group, the *Service d'ordre legionnaire*, or had made public anti-Gaullist speeches. Governors-General Boisson in AOF and Annet in Madagascar, who had ordered their troops to fire at the Gaullist forces when they tried to land in AOF and Madagascar, were dismissed and scheduled to be tried for treason. Boisson died before his trial, and Annet was sentenced to "lifetime national degradation." Léon Cayla, who had also served as governor-general of Madagascar, was sentenced in 1946 to five years imprisonment, 10,000 francs fine, and "lifetime national indignity." Some men who had headed the secretariat of state for colonies under Vichy were also dealt with after the war. Brévié in 1947 was sentenced to ten years' imprisonment, "lifetime national degradation," and confiscation of his property. Admiral Platon was executed by a Resistance group in 1944, and Admiral Bléhaut was sentenced in 1948 to ten years' imprisonment and "lifetime national degradation."[30]

Lesser officials who had collaborated with Vichy, however, were dealt with less severely. Governors who had served the Vichy regime were usually pensioned. The administrators, however, as a rule, were retained, since it would have been impossible to replace them all. Even administrators who were rather closely identified with Pétain were retained and only delayed in their promotion; the Gaullist regime in 1944 knowingly promoted some officials who had compromised themselves with the Pétainist regime.[31] The colonial service, just as the other French bureaucracies, was not—in spite of Resistance demands—heavily purged. Of one million civil servants employed by the central government in France, only 5,000 or one-half percent, were dismissed for collaboration.[32]

Once France was liberated and the war ended, a Constituent Assembly met in Paris. Even before it had drawn up a draft of the constitution, it adopted a number of laws regarding the overseas territories. Following the recommendations of the Brazzaville Conference it abolished forced labor and the system of the *indigénat*. In March 1946 it adopted the Lamine-Gueye law, sponsored by the Senegalese deputy, which proclaimed all the peoples of the overseas territories to be French citizens. These measures were incorporated into the constitution which was eventually adopted.[33] Also, the constitution established local assemblies in the colonies which, as the Brazzaville Conference recommended, had the power to vote the local budget, but were otherwise deprived of any legislative powers.

While adopting the measure of French citizenship the assembly added that the rights connected with citizenship would later be defined. When this was done, only a limited number of inhabitants from the overseas territories, with specific educational and professional qualifications, were given the right to vote in elections. The overseas areas contained a population one and a half times as large as the mainland French population, but the overseas deputies who were to sit in the National Assembly held only seven percent of the total number of seats in the assembly, and the overseas councillors 15 percent of the Council of the Republic.

In addition to the National Assembly and the Council of the Republic, a third chamber, the Assembly of the French Union, was established in which the overseas populations had an equal membership with the metropole. This assembly, however, was of no consequence since it had only consultative powers. Symbolizing the ineffectiveness of the assembly was its location in Versailles, rather than in Paris, which of course was the center of power. The overseas territories had less political weight than had the metropole; the founders of the constitution had heeded the words of Herriot, who had warned of the danger that "France will become the colony of its former colonies."[34]

The Swiss journalist Herbert Luethy, a well-known critic of French institutions, summed up the case against the parliamentarians who had drawn up the constitution of the Fourth Republic:

They decreed in a vacuum that the French empire was "a freely consented Union" without making the least attempt to ask the consent of those concerned; they decreed that all the inhabitants of this empire were French citizens and would have to elect a certain number of deputies to the French Parliament, when these people did not demand the ridiculous honor of governing French domestic affairs, but rather wanted to govern their own affairs and to be citizens of their own countries.[35]

The constitution of 1946, many colonial administrators believed, had abolished the colonial relationship. In fact, there were no longer any "colonies." As Delavignette declared, "There are no longer any colonies.... Tomorrow we shall be the natives of a common French Union."[36] A whole change of nomenclature seemed to confirm this. The ministry of colonies was now the ministry of overseas France, and the Corps of Colonial Administrators became the Corps of Overseas Administrators. It was no longer fashionable to call the populations of the overseas territories "*indigènes*"; instead, they were called "*autochtones*." These changes in name had great symbolic value. Asked when they had entered the colonial administration, several former officials denied that they had ever been in such an administration, saying they had been in "the overseas administration." Added one former official, "I hope you understand the difference."[37]

The administrators identified the emancipation of the colonial peoples with the abolition of all forms of colonial subjugation, but they did not believe that this emancipation required the political independence of the territories. A liberal-minded student at the ENFOM wrote in 1947:

Colonization can... justify itself only if it is a transitory stage and a perpetual becoming, destined to favor the total emancipation of peoples.... The question is not whether there will or will not be an emancipation of the colonial peoples, but rather whether it will be done with us or against us.

Then, he added the hope common to nearly all administrators:

> If our action is efficient and sincere, the natives will understand that the times are no longer favorable to blind nationalism and xenophobia, but to a freely accepted federalism, and, depending on our political intelligence, we may become the center.[38]

Regardless of their political ideas, the French administrators were committed somehow to maintain the bonds between the mother country and the overseas territories.[39] In the end, even independence was favored as an expedient by which to retain French influence. In a special issue, the ministry's information bulletin refuted critics of French overseas rule. "Total evacuation" of the French Union, which contained peoples who were "insufficiently developed," would, it argued, "without fail" mean that "they would fall under the direct or indirect domination of a foreign power."[40] Moutet, who again presided at Rue Oudinot, made it clear that while overseas reforms were desirable, the ties connecting France to its territories were of a permanent nature: "France maintains and means to maintain the rights acquired for her by so many gallant efforts ... overseas by her schools, her administrators, her colonials, her workers, her soldiers, and her policy."[41]

The constitution ensured the control of the metropole over the overseas territories, but it radically altered the role of the overseas administrators. Because the overseas populations were now citizens, the administrators could no longer impose either the code of the *indigénat* system or forced labor. Before the war the administrators had been endowed with judicial powers in addition to their administrative powers. But after 1945 all judicial powers were transferred to the overseas magistrature,[42] and the overseas judges were often bitter rivals of the administrators. In spite of the fact that they had been trained at the ENFOM, they developed few contacts with the cadets going into the administration. They took few courses at the school and spent most of their time completing their law studies and gaining practical experience in the Paris courts. In the final analysis, of course, the clash between the administrators and the judges was determined less by their lack of contact with each other than by the different roles they were filling. For the administrators the smoothness and efficiency of their administration was the prime concern; for the judges the dictates of justice tended to predominate. Members of each branch had harsh words to say about the other. One former judge, in describing some administrators he had known, compared them with "oriental despots ... who were the Stalins of their regions."[43] Many administrators thought of the overseas judges as being "stupid and meddlesome."[44] Without their disciplinary powers the administrators were henceforth unable to force the indigenous populations to cultivate their own fields or to work on projects of public utility. Freed from outside constraint, the local populations in some territories no longer worked, some administrators complained. One official wrote:

> Anarchy rules in the bush where the people do not even cultivate the areas necessary for feeding a family. The old people work alone under the ironic gaze of the young citizens, whose principal activity resides in endless speechmaking. The level of production drops fast. The roads are no longer taken care of. The notion of a general interest has been completely forgotten.[45]

Nevertheless, in 1951 this same official found that the people of his *cercle* had gone back to work, repaired the roads and even built new schools.[46]

In any case, a much more sophisticated program of economic development than had existed before was planned by the Fourth Republic. In 1946, the French government established a massive investment program, the *Fonds d'investissements économiques et sociales* (FIDES). In the ten-year period from 1948 to 1958 it invested a trillion francs, or eight percent of the national revenue, in the overseas territories.[47] To carry out the development projects, a large number of technicians were appointed overseas. Engineers constructed roads, bridges, and public buildings; health officials combatted epidemics; agricultural experts helped develop crops; and census takers recorded the population level. No longer were the administrators the "jacks of all trades"; their tasks became increasingly limited to strictly administrative functions.

By establishing regional assemblies and giving the overseas populations the right to send deputies to the French Parliament, the constitution also diminished the power of the administrators by creating new rivals to their authority—African politicians. The territorial councillors and the deputies to the French National Assembly developed an increasing dominance over the local populations; and they began to supplant the authority of the legal government, the administration.[48]

The political instability of the Fourth Republic meant that the existence of cabinets might depend on the votes of a few overseas deputies in the National Assembly. In order to appease those deputies and win support for the government, the ministers of overseas France often transferred officials who might have incurred the wrath of an overseas deputy. As a result of African pressures, administrators, governors, and even governors-general were often replaced. Under the pressure of local politicians, governors-general and governors also replaced or demoted their subordinates. The extent to which this occurred is suggested by the warning sent in 1949 by Paul Coste-Floret, minister of overseas France. Governors-general and governors, he ordered, must not demote their subordinates before investigating the veracity of complaints made by local politicians or interest groups. Also, the extent to which Rue Oudinot was open to political influence may be seen in Coste-Floret's need to assure the Corps that he would not allow outside influences to be decisive in making promotions or reassignments.[49]

Until 1952 the ministers were not always receptive to the demands of the overseas deputies, but thereafter they became increasingly accommodating. Writing about the period after 1952, an American political scientist has noted that in the Ivory Coast:

> The French government replaced any officials, including governors, who displeased the PDCI [the dominant party in the Ivory Coast]. By 1956 ... administrators knew their jobs depended upon the PDCI, and as a result, backed down or asked the party for help when they had to implement unpopular decisions.[50]

As government coalitions in France shifted, governors and governors-general of the same persuasion as the government were named. In 1948, for example, as a result of a change in government, four out of the five governors-general and thirteen governors were replaced. Before the war the positions of the governors-general (but usually not governors) had been semipolitical posts. But after the war the colonial administration had become more politicized than before. When high officials were looking for young administrators as their collaborators, they chose officials of similar political leanings. ENFOM students were often approached by rival teams of governors, urging them to join a given political party; and administrators who had attached themselves to a governor belonging to the parties in power could expect interesting assignments and quick promotions.

After the war the overseas administration made a concerted effort to ensure continuity of personnel by not displacing functionaries too frequently, but earlier traditions of changing personnel remained. Frequent displacement was also due in part to the introduction of politics into the administration. At the top level it was very serious because it led to instability. In Oubangui, for example, there were nine successive governors between 1946 and 1951, and three governors in Chad between 1949 and 1951.

The instability of the governments of the Fourth Republic meant that any event of the least significance could topple a cabinet. No issues connected with Black Africa ever caused the downfall of a government, but the ministers of overseas France feared such an eventuality. "*Surtout pas d'affaires* (above all—avoid trouble)," was the slogan of the day. Therefore, the ministers of overseas France, unlike their predecessors, kept a tight rein on the overseas administration.

Communications improved in the 1950s and as a consequence the offices at Rue Oudinot could be kept in close touch with officials in Dakar or Brazzaville, the federal capitals with the territorial capitals, and they in turn with the *commandants de cercles*. At the same time, the improved communications limited the freedom of action that the administrators had previously enjoyed, as is illustrated by the experience of an official who served in 1949 in an isolated region in Chad. During the rainy season, the roads eroded and his mail could reach him only by river, taking three weeks from Fort Lamy, the capital. "When the governor sent me instructions with which I disagreed," the administrator told the author, "I would act as if I had never seen them, noting down in the diary of the post, 'mailbag seems to have fallen into river, governor's mail arrived wet and illegible.' "[51] But when the same administrator served in that district a few years later, he was unable to use this stratagem, since his region was now regularly connected with the capital by plane. Earlier he was sure that there would be no inspections of his *cercle* during the rainy season, but with the establishment of air communications he had to take into account the possibility of an inspector's—or even a governor's—arrival on an unannounced visit.[52]

The division of what once had been absolute power, the sharing of authority with other officials, the intrusion of politics into the Corps, and the establishment of more intense supervision by superiors considerably weakened the administrators' freedom of action. They were no longer the "real chiefs of the empire." The administrators, aware of this situation, suffered from what Coste-Floret called a *"crise de confiance."*[53] Coste-Floret while minister of overseas France attempted to strengthen the position of the administrators, but the forces unleashed after 1946 were too strong to restore their former power. A former administrator has described in a colonial novel the experience of a young man entering the service as an administrator after the war. He writes:

He enthusiastically began his career, but he noticed after a few months that he was living at the end of an epoch, and that he arrived too late to enjoy for long the sweet taste of absolute power. If authority survived, it was already a forbidden fruit. The *commandant* exercised less authority every day and the grandeur of the profession disappeared fast, while the duties became heavier.[54]

When two decades earlier, reforms similar to those introduced by the French in Africa had been instituted in British India and the Dutch East Indies, giving greater political authority to indigenous bodies, a corresponding decline in morale had occurred among the members of the India Civil Service and the Dutch East Indies service.[55] De Kat Angelino argued that this decline in morale was due to the British and Dutch administrators' desire to have "a man's full job, a real task, an active share in the process of evolution."[56] With the French colonial service the cause for dissatisfaction was the same. Even if the role of the administrator had legally changed, those who were in the Corps and even those who were just entering it still wanted to think of themselves as the main force shaping the destiny of the overseas territories.

As to the timeliness of the reforms of 1945-1946 administrators themselves have overwhelmingly declared in the affirmative (See Table 11).

Table 11

Attitudes toward the timing of reforms of 1945-1946

Date of entry into *Ecole Coloniale*	Attitude toward timing of reforms		
	Premature	Timely	Too late
1920-1929	5	23	8
1930-1939	12	72	6
1940-1945	4	28	5
1946-1950	6	30	4

The figures show that the bulk of the Corps accepted the reforms. On the other hand, they also show that very few administrators had been impatiently awaiting or agitating for reform. What really occurred was an adjustment by the Corps to what was considered inevitable. A few die-hards in 1965 still regretted the reforms that had been instituted two decades earlier. One administrator wrote: "Even today in 1965 they seem to me to have been premature."[57] An older administrator, who began his overseas service in the 1920s, deplored the abolition of forced labor, since "it made the natives lazy." Still another official wrote, "Democracy is not for export."[58]

The number considering the reforms to be premature closely balanced the number who believed that they should have been instituted earlier. The main argument of the latter school is that expressed by an old official who entered the service in the 1920s: "The reforms should have been carried out before we were forced to grant them." A younger man who entered the service in the early 1940s wrote, "We had to destroy the colonial institutions and build new ones." Two officials, still serving when the reforms were instituted, seem to have been entirely unaffected by them; they did not remember that any had been made.[59] While the different answers may not have been representative of the entire Corps, nevertheless, it is clear that the Corps eventually became reconciled to the reforms.

As a result of reforms with which they had little to do in formulating, the administrators had been deprived of their former positions of omnipotence. This loss of power represented a real crisis to most administrators. Writing in 1945, a high official serving in AOF only dimly perceived the consequences of the reforms which were beginning to be applied.

AOF is in the process of seeing a substitution of a social order founded on the rights of the African for a social order founded on the African's duties and on his need to obey. It is a real revolution whose effects are only imperfectly felt, but which makes the present period rather difficult to define. It seems, however, to be decisive for the future of this country.[60]

The official noted that the administrators were feeling "some bitterness" at the discredit into which they had fallen as a result of being told "that their reign is from now on finished." Although praising the administrators for maintaining "under difficult conditions the functioning of an administration in which they remain the base," the official wrote that "most of them have difficulty in understanding and applying the policy of assimilation that France has very resolutely engaged itself to follow."[61]

Delavignette, serving as high commissioner of the French Cameroons, also seemed to feel that some of his subordinates were having trouble adjusting to the new reforms. He told the administrators in his territory:

If you resent your loss of personal or public authority because there is a representative assembly, because your subordinates are unionized, because the *indigénat* code is suppressed, because you no longer possess judicial powers, because the Cameroons of 1946 no longer is that of 1920, you are really demanding the impossible. Catch up with the times.[62]

French bureaucracy, an eminent sociologist has remarked, is unusually resistant to change. But when faced by crisis and the need to change, it proves remarkably adaptable.[63] This seems to have been true of the Corps of Overseas Administrators. It is true that some of the liberalization occurring in the 1930s, the writings of men like Labouret and Delavignette, and the decisions of the Brazzaville Conference foreshadowed in part the coming changes. But it was one thing to postulate the need for such changes, and quite another to have to live with them once they had been effected.

The adjustment of the Corps to the changes overseas was facilitated by a relatively rapid infusion of new blood into the Corps. Out of 1,620 administrators in the Corps in 1957, 793, just slightly less than half, had been appointed after 1944.[64] These young men were generally able to adjust to the shift away from the authoritarian, paternal type of rule that had been practiced before the war. But there were many influences tending to continue prewar attitudes. During their apprenticeship the young administrators were assigned to learn the profession from their elders, who often inculcated in them their own values. While times had changed, the elders still held fast to doctrines and methods of rule that had become anachronistic. The experience of a young urbanist in Morocco was surely not unique; when he arrived in Morocco in 1946, he remarked, "The first concern of the administration . . . was to give me the circulars of Lyautey about urbanism. 'You have to do nothing but follow them,' I was told in an imperious tone."[65]

Even the most liberal administrators were not immune to the temptation of exercising the kind of unlimited authority that their elders had possessed before the war. At times circumstances also seemed to dictate that the administrator exercise powers that he no longer legally possessed. Administrators were not permitted to build roads with forced labor, but the road needed building, the local populations would not volunteer, and there was no money in the local budget to hire the labor. Clandestinely, the administrator used coercion to build his road.[66] A young administrator who served in Chad after the war noted that there was a divorce between the principles and the facts: "the principles were those of the Constitution and of the reforms of 1946, while the 'reactionary' facts were the slowness in applying the texts and the difficulties of doing so, which led easily to their non-application."[67] The divorce between "principles" and "facts" was most marked until the late 1940s; in the following decade, under closer control of their superiors, the administrators conformed more in their actions to the liberal principles enunciated in Paris.

How could the changes that were envisioned and desired in Paris be forced on the overseas bureaucracy? The governments of the Fourth Republic did so by politicizing the colonial service. Administrators who were promoted or otherwise favored because of their membership in a political party tended to be more loyal to the principles of that party than to the set of ideas held by the Corps of which they were members. Thus some of the solidarity of the Corps was broken. A former administrator, in expressing his attitude toward reform introduced by a Socialist minister of colonies, said that as a Socialist he, of course, had been in favor of it since it had been proposed by a government of his party.[68]

The appointment of "outsiders," of men who had had no previous colonial experience, to the very highest administrative posts again enforced change. Between 1946 and 1957 more men without colonial experience served as governors-general than in the entire period since the post of governors-general had been founded at the beginning of the century. They were undeviatingly loyal to the government that appointed them, and they did not share the values of the Corps.[69]

While changes were introduced into the overseas territories as a result of the laws of 1945-1946, the method of rule through the chief-system was retained. The reforms had been basically assimilationist and presumably were intended to make the overseas populations into Frenchmen with the same rights and privileges as those held by the inhabitants of metropolitan France. If this policy had been followed to its logical conclusion, what was left of the chief-system would have been dismantled. But the needs of effective administration took precedence. And this, it seemed, could be ensured only by retaining the chiefs. The ideas of Eboué regarding the need to respect local institutions were especially influential after the war; Delavignette serving as high commissioner of the Cameroons, advised his administrators to study and to heed the doctrine elaborated in *La Nouvelle politique indigène*. Eboué was also closely studied at the ENFOM.

Reliance on the chief-system was dictated by the lack of sufficient administrators. Even though direct rule had been practiced ever since the first decades of the twentieth century in most regions, in the sense that the administrators had been able to transform the local chiefs into their subordinates, the French administration had never been sufficiently large to dispense with the chiefs themselves. During the war the Corps serving in Africa had gained two hundred additional administrators. In 1949 the Corps of Overseas Administrators, which since 1942 also included the upper officials of the ministry of overseas France and the officials of the Civil Services of Indochina, numbered 2,028 administrators, but as a result of economy measures the size of the Corps was reduced to 1,820 members by 1951, and to 1,600 by 1959. In spite of the growth in personnel over prewar days, many overseas territories were still understaffed. In 1947 the ministry of overseas France had decided to assign 406 administrators to

AOF on active service, but in 1949 there were only 370 serving—forty-six fewer than there had been before the war. Because of the lack of personnel, forty-four *cercle* subdivisions had to be closed down.[70] Of those serving, not all were in the bush; a fairly large proportion, varying from a third to a fourth, occupied desk jobs in the territorial capitals.[71]

The administrative regions were too large and too diverse to allow the administrators to control them without intermediaries. An administrator serving in the Sudan has described the immensity of the region that he administered, together with his assistant:

> [In] a territory of 35,000 square kilometers, which is as vast as Belgium, [we] must administer, counsel, and survey a population of 200,000 illiterates and this through thirty-six traditional *chefs de canton*, of whom only five speak French and two know how to read and write, and they themselves command 875 village chiefs.... Certain villages are 150-200 kilometers away from the administrative center, most of the time inaccessible by car.[72]

Throughout the decades of French rule complaints were made about the lack of contact between the administrators and the indigenous population, but the lack was probably never more evident than in the period after the second world war. The administrators no longer had to fill the many roles that they had filled up to 1945, but they were now busier than ever before. They were occupied with an ever growing amount of paperwork, with coordinating the activities of the technicians serving in their *cercles*, and with solving the conflicts among them.

An administrator who served in Oubangui in the late 1940s found that "with the development of new services the administration becomes heavier and the tasks of office-work absorb increasing time." As a result he no longer went on extensive tours of the villages.[73] As the minister of overseas France stated in 1949, because of the limited effectiveness of the French administrators there could "be no solid territorial command which does not depend on the chiefs."[74]

Before 1914 the colonial administrators had reduced the local chiefs' powers hoping to modernize, to assimilate the colonial populations by direct rule. During the interwar years the administration became cautious, fearing that further evolution of the overseas populations would bring about unrest against colonial rule. Thus rather than encourage the young educated elites, the administration in general backed the traditional chiefs. At the Brazzaville Conference this fact was openly recognized when one participant stated that the administration and the religious missions had been on opposite sides: "Generally, the administrators have taken sides with the traditionalists, the missions with the young."[75] This situation remained virtually unchanged until the early 1950s.

Governor Henri Laurentie (formerly Eboué's right-hand man in AEF), the director of political affairs in the ministry of colonies, seemed to recognize the need for some change in the method of "native administration." In a speech in 1945 he announced that the administrators would henceforth have to pay increased attention to the *évolués*. But he immediately expressed the concern that French officials nearly always felt: the needs of the masses had to be taken into account; they must not be "artificially subjugated by the elites." Laurentie stated that there were two ways to rule: either through the chiefs or through the *évolués*. Since neither was quite acceptable, Laurentie stated that there was a third way: "Let the village speak. We should have confidence in the African countryside from which we can and must draw the new means and men who will create both an authentic and modern political life."[76] Rhetorically, "the third way" sounded attractive, but it seems never to have been a genuine alternative.

Faced with the only two real alternatives, rule through the elite or rule through the chiefs, the administrators chose the latter. They did so not only because this had been their traditional and most convenient method of rule, but also because with Laurentie they saw the *évolués* as an artificial class not possessing the authentic connection with the masses that presumably the chiefs had. In spite of the adoption of assimilation as the overseas policy of the Fourth Republic, the administrators just as in the interwar period continued to be wary of educated Africans. The illiterate peasant appealed much more to his romantic notion of what a "genuine native" was like. This kind of perception also gave his vocation and his country's rule over alien peoples a sense—a civilizing mission—which it otherwise might not have possessed.

Until roughly 1953 political developments within the overseas territories favored a growth in the authority of the chiefs. Formerly the overseas administration had actively opposed the development of mass political parties, going so far as to intimidate the leaders or even to imprison them; and to thwart the mass parties politically, the administrators encouraged the formation of client parties around local chiefs. Pierre Alexandre, an administrator in Togo in the early 1950s, described how the administration used this tactic to fight CUT, the mass party in Togo. The French in strengthening the authority and prestige of the local chiefs thereby allowed them increasing independence. It was this situation "that explains in part," Alexandre wrote, "why I had so much time to involve myself in ethnographic studies; the Uro Esso [local chief] concerned himself to a large extent with the administration."[77]

Out of convenience, the administrators retained the chiefs and showed remarkable reluctance to replace them. Only when a chief had committed a crime or had failed to meet the quotas of production was he dismissed. To all other kinds of abuses the administration was blind. "We were then more concerned with production than with principles," remarked a former administrator who served in Upper Volta.[78]

A possible alternative to the chief-system would have been to institute local government, with town and village councils. But with the exception of the communes of Senegal, none of the municipalities in French Black Africa enjoyed genuine local rule. The more urban areas did have city councils, but they were elected in such a way as to give the French settlers predominance on the councils, and the local administrator who served as mayor could override council decisions. It is not surprising that the French, who by tradition have not favored the development of local rule at home, would be reluctant to encourage it in their overseas territories. And control of the local population seemed much easier to maintain through the chiefs.

Administrative expediency dictated the use of the chiefs, but in their own right the chiefs did not possess any power. After 1953, when the French administration began cooperating with the mass parties, and especially after the reforms of 1956-1957, when most of the parties began to win control over the internal administration in the overseas territories, the authority of the chiefs waned. The mass parties were hostile to the chiefs since the latter usually had been the mainstay of the French administration. With the change in policy, the administrators, on orders from Paris, usually cooperated with the African politicians. The administrators thus abandoned the chiefs, and, in fact, declared them superfluous. At a conference of French administrators in Guinea in 1957 each administrator, discussing the role of the local chiefs in his region, dismissed them as useless. Of the twenty-one chiefs in one *cercle* two were imprisoned and one was out of jail on provisional liberty. "In reality," concluded the administrator of that region, " ... the chiefs have been absolutely inefficacious, they don't serve any purpose." Discussing the need to replace the old chiefs, the administrator of a *cercle* subdivision declared that in his five *cantons* there was only one chief who was intelligent, the rest ought "to be liquidated."[79] The administrators had deliberately stopped having contacts with the *chefs de canton*. One *commandant de cercle* declared that "for eight months I have had no contact with a *chef de canton*. For me, if they exist or don't, it is the same thing."[80]

Before the early 1950s there were few political reforms. The changes that had been instituted in 1945-1946 were considered to have satisfactorily regulated the legal relationship between France and her overseas territories. In any case, the overseas administration saw the economic and social problem of underdevelopment as the main problem besetting the territories. A meeting of governors-general in 1946 unanimously advised Rue Oudinot to give priority to economic over political issues.[81] Four years later François Mitterrand, a minister known for his liberal leanings, announced "I do not think that there is a political problem in French Africa.... There is, on the contrary, an essentially economic problem."[82]

In 1952-1953, however, Mitterrand did recognize that a political problem was besetting the French possessions in Black Africa. In nearly all the African territories mass political parties connected with Houphouet-Boigny's *Rassemblement démocratique africain* had developed. By their vehement anticolonialism these parties were causing the French government considerable embarrassment and difficulty. Mitterrand made an agreement with Houphouet that the French would cease their harassment of the mass parties if in exchange the RDA would abandon its anticolonial propaganda. The governors were suspicious of the RDA and were unwilling to allow Houphouet's representatives into their territory to give the order to stop opposing the French administration.[83] The older administrators also hesitated to cooperate with the former opponents of French rule; only the younger officials, Mitterrand noticed, were able to adjust to a new policy.[84] In any case, the orders from Rue Oudinot prevailed.

Within the Corps itself new currents developed, as a number of administrators became cognizant of the need for reforming the imperial structure. The defeat of the French at Dien Bien Phu and the outbreak of war in Algeria, within a few months of each other, were serious blows to those who believed in the institutions that had been built overseas. Speaking for many of his comrades, an administrator who had entered the overseas service in the late 1940s wrote of the events of 1954, especially of Dien Bien Phu:

For a colonial administrator who had studied, lived, worked, sweated for the greatness of the French empire, it was Agincourt, Trafalgar, and Waterloo all at once. It was a whole world which collapsed.[85]

The outbreak of the Algerian war seemed to presage trouble for the Black African territories. Pierre Gentil, an administrator serving in AEF, warned that just as the Algerians had gained experience fighting colonial wars in helping the French try to suppress the Indochinese, the soldiers from Black Africa fighting in Algeria "may become the revolutionary militias of Senegal and the Congo."[86] Timely reforms in Black Africa would be the only way of staving off revolt.

In other ways the revolt overseas liberalized the attitudes of the Corps in Africa. Between 1946 and 1955 about 300 officials from Indochina were transferred to Africa. In Indochina many officials had witnessed how their government by its intransigence had lost its Asian possession. If this experience was not enough, they had also witnessed the disintegration of other European empires in neighboring territories: in 1947 British rule had come to an end in India, and the following year the Dutch had been forced to recognize the independence of Indonesia. Obviously not all administrators who had served in Indochina were liberal-minded, but there was a sizable number who because of their Indochinese experience hoped through a policy of flexibility to preserve French Africa.[87] Also, most of the graduates of the ENFOM in the 1950s were liberally inclined and were well aware of the need to reform the overseas institutions. (*See previous chapter*.)

Beginning in 1954 reforms foreshadowing innovations in the territories occurred. The powers of municipal bodies in the overseas territories were enlarged and the number of African deputies elected to Parliament was increased. Under pressure from the United Nations and for fear of losing the Ewé population of Togo to neighboring Gold Coast, which was on the road to independence, the French in 1955 permitted the establishment in Togo of what amounted to self-government. The territorial assemblies were vested with legislative powers, a Togolese cabinet was established, and it controlled the French administration. Pierre Henri Teitgen, minister of overseas France, expressed the wish to see similar reforms instituted in the various overseas territories.[88] It seemed logical that the territories which by their history and legal ties were more closely connected to France than was Togo, a mandate territory, should be at least as liberally treated as Togo had been. And this was the argument of African deputies and some colonial officials.

In October 1955 Teitgen sent a lengthy report to the president of the Republic and to his cabinet colleagues on the need for reform in the political structure of the territories; the report was entitled *"Sur les principaux problèmes actuels des territoires de l'Afrique noire."* The reason that no solution to the colonial problem had been found, the report stated, was that French policy had been torn between the alternatives of assimilation and separatism. "Integral assimilation is at the same time unacceptable to the Metropole and contrary to the legitimate aspirations of the overseas populations who wish to see their particular personalities respected," the report stated. Separatism was unacceptable; federalism was impossible because of the incapacity of the overseas territories to be economically independent. The only solution was an elastic one to which all territories, so different in their economic, political, and social conditions, could adjust. The immediate solution would presumably consider the interests both of France and of its overseas territories; this could be achieved by continuing to include the overseas territories as part of France. The report clearly upheld the structure established in 1946, but it favored an important increase in the powers of the territorial assemblies.

The personality of the overseas territories must be respected and therefore one must give to the territorial authority, representative of the population, powers to solve strictly territorial problems not affecting the entire Republic.[89]

The report suggested that the assemblies be made more democratic by getting rid of the double electoral college (which gave the minority of Europeans the same electoral weight as the indigenous population), and by the establishment of universal suffrage.[90] Finally, Teitgen demanded increased Africanization of the civil service and an intensified program of social and economic improvement overseas.[91]

Teitgen publicly spoke out for his program, declaring that although overseas parliamentarians were proud to participate in the public affairs of the Republic, their main desire "is to gain political control over their domestic affairs."[92] The colonial peoples desired neither assimilation nor secession; the solution was the creation of a truly federal system.[93]

Teitgen did not have the opportunity to see his suggestions adopted; rather it was a successor—the Mollet government—dominated by the Socialists, which put them into effect. That government faced a Parliament that was generally favorable to reform of the overseas institutions. The Parliament was aware of the need for quick reform, and since in the past it had proved unable to agree on the details of most overseas reforms, it indulged in what was probably an unconstitutional act: it authorized the minister of overseas France to make the reforms.[94] That authorization drew up the framework within which the reforms were to be instituted and was thus known as a *loi-cadre*. The *loi-cadre* itself introduced universal suffrage and got rid of the double electoral college in the overseas territories.

Both Parliament and the administration at Rue Oudinot thought of the overseas territories as forming a bloc. When the British introduced reforms, they did so for each colony individually. There was no overall plan made in London imposed on all of them simultaneously. The British developments have the appearance of having been more empirical, more in tune with the local needs of each colony; the French seem to have been more "Cartesian," more abstract in their overseas reforms. But the French, of course, had to face a difficult legal obstacle. Had not the constitution declared that all the former colonies in Africa which had been administered by the ministry of colonies were overseas territories, an integral part of France? No legal distinctions had been drawn among the overseas territories. If Chad had not been treated as generously as Senegal had been, the result might have been an uprising in Chad.

The reforms introduced in the spring of 1957 took their name from Gaston Defferre, the Socialist minister of overseas France. They gave important legislative powers to the territorial assemblies and empowered them to elect a government council of six to eight ministers. The member of the council elected with the highest number of votes would serve as vice-president of the council. The presidency was to be occupied by the French governor, who held substantial reserve powers in his hands. But the governor was not, as previously, all-powerful: his decisions had to be made in council. The powers to be divided between the governors and the councils were unclear, and the vice-presidents of the councils quickly emerged as the most important figures. In July 1958 the vice-presidents were made presidents of the councils, and the governors presided over the meetings of the councils only when administrative matters were discussed.[95]

Generally, the Corps seemed to favor the Defferre reforms. When asked later about their attitudes toward the *loi-cadre*, most administrators claimed that they had thought it a timely reform, with smaller minorities thinking that the reforms were either premature or too late (see Table 12).

Table 12

Attitudes toward reforms of 1956-1957

Year of entry into *Ecole Coloniale*	Attitude toward timing of Defferre laws		
	Premature	Timely	Too late
1920-1929	8	12	8
1930-1939	20	54	18
1940-1949	18	74	20
1950-	2	16	6
Total	48	156	52

Most administrators believed that the *loi-cadre* was necessary in order to prevent a secessionist movement similar to that which had marked Indochina and was then taking place in Algeria. Four administrators in October 1965 asserted their belief that without the *loi-cadre* there would have been major bloodshed.[96]

Many openly favored reforms. Georges Rey, a former bush administrator and governor, hailed them as "a revolution in the concept of relations between the metropole and the territories of Black Africa." He called on "all Frenchmen living in Africa" to "devote their energies and intelligence so that this evolution will be a success."[97]

It had become increasingly difficult for the French authorities to enforce their rule; the *loi-cadre* conveniently shifted responsibility to African politicians.[98] It was with some satisfaction that French officials in Chad saw the African politicians, who had previously attacked them for being arbitrary and authoritarian, use armed guards to collect the year's taxes in Fort Lamy, the territorial capital.[99]

A journalist, Pierre Paraf, visiting AOF in 1957, found the governors-general and the governors operating within the provisions of the *loi-cadre*. But "in descending the stairs of the hierarchy," he found more resistance. Old and even young administrators seemed to entertain authoritarian views, and expressed unhappiness at seeing French authority diminished.[100] At the same time, however, Paraf found that there were many younger administrators who wished to see the reforms extended to making Africans heads of the councils and to increasing the powers of the territorial assemblies.[101] But in all cases, even if there was some private disagreement, all administrators loyally carried out the reforms.

One of the provisions of the *loi-cadre* was an increased Africanization of the overseas bureaucracy, including the Corps of Administrators of Overseas France. For practical training, African civil servants were assigned as assistants to *commandants de cercles* and were taught the intricacies of regional administration. In 1956, for example, there were six such trainees in the Ivory Coast.[102] The process of Africanization was slow, for the French, unlike the British, did not foresee that their rule was rapidly coming to an end. Because it was assumed that French rule would continue for a long time, they did not want to put men whom they considered insufficiently prepared into administrative posts. Very rigid standards were maintained in bringing Africans into the Corps, either by on-the-job training or through the ENFOM. The liberal governor of Guinea, Jean Ramadier, was one of the few who was aware of the need for rapid Africanization of the administration. In 1957 he told his *commandants de cercles* that it was necessary to create a trained African personnel, since it was possible that Guinea would become independent.[103] Even he, however, could not have realized that within a year his territory would become a sovereign state.

The reforms in 1957 did not make most French administrators fearful for their future careers. They looked forward to long and uninterrupted service overseas. Speaking before the *Académie des sciences d'outre-mer* in 1957, an administrator noted for his perspicacity stated that in Togo, where he was serving, the administrators would be needed for a long time, to serve as neutral arbiters between the various feuding ethnic groups.[104]

In the British colonial service, the officials expected, and indeed were informed upon recruitment, that they should not anticipate a full career overseas, for the administration would gradually be Africanized.[105] But the French had very different expectations; almost without exception the students entering the ENFOM in 1958 thought they would have a lifetime career. They recognized that their functions and powers might change drastically, but they believed that they would remain overseas in some capacity.

At the time it was instituted the *loi-cadre* was not considered to be the first step toward independence; rather, in Defferre's words, it was designed "to maintain and reinforce for many years to come the necessary union between metropolitan France and the peoples of the overseas territories."[106]

The French recognized that they were living in an era of decolonization; after all, the Gold Coast was to receive its independence in 1957, and several other British possessions were scheduled to follow suit. In the United Nations, increasing attacks were made against the maintenance of colonial empires. By 1958 most administrators had perceived that some degree of decolonization had become inevitable. It seems that as much as 90 percent of the Corps had become convinced of this necessity by that date (see Table 13).

But, as the French saw it, decolonization did not necessarily mean the granting of independence to the overseas territories; it could also be achieved through the establishment of a loose union in which all forms of French subjugation were abolished. A genuine French community, some thought, might develop with the eradication of all colonial relationships. One former administrator has described his belief that social progress in the overseas territories would have made it possible for the formation of a federation based on equality:

We were closer to our fellow citizens in Africa than the inhabitants of Vermont were to those of New Mexico a century ago. With the acceleration of history, nothing hindered us from thinking that decolonization would occur with the progressive disappearance of the notion of colonizer and colonized.[107]

Table 13

*Attitudes toward decolonization**

Date decolonization was recognized to be inevitable	Number of administrators recognizing it was inevitable
1920-1929	5
1930-1939	6
1940-1944	12
1945	41
1946	39
1950	28
1952-1954	23
1955	24
1956-1957	27
1958	23
1960	5

*One-third did not answer the question regarding the date when they decided that decolonization would be inevitable, or were so vague that their answers could not be readily tabulated.

Most administrators were aware of the need for decolonization in the sense of abolishing all remnants of French subjugation in the overseas territories, but they tenaciously held to the idea that the bonds between France and the overseas territories could somehow be preserved. Even the African deputies who sat in the French Parliament hesitated until 1960 to opt for full political independence.[108] Senghor told the French National Assembly in January 1957:

We do not wish to leave the French compound. We have grown up in it and it has been pleasant to live in it. We simply want to build our own house which will enlarge and strengthen the family compound, or rather the French hexagon.[109]

To preserve the links between France and her territories, a federation based on equality was proposed by many. François Mitterrand, the former minister of overseas France, warned that only a federation within a "fraternal and egalitarian community" would preserve French power from "the plains of Flanders to the forests of Equatorial Africa." The argument was basically utilitarian. Without a French Africa, Mitterrand prophesied, "there will be no history of France in the twenty-first century."[110] African politicians came out in favor of a "Franco-African community" but they demanded that their right to independence should first be recognized. Once this was recognized, then presumably the territories could join France as equals in a federation. The constitution of the Fourth Republic, however, seemed to pose serious problems for such a solution. For had the constitution not declared that France and her overseas territories together formed an "indivisible Republic"? Therefore, the right to independence could be recognized only with great difficulty.

The coming to power of de Gaulle in June 1958 brought a convenient solution to the knotty problem, for the constitution of the Fourth Republic was set aside. De Gaulle, like the leaders of the Fourth Republic, was interested in preserving the overseas territories for France. To mollify the populace of the territories, he reluctantly recognized the right to independence of the territories. When the referendum for the new constitution of the Fifth Republic was held in October 1958, the overseas populations had the option of becoming independent by rejecting the constitution or of voting for it and thereby becoming members of what was to be known as the French Community. If they rejected membership in the French Community and opted for independence, then, in the words of de Gaulle, they would have to take the consequences. This meant in effect that those territories voting for independence would be deprived of all French economic aid. In the face of this serious threat, no territory except Guinea voted for independence. The referendum was a clever attempt to demonstrate that the Community was a union which had been freely accepted by the territories. It was also an attempt to put an end, once and for all, to the agitation for independence.

De Gaulle's main aim was to preserve French influence in the overseas territories. The new constitution of 1958 gave the territorial populations the right to decide whether they wished to become fully integrated with France by becoming *départements*, or to remain territories, or to become member states of the French Community. In Africa all the territories except French Somaliland voted for the third alternative. The assemblies in the member states had full legislative powers, and the administration was now fully under the authority of the local state government rather than that of the minister of overseas France. Indeed, there was no longer any ministry at Rue Oudinot; it had disappeared in 1959. And the Corps of Colonial Administrators was abolished by simple decree. The service whose members had been the "real chiefs" of the French empire for seventy years had come to an end. The instrument of French rule—with all its benefits and weaknesses—lay dissolved.

Legally the French Community was a loose confederation; nevertheless, it clearly was still dominated by the French. The African political leaders found the Community too restrictive and wanted full independence. But independence was incompatible with membership in the Community; the state leaving the Community would, like Guinea, be cut off from French economic aid.

De Gaulle had meant Guinea to be a warning example to members in the Community. But to him it also had its lessons. By brutally cutting off economic aid, de Gaulle had forced Guinea to rely on Soviet and American aid. Thus French influence in that area had been eclipsed.

In the autumn of 1959 Senegal and the Sudan, having formed the Mali federation, asked that they be granted independence while still being allowed to remain members of the French Community—that is, still be allowed to receive French economic aid. Realizing that the independence movements had become too strong to be repressed, and drawing on the Guinean experience, de Gaulle acceded to the Malian request at the end of 1959. Mali would be independent, but by allowing it to remain in the French Community, de Gaulle ensured that it would remain open to French influence.[111] In 1960 Madagascar and four states within the former AEF were also granted independence while being permitted to remain within the Community, which, now stripped of its meaning, became known as the "*Communauté renovée*." The Ivory Coast was granted independence in 1960 and guaranteed financial aid without even having to accept nominal membership within the Community. Thus even this last vestige of a common institution lost its relevance and disappeared.

For the Corps of Overseas Administrators, independence came quickly and unexpectedly. Even for the British colonial service it was somewhat of a shock to see how speedily decolonization could occur. But at least the granting of eventual independence was part of British colonial doctrine. French doctrine had stressed the indissolubility of the bonds connecting the metropole to the overseas territories. The reforms in the British Empire after World War II were clearly intended to prepare the possessions for independence, but the reforms in the French empire were intended to avoid independence, to win permanently the loyalties of the overseas populations to union with France.[112] In the end even independence was given not for its own sake but in order to preserve French influence overseas. As one former administrator put it, "The question was not whether there would be independence; rather, the question was whether it would be achieved against us, or with us."[113] Many administrators found "independence in friendship" a way of preserving French influence. Others saw no reason for independence, bitterly accusing their country of having abandoned the overseas populations. Many of these die-hards described the granting of independence as nothing more than the delivery of the masses into the hands of ruthless African politicians.[114]

The administrators were nearly evenly split between those thinking that outside international forces had made decolonization necessary and those thinking that indigenous forces within the overseas territories had made the granting of independence mandatory. Seventy-four administrators found international pressures to be the main cause, seventy-six thought indigenous pressures the prime cause, while thirty-nine opted for the simultaneous influence of international and indigenous forces. The evidence collected suggests that the younger men were somewhat more aware of the development of nationalist movements in the overseas territories than were the older. Among the older generation, some tended to be nearly paranoiac, subscribing to a plot theory against the French empire.

Table 14

The prime cause for decolonization as seen by different age groups in the Corps

Year of entry into *Ecole Coloniale*	Internal forces	International forces	Both forces simultaneously
1920-1929	8	11	4
1930-1939	21	37	8
1940-1949	32	26	25
1950-1959	13	2	2

Some of the older administrators stated that decolonization had been caused by the "cheap demagoguery of the USA and the USSR." One former official put the entire burden on "the sick mind of F. D. Roosevelt." The younger men to a greater extent saw decolonization as a logical development, resulting from the spread of higher education in the overseas territories and the development of the new elites. When ascribing external forces as the main cause for decolonization, they were more inclined than were their elders to discuss the examples of the wars in Indochina and Algeria, the granting of independence to the British dependencies, or the manifesto of the Bandung Conference.

In the last analysis, perhaps, it was not the age of the administrators that determined their attitudes but rather the length of time they had spent in the bush. The officials in the bush were less aware of the temper of the elites than were their colleagues in cities. To them what counted was the huge mass of illiterate peasants in the countryside, not the speeches of politicians in the territorial capital or in Paris. Wrote one former bush administrator, "the problem of political liberty in my eyes and in that of many of my colleagues was secondary to that of the physical and agricultural conquest of the country by its inhabitants."[115] But to the administrators serving in the territorial and federal capitals the political evolution of the territories was far more apparent. They were in daily contact with the local politicians, and they were more aware of the climate of opinion among the younger educated elites. The officials in the territorial capitals understood that these new forces had to be taken into account, that they could not be ignored.[116]

Regardless of why they thought independence had become inevitable, most administrators were reconciled to the fact that, indeed, it had become an inevitable movement. But only a few thought that the granting of independence, when it did occur, was timely. Most believed that the French physical presence should have continued for another generation. Presumably twenty years would have permitted the economic development of the territories, and would have laid the foundation for stable and democratic societies. Such a view probably overestimated the extent to which the French administration was able to effect change. Events throughout the world have revealed that more than administrative fiat is necessary for economic development and political institutions that are both stable and democratic.

IX The Legacy

Once the new states had achieved independence they began to Africanize their administrations. In Senegal, all the French *commandants de cercles* handed over their power to Senegalese officials, many of whom they had helped to train, and in all cases the transferral of authority was carried out in an orderly manner. In some of the lesser developed countries, French administrators continued to rule until 1962-1963. By that date, however, Africanization of the regional administration had occurred. In Senegal, Africans taking over authority publicly recognized the contributions of their French predecessors; the first Senegalese governor of the Casamance region in March 1960 spoke enthusiastically of his predecessor as having served "with much devotion of heart."[1] A member of the Senegalese cabinet, supervising the transferral of power from a French to a Senegalese administrator in eastern Senegal, made the following peroration about the members of the French colonial service:

> For more than a century French administrators have directed Eastern Senegal, they have built the schools and dispensaries, they have built roads, dug wells and have succeeded in making ... [this] region a developed area. I wish, in the name of the Republic, to give them vibrant homage for the work they have accomplished here with much devotion and disinterestedness, because they believed in their mission and had confidence in our country and its men.[2]

For the French administrators independence meant an end to the career that they had intended to pursue for a lifetime. For them independence was, of course, a painful episode. Considering the circumstances, however, the administrators were treated in the most generous manner possible by the French government. Some former administrators think that their favorable treatment was a reward for the Corps' loyal service to the French state. This may be true, but one must note that many influential members of the Corps had important contacts both with Parliament and with the de Gaulle government. One of the main guardians of the corporate interest of the administrators, the alumni association of the ENFOM, had the adroitness to prevail upon Prime Minister Michel Debré to become its honorary president.

Having abolished the Corps of Overseas Administrators in 1959, the government offered the administrators three alternatives. The one chosen by a majority of the members of the Corps was integration into the metropolitan civil service. Those not taking this alternative and not wishing to retire could enter either of two newly formed Corps. One, the Corps of *conseillers des affaires d'outre-mer*, was under the ministry of state for the overseas departments and territories, but most of its members worked for the ministry of cooperation, the special ministry then in charge of channeling aid to the former French territories in Black Africa. The other Corps was that of the *administrateurs des affairs d'outre-mer*, which was reserved for senior officials, also acting as advisers to the African states, but entitled to retire with five years' full pay whenever they wished.[3]

In the British colonial service the administrators had to decide whether they wanted to retire under a lump sum scheme, or, if offered the opportunity by the new states, become part of their civil service. Given only those alternatives, nearly all British officials returned to Great Britain, or emigrated to North America or Australia. But French officials could reserve the right to be integrated into the metropolitan civil service while serving for an indefinite period in the former overseas territories *en service détaché*. This arrangement encouraged hundreds of French administrators to remain in the former territories. Although withdrawn from local administration, a large number of French administrators continued to play important roles in the central administrations of the newly independent states; in some they even became cabinet ministers. In the Ivory Coast and in Senegal former French administrators became ministers of finance, in Chad one became minister of information and tourism. In some states they helped draw up the constitution; in one a French administrator designed the national flag.[4]

A large number of administrators remained overseas because of the flexible alternatives offered them. Also, the newly independent states found it convenient to employ the French officials since their salaries were carried by the French technical assistance budget. Except for a small monthly fee for each expert, the new governments were not required to pay pensions or other expenses.[5] In the British territories some colonial officers were retained, but it was at far greater cost to the independent states, than in the case of the French, and it lasted for a shorter period than in most of the former French territories.

The French method of ensuring the continuation of efficient

administration in the successor states has generally won praise from outside observers.[6] In 1967 the alumni association of the ENFOM listed 186 of its members still serving in the successor states as technical assistants,[7] and forty-five former administrators served in Paris in the secretariat of foreign affairs in charge of cooperation.

In a number of cases, especially in the first few years after independence, the former administrators performed as advisers very much the same function they had in the colonial period. Although the African minister made the final decision, in many cases he relied heavily on his French adviser. In Gabon, the American ambassador found to his consternation that he could not hold a private discussion with the minister of education; a partition which did not go entirely to the ceiling separated the minister's office from that of his French administrative assistant.[8] The latter presumably overheard all discussions and then advised the minister. Also, because of lack of interest or of expertise, African ministers, it is alleged, often delegated their authority to the French advisers, who thus were vested with nearly as much power as they had held in the colonial era.

Other ex-administrators retained considerable power in the former colonies by being appointed into the diplomatic corps as French ambassadors to the independent state. Some served as ambassadors to the areas they had previously helped administer; for example, in 1962 the French ambassadors to Niger and Gabon were its former governors. In June 1965 three former administrators were serving as ambassadors to states that had formerly been under French rule: Gabon, Dahomey, and Togo. Former administrators have also served as ambassadors to foreign countries with no previous colonial ties to France: in 1967 the French ambassadors to Malaya and to Albania and the permanent representative to the Council of Europe were former administrators. Indeed, a very large number of former administrators have served in the French diplomatic corps; the alumni association of the ENFOM in 1967 listed ninety-two of its members as serving in embassies and consulates, of whom one fourth were assigned to the French African states, and more than half, to the central administration of the Quai d'Orsay.

In France the former administrators occupied important posts. Approximately 350 former overseas functionaries entered the Corps of Civil Administrators, which fills the higher executive positions within the metropolitan civil service. The ministry of finance and economic affairs had sixty civil administrators formerly belonging to the Corps of Overseas Administrators, the largest number of any of the ministries. The rest were scattered among numerous ministries and public agencies. Some of the very top posts within the French administrative system were occupied by former overseas administrators. In 1967, thirty members of the prefectoral corps, of whom four were prefects, were former administrators; eleven were members of the *Conseil d'état*; one, of the *Cour de cassation*; and eight, of *Cour des comptes*. In 1964 two former administrators occupied cabinet posts. Pierre Messmer was minister of the armed forces and Jean Sainteny minister of veterans and war victims. The latter left his post in 1966, but another former overseas official, Yvon Bourges, joined Messmer in the cabinet as state secretary in charge of information. In the 1968 elections eleven ex-administrators were elected to Parliament, most of whom belonged to the UDR, the government party.

In other ways too, former members of the Corps played an important role in French life. Several were overseas, working for private organizations involved in business or having cultural or social functions. In France in the private sector former administrators occupied the most diverse posts imaginable. One was an executive of a packaging firm, another headed a private detective agency, a third was a monk. Former administrators also served actively in international organizations; in 1967 the alumni association of the ENFOM listed sixty-five of its members as working for international organizations, of whom twenty were employed by the United Nations.

Many Africans who had served in the Corps were appointed after independence to important posts in their countries. In 1967 two of the cabinet ministers in the Central African Republic (formerly Oubangui-Chari), two in the Ivory Coast cabinet, and one in the Senegalese cabinet were former African administrators. Because of their close ties with France several Africans who had been members of the Corps served as ambassadors to Paris; in 1964 they represented Chad, Mali, and Togo. Others served as their country's ambassadors to other nations: the ambassador of the Ivory Coast to Morocco, the permanent representative of the Central African Republic to the United Nations, and the ambassador of Niger to Belgium were all formerly members of the Corps. The personnel of the Corps thus still plays an important role in France, in the former colonies, and in the world as a whole.

It is striking that in most instances the French administrative pattern has been retained in the successor states. The names of the administrative units have changed in some areas; for example, there are no longer *cercles* in some states, but rather regions or prefectures. The boundaries of some of the administrative regions have been redrawn, but the basic hierarchical structure has been retained. The orders go out from the capital to the regional representatives of the central government who then pass them finally down to the village level. In Senegal, for example, the country has been divided into seven regions, administered by governors; each region is divided into several prefectures. The prefects keep in touch with the *chefs d'arrondissements*, the administrative equivalent of the former *chefs de cantons*. Most of the traditional chiefs were initially retained, although many of them were appointed to different areas. Of the eighty-four *chefs d'arrondissements* appointed in 1960, forty-nine had been *chefs de cantons* and sixteen had been assistant chiefs. By 1965 fewer of the traditional chiefs, only half, served as *chefs d'arrondissements*.[9]

In all the French-African states the chiefs have become full-fledged government functionaries. They no longer are cast in their ambiguous role of the colonial period, when they were considered both the traditional representatives of their people and agents of the government. As the Senegalese minister of interior declared in 1960, "It is not because of their family influence in the region that they can administer, but rather because of their personal qualities. They should be able to serve in any region just like any other functionary."[10]

In Senegal many of the *chefs de cantons* were retained, but in some of the other French successor states, such as Mali and Guinea, all the former *chefs de cantons* were dismissed. The local regional chiefs were elected by members of the ruling party. And the chiefs did not regain any of their former powers after independence; on the contrary, the African countries have carried out more fully the process begun by the French of destroying the traditional power of the chiefs and transforming them into government auxiliaries.

Originally, there was some reaction against the omnipotence that administrators had enjoyed in the colonial period. In Senegal, regional assemblies were established with which the regional governors had to share power. Also, municipal powers were increased, and the role of the representatives of the central government in the municipal councils was significantly reduced. But experience showed that the most efficient personnel was in the central administration, and that the regional and municipal bodies were often inefficient and even corrupt. Therefore, in 1966 the Senegalese government strengthened the prerogatives of the central administration by enlarging its powers of control and inspection over the regional and municipal bodies. Centralization had originally been described as a colonial atavism, but the Senegalese government found it the only method of ensuring the continuation of a reasonably efficient administration. Other French-African states tried experiments similar to those in Senegal, and as in Senegal, nearly all of them by 1966 had strengthened their control over regional and communal governments, thus returning to an administrative system more like that of the colonial era.[11]

Each of the French-African states has fallen under the control of one political party. As a result, the administration has been politicized, and many officials seem to have been appointed or promoted merely because of their political loyalties. In Guinea where politicization of the administration has gone furthest, civil servants and party officials are often considered to be interchangeable. A Guinean official declared that "the administrator who is governor of a region should be able to perform the political functions of the party leader at the regional level and vice versa."[12] But in most of the African states a division has been preserved between administrative and political functions, because administrators faced with distinctly administrative problems find it necessary to preserve a separation between these two spheres of activity. A regional governor in Senegal, who was at the same time a high party official, complained of his troubles with local political party members and stated his determination to keep them from meddling in what was strictly administrative business.[13] Some of the former French administrators regret the politicization of the administration in Africa,[14] but in fact the French Corps of Overseas Administrators had faced similar problems toward the end of the colonial period, certainly as early as the 1950s.

French administrators erroneously feel that they have left behind a tradition of nonpolitical administration;[15] for they have really left to the successor states the tradition to politicize administration. Only the British administrators left a tradition of strict neutrality in political affairs in a relatively pure form to its successor states. Again this is not necessarily a reflection of the different colonial services as much as of the different national traditions.

While administration both in Britain and in France has tended to be politically neutral, nevertheless certain segments of the French administration have played distinctly political roles: for example, in the case of the prefectoral corps. The French overseas administrators seem to have emulated prefects of the nineteenth and even in some cases of the twentieth century in their manipulation of elections, in their repression of opposition candidates, and support of candidates friendly to the government. It might be considered somewhat unfair to blame the politicized administration in the French successor states on the colonial tradition, for in the former British territories—heirs to a different tradition—there also has developed a politicized administration, although it seems to be less pronounced than in the former French territories.

Writing about the general effects of European rule, James Coleman has remarked:

As there was no provision for alternation in governments, colonial officials tended to be regarded as agents of the prevailing power group and not as independent and neutral civil servants. Insofar as the colonial experience produced such perspectives—and there were exceptions—it tended to weaken respect for the laws and regulations governing the public service.[16]

After 1945 the French administrators lived in a transitional era; and their successors also are performing their tasks in a period of relative instability.[17] But with the spread of education and the development of national schools of administration (there is one in nearly every former French territory), probably a civil service tradition will emerge which will tend to be more committed to administrative efficiency than to political expediency.[18] The force of French tradition and the example of administration within France may, however, lead to the continued retention by the administration of a certain political role.

The lack of well-trained personnel and of a genuine civil service tradition has meant that many of the successor states have suffered from corrupt and inefficient administration. The dishonesty and inefficiency of the Senegalese administration has been criticized by the Senegalese themselves. A high official of the Senegalese Supreme Court in 1967 described "*le building administratif*," housing most of the government services, as "the place where people come, go, gossip a lot, and hardly work."[19] Another Senegalese denounced the Senegalese civil service as inefficient and uninterested in "promoting the common good."[20]

In the Central African Republic, Michel Legris, a correspondent for *Le Monde*, reported in January 1966 that more than twenty prefects and subprefects had been arrested since 1963 for embezzlement. A few had to be released "since they are needed." Corruption was so rampant that the inspectors of administrative affairs have been suspected of following an unwritten rule that they report only officials having a deficit above 250,000 CFA francs ($1,000). The fate of dishonest prefects seemed to be so well known that students in the Central African Republic, when asked which profession they would like to enter, stated, "I don't want to be a prefect, I don't want to be a subprefect, because I don't want to go to jail."[21]

The very top echelons of the civil service in the French-African states are usually filled with conscientious, educated, and hard-working men. But nearly all of them are employed in the capital cities, while serving below them in the central ministries and in the interior are men who are less well qualified. A French observer, writing about the middle and lower levels of the civil service in Niger in 1964, commented:

The cheerful indifference of the lower and middle grade official is not a disease confined to Niger.... For thirty months or so it has been afflicting most of the young independent African states. And in Niamey as in

Senegal, Dahomey, or the Congo many officials discharge their duties capriciously without worrying about efficiency or production.[22]

The officials are often insufficiently imbued with an administrative tradition. Thus, in Senegal, the prefects have been somewhat unaware of the value of regular written reports to the central government. In 1965, of the 162 written reports that they were supposed to send to the ministry of interior in the first six months of the year, only sixteen were received. Thus the Senegalese ministry of interior sometimes had difficulty in knowing what was occurring in some of the districts and as a result of this lack of information found it difficult to plan or to create a coherent policy for the whole country.[23]

Throughout the colonial era there tended to be insufficient contact between the administrators and the people they ruled, and independence has not entirely solved the problem. A chasm still exists between the representatives of the government and the local inhabitants, especially in rural areas—a chasm caused in part by the dramatic difference in living style between the government functionaries and the majority of the population.[24]

In the independent African states the high salaries paid functionaries in the colonial era have, in part, been retained. In spite of repeated efforts to economize, the countries have been unable to resist the demands of the civil servants to retain high salaries. Remuneration of civil servants was so high in Senegal and Dahomey that two-thirds of the national budget was absorbed by salaried functionaries. The regional administrators in Senegal were paid less than the French administrators had been paid; in 1960 their salaries varied from 15,000 to 25,000 CFA francs monthly ($60-$100), but nevertheless it provided a strikingly higher standard of living than that enjoyed by the Senegalese peasant who was fortunate to earn in a year what the local administrator earned in a month.[25] In 1969 the total benefits of Senegalese administrators varied from 64,598 to 152,033 CFA francs monthly ($258-$608).[26]

African administrators prefer living in urban areas, where they can lead a more European style of life, to serving in the interior. While most of the French administrators tended to glorify bush administration, and expressed a certain contempt for desk posts in the colonial capital and in Paris, their African successors tend to long for posts in the capital. An unusually high proportion of all functionaries are located in the national capitals because governments have had difficulty convincing officials to serve inland. In Senegal, President Senghor in a public speech denounced those functionaries refusing to serve their fellow citizens and threatened that officials "not joining the post to which they had been assigned would be automatically dismissed."[27] But neither this speech nor other efforts have been very successful. In 1965, 41.2 percent of all Senegalese functionaries were located in Dakar.[28] The African functionaries behave very much like their counterparts in France, who have a certain contempt for the "provinces." But in comparison with their predecessors—the members of the Corps of Overseas Administrators—the African functionaries are inclined to be somewhat sedentary and insufficiently concerned with the bush. In Senegal, a circular ordering the prefects to spend ten out of every thirty days on tour of their regions was never implemented.[29] Of course, with time, this situation will probably change. As a former French administrator has remarked, "it will have to change."[30]

Perhaps the younger generation of men currently entering the administration will speed the trend. In 1961, 72.1 percent of Africans studying in France intended to enter government service.[31] Among them a very small number made their choice because of the financial security or material comforts involved in government service. Most of them stated that they wished to enter public service because it would permit them to serve their people.[32] Undoubtedly a certain amount of time will have to pass before one can tell whether these answers were mere rationalizations for choosing a comfortable position, the product of youthful idealism, or really represented a profound commitment to the rural masses of their states.

The poor quality of administration has become acute only because of the lack of genuine traditions of local government. French rule carries much of the blame, for direct rule destroyed the traditional means of government, substituting for the local institutions a reasonably efficient and well-trained administration recruited in France. Independence meant that the new states would have to have an equally efficient administrative apparatus, and there really was no alternative to a modern administration, since the time for a possible restoration of traditional authorities was long past. In any case, the independent African states did not wish to resuscitate the power of ancient chiefdoms. They wanted to assert the power of the central government over the countryside; in so doing they found relatively little resistance from the traditional structures, unlike their English-speaking neighbors. None of the French-speaking African states experienced the same degree of violent struggles between central government and traditional power that until recently racked Ghana and Uganda. The French spared their successors those struggles, having to a large degree successfully overcome traditional power nearly half a century earlier. By crushing the traditional political structures and ignoring ethnic divisions, the French left behind relatively more homogeneous areas.

Although a certain amount of ethnic strife persists in the French-speaking African states, it seems less pronounced than in their neighboring English-speaking countries. It is somewhat premature to make a definitive judgment, but it seems at present that the French policy of direct rule has prepared the colonies better for national unity after independence than have the British.

The French imposed a certain uniform method of administration on all the territories. In the British territories administrators might be serving for twenty years in one post; in the French colonies the personnel was frequently rotated. The institutions in all French colonies were similar; eventually all the French territories were given the same political institutions.

After independence the French successor states continued to have similar institutions. They all have adopted governments styled on the presidential regime of the French Fifth Republic. They have kept most of the administrative features of the colonial period; and their administrative personnel is trained in their own national schools of administration, which are all modeled on the *Ecole nationale d'administration* in Paris, or on the *Institut international d'administration publique*. Although the French did not succeed in joining the colonies to France, Pierre Alexandre has suggested that they did assimilate the different territories to each other by a process he has called "lateral assimilation."[33] After independence this process continued. More than in the British territories, there seems to be ground for the development of some sort of political bond among the former French territories in Africa. In 1961, 87 percent of the African students in France favored such a development (53.5 percent favored a federation, 33.5 percent a confederation.)[34]

In 1960-1961 a common organization was formed by Madagascar, the Cameroons, the former AEF states, and the former AOF states, with the exception of Mali and Guinea which remained aloof for ideological reasons. Together those states formed a consultative group known as the UAM (*Union africaine et malgache*), which in 1965 changed its name to OCAM (*Organisation commune africaine et malgache*). The members of the organization have in common the fact that they were once part of the French empire in Africa.[35] French language and culture also connect them. At the conference of ministers of education of the UAM in 1964, the minister of national education of Madagascar observed:

French language and culture constitute the most solid cement of our national unity and on the international level they are also the base of our mutual understanding, the guarantee of friendship, and one of the essential factors for African unity.[36]

Other groupings also related to the colonial past and to regional proximity have developed. The Ivory Coast, Upper Volta, Dahomey, and Niger had already formed in 1959, even before achieving independence, the so-called *Conseil de l'entente*. In 1965 a common nationality was proclaimed in the four states, giving the citizens of each state equal access to public service in all four nations. This move may, however, have been too precipitate, for it raised strong opposition and was therefore not implemented. Another organization devoted to the possibility of joint economic development is the *Riverains du Sénégal*, consisting of the nations bordering on the Senegal River (Mauritania, Senegal, Mali, and Guinea); it was formed in 1964. The common colonial past and the use of the French language played an important role in the development of those organizations. Lately President Léopold Senghor has become the spokesman for the establishment of a Francophone commonwealth, connecting not only Black African states, but also the Maghreb and France.[37]

Independence has by no means broken the close ties between the French and their former colonies. The legacy of assimilation has continued. France more than any other former colonial power feels committed to aiding her ex-dependencies. The French government gives her former colonies in Black Africa more aid than does Britain to her entire commonwealth, which contains fifteen times as large a population.[38]

The aim of assimilation, in the sense of wanting to join the overseas populations to France culturally, still persists. Although economic and political imperialism belong to the past, the French government still carries on a policy of "cultural imperialism." In a debate on aid in the National Assembly in June 1964, the French prime minister, Pompidou, said:

Of all countries, France is the one that cares most about exporting its language and culture. This characteristic is genuinely specific to us. When a Frenchman travelling abroad meets someone who speaks French, who has read French authors, he feels as if he has found a brother. This is a need of our thought, perhaps of our genius. Our cooperation is undeniably oriented, and ought to be so, towards this expansion of our language and our culture.[39]

The success of the French language and culture is seen by many thoughtful Frenchmen as being dependent on the economic and social success of the newly independent states. French culture is closely identified with the present rulers of the African states; their failure to achieve social and economic justice for their peoples, Delavignette warned in 1965, may create a reaction against French culture.[40] The director of cultural cooperation of the ministry of cooperation said in March 1965:

> The attraction that French exercises on young Africans today is directly connected to their hope of achieving a better life.... The future of French would be compromised if Africa fell into misery and chaos. A fundamental tie connects the use of our language and a certain mode of life.[41]

In his memoirs, published in 1970, de Gaulle made clear that the main reasons the ex-dependencies received economic aid was "so they will speak our language and share our culture."[42]

The French administration never did succeed in assimilating the overseas populations; only a restricted elite was successfully assimilated. Through education and participation in French political life after the second world war, an elite developed overseas which identified very closely with France. Independence has by no means put an end to this assimilationist phase. The younger generations continue to identify closely with France; few wish to see France reduced to a second-rate power like Spain or Italy.[43] Among their reasons for wishing France to remain a great power, African students wrote:

> In spite of the colonial fact, I have a certain esteem and even gratitude for France. (Senegalese student)
>
> That would be a shame because France has a brilliant past; it was the carrier of democracy (1789). (Guinean student)
>
> It is a people which by its sons (Robespierre, Descartes, etc.) has done much for humanity. I do not have the right to wish it evil. (Senegalese student)
>
> In spite of it all, an eternal bond connects us with France by its culture, its civilization, and its language which has become the national language in each former colony. (Malian student)
>
> I am of French education and culture. (Dahomean student)[44]

Not only the political leadership but also the students, most of whom are in opposition to their home governments, favor continued close ties between France and their countries.[45]

In the colonial era, the effort to assimilate the colonial populations, in the sense of raising them economically and culturally to the French level, failed. But the heirs of the French are continuing that particular phase of the assimilationist tradition. The leaders of the independent states are committed with less ambiguity than were their predecessors to a program of economic development on Western patterns. Although the academic standards seem to have been lowered under the pressure of numbers, the new states have developed a program of mass education. While in the Ivory Coast only 24 percent of the children between the ages of six and fourteen attended school in 1959, 44 percent attended in 1965; in Chad the number of students receiving elementary education tripled in the same period.[46] The curriculum is entirely in French and with a few exceptions, namely in the teaching of history and geography, the education is largely modeled on the curriculum of French schools.

With the help of foreign (mainly French) economic assistance, and a substantial effort on their own part, the African states are continuing their effort to modernize themselves.[47]

In many ways administrations in the African countries have to face some of the same problems that faced the French colonial service. Like Faidherbe and his immediate successors, the African governments are faced with the problem of finding efficient and honest functionaries. Although the French by 1920 had succeeded reasonably well in creating an efficient bureaucracy, they were less successful in relating effectively to the needs of the local populations. That problem still seems to persist, to a certain extent, in the independent states.

Coups d'états, social revolts, ethnic strife, and economic decline have beset a number of the French African states. Nevertheless, regardless of the changes in regimes, the announced aim of each new government has been the same: to unite and to ensure the economic modernization of its country. Thus some of the aims that the administrators had hoped to achieve are still being pursued today. But the very difficulties that the independent countries have in fulfilling national unity and prosperity show that the legacy left by fifty—in some places seventy—years of rule is precarious. Only the future will tell whether French rule was a short parenthesis in the history of Africa, or the harbinger of a new and different world.

Appendixes
Notes
Bibliography
Index

Appendix I

Undersecretaries and Ministers
in Charge of Colonial Affairs

Louis Pothau	15 February 1871–25 May 1873
Charles de Dampierre d'Hornoy	25 May 1873–22 May 1874
Martin Fourichon	5 March 1875–23 May 1877
Albert Gicquet	23 May 1877–23 November 1877
Albert Roussin	23 November 1877–13 December 1877
Louis Pothau	13 December 1877–4 February 1879
Jean Jauréguiberry	4 February 1879–23 September 1880
Louis Pothau	23 September 1880–4 November 1881
Félix Faure	14 November 1881–30 January 1882
Albert Berlet	30 January 1882–22 September 1883
Félix Faure	22 September 1883–28 April 1885
Armand Rousseau	28 April 1885–15 January 1886
Jean de la Porte	15 January 1886–7 June 1887
Eugène Etienne	7 June 1887–5 January 1888
Félix Faure	5 January 1888–19 February 1888
Jean de la Porte	19 February 1888–14 March 1889
Eugène Etienne	14 March 1889–8 March 1892
Emile Jamais	8 March 1892–18 January 1893
Théophile Delcassé	18 January 1893–3 December 1893
Maurice Lebon	3 December 1893–20 March 1894
Ernest Boulanger[1]	20 March 1894–30 May 1894
Théophile Delcassé	30 May 1894–26 January 1895
André Chautemps	26 January 1895–1 November 1895
Pierre Guieyesse	4 November 1895–29 April 1896
André Lebon	29 April 1896–31 May 1898
Georges Trouillot	28 June 1898–1 November 1898
Antoine Guillain	1 November 1898–22 June 1899
Albert Decrais	22 June 1899–7 June 1902
Gaston Doumergue	7 June 1902–24 January 1905
Etienne Clémentel	24 January 1905–14 March 1906
Georges Leygues	14 March 1906–25 October 1906
Raphaël Milliès-Lacroix	25 October 1906–24 July 1909

1. First one to serve as minister after the undersecretariat of colonies was elevated to a ministry.

Georges Trouillot	24 July 1909–3 November 1910
Jean Morel	3 November 1910–2 March 1911
Adolphe Messimy	2 March 1911–27 June 1911
Albert Lebrun	27 June 1911–12 January 1913
René Besnard	12 January 1913–21 January 1913
Jean Morel	21 January 1913–9 December 1913
Albert Lebrun	9 December 1913–9 June 1914
Maurice Manoury	9 June 1914–13 June 1914
Maurice Reynaud	13 June 1914–26 August 1914
Gaston Doumergue	26 August 1914–20 March 1917
André Maginot	20 March 1917–12 September 1917
René Besnard	12 September 1917–16 November 1917
Henry Simon	16 November 1917–20 January 1920
Albert Sarraut	20 January 1920–29 March 1924
Jean Fabry	29 March 1924–14 June 1924
Edouard Daladier	14 June 1924–17 April 1925
André Hesse	17 April 1925–29 October 1925
Léon Perier	29 October 1925–19 July 1926
Dariac	19 July 1926–23 July 1926
Léon Perier	23 July 1926–11 November 1928
André Maginot	11 November 1928–3 November 1929
François Piétri	3 November 1929–21 February 1930
Lucien Lamoureux	21 February 1930–2 March 1930
François Piétri	2 March 1930–13 December 1930
Théodore Steeg	13 December 1930–27 January 1931
Paul Reynaud	27 January 1931–20 February 1932
Louis de Chappedelaine	20 February 1932–10 May 1932
Albert Sarraut	3 June 1932–6 September 1933
Albert Dalimier	6 September 1933–26 October 1933
François Piétri	26 October 1933–26 November 1933
Albert Dalimier	26 November 1933–30 January 1934
Henry de Jouvenel[2]	30 January 1934–9 February 1934
Pierre Laval	9 February 1934–13 October 1934
Louis Rollin	13 October 1934–24 January 1936
Jacques Stern	24 January 1936–4 June 1936
Marius Moutet	4 June 1936–18 January 1938
Théodore Steeg	18 January 1938–13 March 1938
Marius Moutet	13 March 1938–10 April 1938
Georges Mandel	10 April 1938–18 May 1940
Louis Rollin	18 May 1940–16 June 1940

2. Only one to use the title of "Ministre de la France d'Outre-Mer" before World War II.

Appendix II

Letter and questionnaire sent to former administrators
(Translation follows)

Paris, le 1er Octobre 1965

Monsieur,

Vos aimables réponses à ce questionnaire m'aideront à écrire une thèse de doctorat en histoire moderne pour l'Université de Stanford, Californie—sur "Les Administrateurs Coloniaux Français, 1887-1960."

Ce questionnaire a été dressé pour connaître des généralites et ne vise pas des personnes individuelles. Il est évident que ce questionnaire est anonyme et que toute information individuelle sera utilisée avec la plus grande discrétion.

Je vous serais reconnaissant de remplir ce questionnaire aussi complètement que possible. Cependant s'il contient des questions auxquelles vous préférez ne pas répondre, il vous est très possible de laisser des blancs.

Je vous remercie, Monsieur, de bien vouloir m'aider dans ce travail, et vous prie d'agréer, l'expression de mes sentiments distingués.

William B. Cohen

1) Votre année d'entrée a l'ENFOM? _____
2) Dernière année de service Outre-Mer? _____
3) Quel grade aviez-vous lorsque vous avez quitté définitivement l'Outre-Mer? _____
4) Lieu de naissance? _____
5) Profession du père _____
6) Avez-vous été marié? _____
7) Quels motifs vous ont fait choisir la vocation d'Administrateur de la France d'Outre-Mer?
   _____
   _____

8) Comment jugez-vous rétrospectivement, la préparation professionnelle que vous avez reçue à l'ENFOM?
   _____
   _____
   _____

9) Quels sont les cours qui vous ont le mieux préparé? _____
   _____ 10) Lequel le moins? _____
11) Quelle personne pensez-vous, a eu la plus grande influence sur vous à l'ENFOM? _____
12) Quels livres ou quelles personnes vous ont influencé à choisir votre carrière? _____
13) Quels livres ou quelles personnes vous ont le plus influencé quant à la manière dont vous avez exercé votre métier? _____
   _____
14) Avez-vous servi en brousse ou en chef-lieu? _____
    Si dans les deux, lequel vous a plu davantage? _____
    Pourquoi? _____
15) Lesquelles des réformes de 1946 vous ont apparu comme nécessaires?
    _____
    Lesquelles comme prématurées? _____
    Lesquelles vous ont semblé venir trop tard? _____
    Lesquelles vous ont paru malheureuses? _____
16) La loi cadre Defferre de 1956-57 vous a-t-elle apparue comme nécessaire? _____
    Comme prématurée _____

Vous a-t-elle semblé venir trop tard? _____
Vous a-t-elle parue malheureuse? _____

17) Est ce que vous pensez actuellement que la décolonisation a été un processus inévitable? _____

   Pourquoi? _____
   _____

18) En quelle année avez-vous pensé que la décolonisation était devenue inévitable? _____ Pourquoi? _____
   _____

19) Est ce que vous pensez que vous avez eu suffisament d'indépendance à l'égard de votre supérieure pour gérer votre cercle ou circonscription selon vos voeux? _____
   _____

20) Quelles personnes (inspecteurs des colonies, magistrats, membres du service techniques, supérieures hiérarchiques, ou politiciens autochtones) vous ont entravés le plus dans la direction de votre commandement? _____

21) Si vous avez servi avant et après le Seconde Guerre Mondiale, trouvez-vous qu'il existait une différence entre les méthodes d'administration des deux époques? Laquelle? _____
   _____

22) Rétrospectivement, auriez-vous choisi la vocation d'administrateur colonial? _____

23) Si vous n'auriez pas choisi la vocation d'administrateur colonial, quelle autre vocation auriez-vous choisi? _____

24) Que pensez vous du jugement d'un journaliste français qui a écrit que les administrateurs coloniaux n'ont pas eu l'Etat qu'ils méritaient?
   _____

(Translation of letter)

Paris, October 1, 1965

Dear Sir:

Your kind answer to this questionnaire will help me write a Ph.D. thesis in modern history for Stanford University on "The French Colonial Administrators, 1887-1960."

This questionnaire has been drawn up for the purpose of acquiring only general information. It is obvious that the questionnaire is anonymous and all answers will be treated with the greatest discretion.

I would be grateful if you could fill out this questionnaire as completely as possible. However, you should not feel obligated to answer every question.

I wish to thank you for helping me.

Sincerely yours,

William B. Cohen

(Translation of questionnaire)

1) Year of entry to the ENFOM   2) Last year of service overseas
3) What rank did you have when you left the overseas service?
4) Place of birth
5) Father's profession   6) Have you been married?
7) What motives inspired you to become an overseas administrator?

8) How do you in retrospect judge the professional training which you received at the ENFOM?

9) Which courses prepared you best?
    10) Which the least?
11) Who had the greatest influence on you at the ENFOM?
12) Which books or persons influenced you in choosing a career?
13) Which books or persons influenced you the most in your profession?
14) Did you serve in the bush or the colony's capital?
    If both, which one did you prefer?
    Why?
15) Which of the reforms of 1946 seemed to you necessary?
    Which premature?
    Which seemed too late?
    Which seemed undesirable?
16) Did you find the *loi-cadre* Defferre of 1956-57 necessary?
    Did it seem premature?
    Did it seem too late?
    Did it seem undesirable?
17) Do you now think that decolonization was inevitable?
    Why?
18) When did you think that decolonization had become inevitable?
    Why?
19) Do you feel that your superior permitted you sufficient independence to run your region as you saw fit?
20) Who (colonial inspectors, judges, technicians, administrative superiors, or local politicians) meddled the most in your administrative affairs?

21) If you served before and after World War II did you find that there was a difference in the methods of administration?

If so, what?

22) Knowing what you now know, would you have become a colonial administrator?

23) If you would not have become a colonial adminsitrator, what profession would you have chosen?

24) What do you think of a French journalist's verdict that the colonial administrators did not have the State support they deserved?

Appendix III

Average number of years spent by administrators in the colonies

Only averages for colonies in AOF and for Madagascar have been computed; my data for the other colonies are insufficient to be useful. The figure gives the average of the total number of years spent in a colony, including any immediate service prior to entering the Corps, such as service as agent of native affairs.*

	Dahomey	Guinea	Ivory Coast	Madagascar	Mauritania	Senegal	Upper-Senegal-Niger**			Average
1880-1919	7.3	7.5	6.3	7.7	4.3	6.4	8.2			7.0
1920-1939	6.0	7.9	5.6	8.2	3.5	5.4	Niger	Sudan	Upper Volta	5.4
							4.6	5.4	4.1	

*It was not common for administrators to come back to a colony after serving elsewhere for several years. The average number of consecutive years would obviously be lower than the figures in the table, but not significantly; between .1 and .2 lower.

**After 1920 Upper-Senegal-Niger were divided into the colonies of Niger, Soudan, and Upper-Volta.

Appendix IV

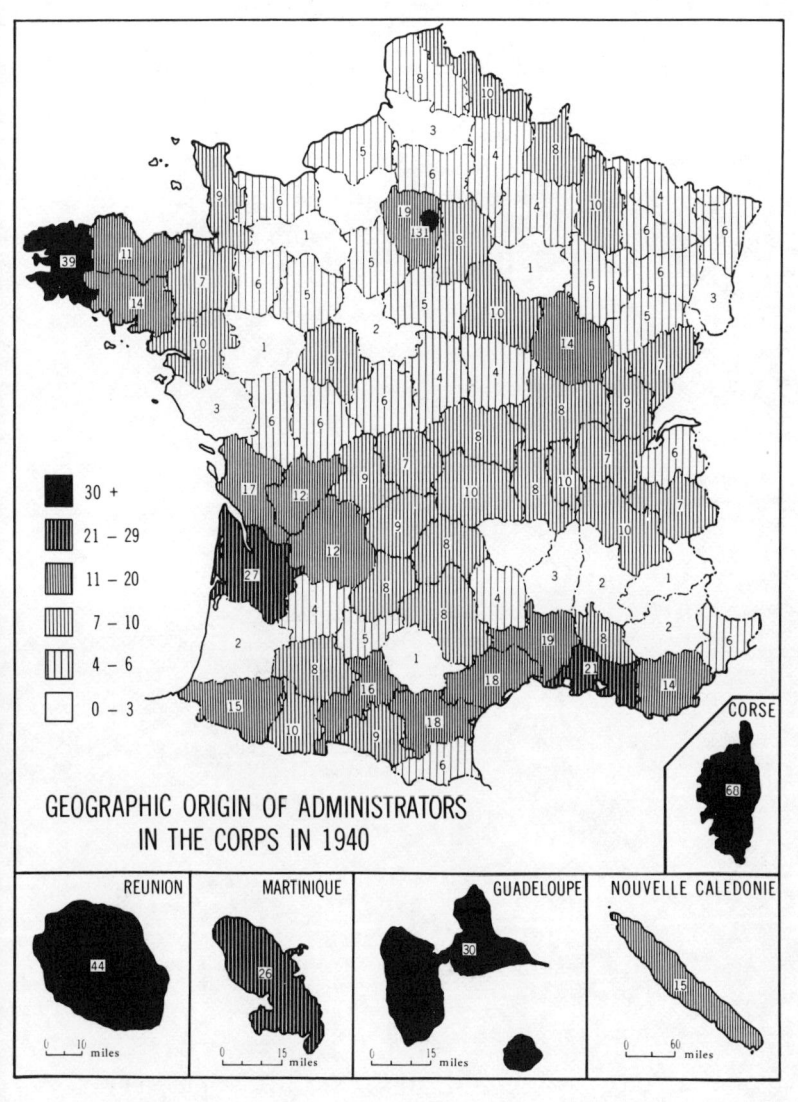

Appendix V

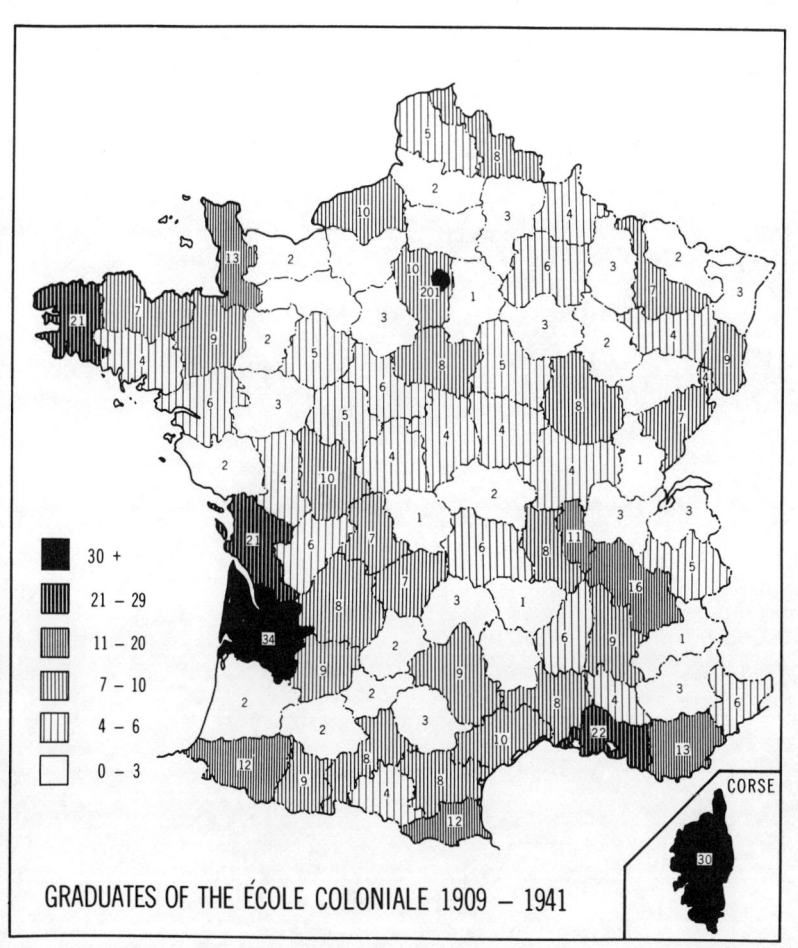

Notes

Preface

1. A good beginning in this field is Martin A. Klein, *Islam and Imperialism in Senegal: Sine-Saloum, 1847-1914* (Stanford, Calif., 1968), and Brian Weinstein, "Governor General Félix Eboué–A Short Biography" (unpublished manuscript, 1969).

Chapter I: Founding an Overseas Administration

1. For training programs of various colonial services, see A. Lawrence Lowell, *Colonial Civil Service* (New York, 1900).
2. For a description of the Algerian resistance to the French before 1840, see Charles A. Julien, *Histoire de l'Algérie contemporaine*, vol. I (Paris, 1964), 106-163.
3. F. Hugonnet, *Souvenirs d'un chef du bureau arabe* (Paris, 1858), p. 5.
4. On the *bureaux arabes*, see Roger Germain, *La Politique indigène de Bugeaud* (Paris, 1955); also Julien, *Histoire de l'Algérie contemporaine*, pp. 333-341; General M. Boucherie, "Les Bureaux arabes," *Revue de défense nationale* (July 1957), pp. 1052-1066.
5. Faidherbe, quoted in A. P. Thornton, *Doctrines of Empire* (New York, 1965), title page.
6. "Mémoire sur la colonie du Sénégal," August 1856, in Sénégal, I, 43, Archives nationales, France, Section outre-mer (henceforth cited as ANSOM).
7. Faidherbe to minister of navy, St. Louis, October 14, 1859, Sénégal, I, 46, ANSOM. In speaking of an educational program for Senegal, Faidherbe also wrote, "In this as in many other matters, we have only to imitate what was done in Algeria." Quoted in P. Cultru, *Histoire du Sénégal du XVe. siècle à 1890* (Paris, 1910), p. 365.
8. Quoted in I. M. Brunel, *Le Général Faidherbe* (Paris, 1890), p. 135.
9. *Arrêté*, January 22, 1862, in *Feuille officielle du Sénégal* (Saint Louis, 1862), pp. 284-286.
10. *Ibid.*
11. Faidherbe to minister of navy, September 11, 1863, in Sénégal, I, 50, ANSOM.
12. "Mémoire sur la colonie du Sénégal," Sénégal, I, 43, ANSOM.
13. *Ibid.*
14. *Ibid.*
15. Faidherbe to minister of navy, St. Louis, October 14, 1859, in Sénégal, I, 46, ANSOM.
16. Quoted in Anon., *Marine et colonies: Opinion d'un marin, ancien gouverneur de colonie* (Paris, 1886), p. 47; author's italics.
17. Jauréguiberry to minister of navy, January 8, 1862, in Sénégal, VII, 13, ANSOM.

Notes to pages 14-20

18. Frederic Carrère and Paul Holle, *De la Sénégambie française* (Paris, 1855), p. 341.
19. Jauréguiberry to minister of navy, October 16, 1862, in Sénégal, VII, 13, ANSOM. Governor Pinet-Laprade also shared this view: Pinet-Laprade to minister of navy, June 27, 1866, 2B33 *bis,* Archives nationales, Sénégal (henceforth cited as ANS).
20. Naval ministry memorandum, n.d. (presumably written in 1869), in Sénégal, II, 4, ANSOM.
21. Quoted in A. D. A. De Kat Angelino, *Colonial Policy* (Hague, 1931), I, 6.
22. J. M. Compton, "Open Competition and the Indian Civil Service, 1854-1876," *English Historical Review* LXXXIII (April 1968), 267.
23. Brière de l'Isle to minister of navy, April 7, 1879, in 2B52, ANS. Eugène Etienne, undersecretary of colonies, made a similar description of the men overseas in 1887: "Mostly, the overseas functionaries coming from the metropolitan bureaucracy go abroad only to get higher pay, or, if they have had no previous government service, they desire to leave France only because they don't know what to do at home." Etienne to Governor General Ernest Constans, Paris, November 19, 1887, Indochine A 11(9), ANSOM, quoted in Herward Sieberg, *Eugène Etienne und die französische Kolonialpolitik (1887-1904)* (Cologne, 1968), p. 45.
24. Brière de l'Isle to minister of navy, July 8, 1879, in 2B52, ANS.
25. Circular of *directeur de l'intérieur* to *commandants de cercles,* November 30, 1885.
26. General inspector of navy to minister of navy, June 7, 1874, in Sénégal, VII, 14, ANSOM.
27. Gallieni to governor of Senegal; Kita, March 15, 1887, in Sénégal, VII, 15 *bis,* ANSOM.
28. Personnel File EE II 9 (4), ANSOM.
29. Personnel File EE II 140 (1), ANSOM.
30. Personnel file of Georges Ehrmann, ANSOM.

Chapter II: The Years of Experimentation

1. *De la colonisation chez les peuples modernes,* 5th ed. (Paris, 1902), II, 695-696.
2. *Ibid.,* II, 692.
3. Albert Duchêne, *La Politique coloniale de la France* (Paris, 1928), pp. 34-35.
4. Albéric Neton, *Delcassé* (Paris, 1952), pp. 119-120.
5. With the exception of thirteen months (August 1882 to September 1883) when the colonies were again put under the responsibility of a civil servant with the title of director, this system of organization was to last until 1894. For two brief periods, in 1889 and again in 1894, the undersecretariat of colonies became again an undersecretariat in the ministry of commerce, then known as the ministry of commerce and colonies.
6. J. Chailley, "Chroniques," *Quinzaine coloniale,* January 10, 1908; quoted in Jacques Chastenet, *La République des républicains* (Paris, 1954), p. 267. The only scholarly study of Etienne is Sieberg, *Eugène Etienne und die französische Kolonialpolitik.*
7. François Berge, "Le Sous-secrétariat et les sous-secrétaires d'état aux colonies: Histoire de l'émancipation de l'administration coloniale," *Revue française d'histoire d'outre-mer* XLVII (1960), 361.
8. Duchêne, *La Politique coloniale de la France,* p. 290.
9. In 1909 the ministry of colonies was moved to a more spacious building across the Seine, located at Rue Oudinot. The ministry was to remain there until it was abolished in 1959.

Notes to pages 20-28

10. Note by Faure, June 1898, when Delcassé became foreign minister; quoted in Berge, "Le Sous-secrétariat," p. 368.
11. Duchêne, *La Politique coloniale,* pp. 112-131.
12. See, for instance, Jean Blancsubé, *Projet d'organisation d'un ministère des colonies* (Paris, 1883); Anon., *Les Fonctionnaires des colonies en avant, par un voyageur* (Paris, 1884); Anon., *Marine et colonies: Opinion d'un marin, ancien gouverneur des colonies* (Paris, 1886).
13. Gallieni to Etienne, Siguiri, Sudan, February 10, 1888 (*Nouvelles acquisitions,* France, 24327, Bibliothèque nationale, manuscript division.)
14. Pierre Ma, *Organisation du ministère des colonies* (Paris, 1910), pp. 7-8.
15. Neton, *Delcassé,* p. 125.
16. Berge, "Le Sous-secrétariat," p. 324.
17. Decree, September 2, 1887, *Journal officiel de la République Française: Lois et décrets* (Paris, 1887), p. 4086 (henceforth the *Journal officiel* will be cited as *J.o.*).
18. *Ibid.*
19. Decree, December 12, 1888, *J.o.: Lois et décrets* (Paris, 1888), p. 5365.
20. Paul Tisseyre Ananké, *L'Assiette au beurre coloniale* (Paris, 1911), p. 34.
21. 1C 21, Archives de l'Afrique occidentale française, Dakar (henceforth cited as AAOF).
22. Victor Margueritte, "De la justice," *Annales coloniales* XIII (June 1, 1912).
23. Robert Delavignette, *Freedom and Authority in French West Africa* (London, 1950), p. 27.
24. A. H. Canu, *La Pétaudière coloniale* (Paris, 1894), p. 86.
25. Lucien Hubert, *L'Eveil d'un monde* (Paris, 1909), p. 73.
26. Georges Hardy, *Ergaste, ou la vocation coloniale* (Paris, 1929), p. 9.
27. *Echo de Paris,* May 6, 1931; quoted in Jean Suignard, *Une Grande administration indochinoise* (Paris, 1931), p. 54.
28. Hubert Deschamps, "La Vocation coloniale et le métier d'administrateur," *Afrique française,* supplement, XLI (September 1931), 498.
29. Robert Heussler, *Yesterday's Rulers* (Syracuse, N.Y., 1963), *passim.*
30. *Bulletin de l'Association professionnelle des administrateurs coloniaux,* no. 15 (September 30, 1910), 2-3. (Henceforth cited as BAPAC.)
31. See next chapter for a discussion of the *Ecole Coloniale.*
32. For material on opposition to the school, see newspaper clippings in scrapbook edited by the institution entitled *Documents divers.* It is available in the library of the *Institut international d'administration publique,* Paris. For opposition from the Lyon Chamber of Commerce, see John F. Laffey, "Roots of French Imperialism in the Nineteenth Century: The Case of Lyon," *French Historical Studies* VI (April 1969), 87-88.
33. Emile Boutmy, *Le Recrutement des administrateurs coloniaux* (Paris, 1895).
34. *Récueils des délibérations du congrès colonial national, Paris, 1889-90* (Paris, 1890), *passim.*
35. 1C 374, AAOF.
36. An example of such pressure is the letter sent by the *Association professionnelle des administrateurs coloniaux* to the minister of colonies, April 5, 1909; printed in BAPAC no. 10 (June 30, 1909), 2.
37. C. Pillias, "Composition du corps des administrateurs des colonies," *BAPAC* no. 1 (July 13, 1907), p. 1.
38. *Ibid.*
39. EE II 1242 (3), ANSOM.
40. Jules Champon file, ANSOM.
41. Pillias, "Composition du corps des administrateurs des colonies," p. 1.
42. EE II 1124 (4), ANSOM.
43. 1C 1039, AAOF.
44. 1C 1068, AAOF.

Notes to pages 28-38

45. Files available of administrators who had previously been agents reveal that of 89 agents appointed from 1890 to 1900, 36 percent had at least a secondary education, while of 183 agents appointed during 1906-1914, 68 percent had a *baccalauréat* degree or higher.
46. Henri Raybaud file, ANSOM.
47. Letter from Lyautey to Chailley-Bert, Fort Dauphin, December 30, 1901, in *Lettres du sud de Madagascar, 1900-1902* (Paris, 1935), p. 212.
48. Pillias, "Composition du corps des administrateurs des colonies," p. 1.
49. For a discussion of the Congo scandal, see Félicien Challaye, *Souvenirs sur la colonisation* (Paris, 1935); Jules Saintoyant, *L'Affaire du Congo, 1905* (Paris, 1960).
50. In a letter of instructions from Clémentel to Brazza, reproduced in *Afrique française* XV (April 1905), 175.
51. Victor Augagneur, "Le Recrutement des administrateurs coloniaux," *Annales coloniales* XIII (April 6, 1912), 1.
52. Decree, June 5, 1913, *Journal officiel, AEF*.
53. Ralph A. Austen, *Northwest Tanzania under German and British Rule* (New Haven, Conn., 1968), p. 63.
54. Thus a governor vaunting the qualities of one of his subordinates serving in the bush wrote of him: "He speaks German and English as fluently as French; he reads, writes, but speaks with some difficulty Chinese." 1C 660, AAOF.

Chapter III: Beginnings of the *Ecole Coloniale*

1. Joseph Chailley-Bert, "Recrutement des fonctionnaires coloniaux," *Comptes rendus, Institut colonial international* (Paris, 1895), pp. 289-309; M. J. Silvestre, "Le Recrutement des fonctionnaires de l'Indochine française," *Congrès colonial international de Paris, 1889* (Paris, 1889), pp. 231-247. The heavy workload at the *collège,* one writer suggests, may also have had something to do with the brevity of its existence: courses on traditional Vietnamese administration, botany, practical construction, and a general course on Cambodia. Milton E. Osborne, *The French Presence in Cochinchina and Cambodia—Rule and Response (1859-1905)* (Ithaca, N.Y., 1969, p. 43).
2. Debate, February 13, 1888, *J.o., Chambre des députés: Débats* (Paris, 1888), p. 398.
3. One historian of French colonization claims that the Dutch school at Delft was "directly the French model." Stephen H. Roberts, *The History of French Colonial Policy, 1870-1925* (London, 1929), I, 161. He fails, however, to document this point satisfactorily. Unfortunately, I have found no material regarding this problem in the archives.
4. *Colonisation de l'Indochine: L'Expérience anglaise* (Paris, 1891); *La Hollande et les fonctionnaires des Indes Néerlandaises* (Paris, 1902).
5. *Le Libéral de l'Est* (Belfort), August 19, 1886. There had been earlier attempts at educating young men in France for the purpose of gaining influence in their homelands. During the late seventeenth century an army officer brought back to France a young African named Aniaba, allegedly Prince of Assinie, on the Ivory Coast. The officer gave him an education and the Bishop of Meaux, Bossuet, baptized him into the Christian faith with Louis XIV standing as godfather. The "Prince" lived several years in France, but when he was brought back to Assinie, the French attempt to use him in establishing a commercial foothold and Christianizing his homeland failed dismally. Shelby T. McCloy, *The Negro in France* (Lexington, Ky., 1961), pp. 16-17; and Henri Mouëzy, *Assinie et le royaume de Krinjabo* (Paris, 1953), pp. 25-39. I am grateful to Mr. Thomas Cassily for bringing the latter reference to my attention.

Despite the discouraging example of "Prince" Aniaba, during the next century a

Notes to pages 38-46

missionary in French India, the Reverend Charles de Montalembert, suggested the founding of a college for young Indians who would study in France; upon their return to India, they would occupy the highest functions "from which they will spread our influence." Quoted in Victor Morel, "L'Ecole Coloniale," in J. Charles-Roux et al., eds., *Colonies et pays de protectorat, exposition universelle* (Paris, 1900), p. 413.

6. In the 1850s Faidherbe had founded in Senegal a school for chiefs' sons called *Ecole des ôtages*; it is possible that the undersecretariat envisioned the *Ecole Coloniale* as fulfilling for the entire empire what Faidherbe's institution was doing for Senegal.
7. Decree, November 23, 1889, *J.o.: Lois et décrets* (Paris, 1889), p. 5861.
8. "De l'influence de l'éducation et des institutions européennes sur les populations indigènes des colonies," *Congrès colonial international de Paris, 1889*, pp. 49-76.
9. "Rapport présenté au conseil de perfectionnement de l'Ecole Coloniale par M. Ouachée," polygraph copy (Paris, 1900); available at the library of the *Institut international d'administration publique*, Paris.
10. *Ibid.*
11. Cited in Société des anciens élèves de l'Ecole Coloniale, *L'Ecole Coloniale et ses élèves, 1885-1905* (Paris, 1905), p. 31.
12. *Ibid.*
13. "Rapport au conseil d'administration sur le fonctionnement de l'Ecole Coloniale par M. Aymonier, directeur, 1891-1892," polygraph copy; available at the library of the *Institut international d'administration publique*, Paris.
14. *Bulletin officiel des colonies* IV (Paris, 1890), 313.
15. *Quinzaine coloniale* VII (January 10, 1900), 3.
16. EE II 1232 (7), ANSOM.
17. Société des anciens élèves, *L'Ecole Coloniale et ses élèves*, p. 58.
18. *Rapport sur le fonctionnement de l'Ecole Coloniale, 1898-1899* (Paris, 1899), p. 9.
19. Even before World War I, interviews played an important role in the recruitment of the British colonial service. Heussler, *Yesterday's Rulers*, pp. 22-26.
20. On *concours*, see Roy Jumper, "Entrance Examinations for the French Administrative Service," *Personnel Administration* XVIII (September 1, 1955), 31-37, 47; Michel Crozier, *The Bureaucratic Phenomenon* (Chicago, 1964), pp. 238-244.
21. Heussler, *Yesterday's Rulers*, pp. 17-26.
22. W. R. Sharp, *The French Civil Service* (New York, 1932), p. 140.
23. Ecole Coloniale, *Année scolaire, 1902-1903, rapport sur le fonctionnement de l'Ecole* (Paris, 1903), p. 7.
24. "Rapport adressé au président du conseil d'administration de l'Ecole Coloniale sur le concours d'admission de 1899," polygraph copy (Paris, 1899); available at the *Institut international d'administration publique*, Paris.
25. *Ibid.*
26. I am grateful to Robert Delavignette for furnishing me with information about Dislère.
27. See Carl J. Friedrich, "The Continental Tradition of Training Administrators in Law and Jurisprudence," *Journal of Modern History* XI (June 1939), 129-148.
28. Of all the directors of the *Ecole Coloniale* until World War II, Robert Delavignette was the one who most de-emphasized the study of law; nevertheless, he made all the above-mentioned claims for the usefulness of legal studies. Interviews in 1965.
29. "Rapport présenté au conseil d'administration de l'Ecole Coloniale, 1899-1900," polygraph copy (Paris, 1900); available at the library of the *Institut international d'administration publique*, Paris.
30. Already in 1895 the criticism had been made that the *Ecole Coloniale* was

Notes to pages 46-51

        training within the walls of the same institution men for such diverse tasks as administration in Africa and in Indochina. Boutmy, *Le Recrutement des administrateurs coloniaux*, pp. 38-40.

31. It was claimed in 1913 that an administrator in Indochina could expect to be promoted to administrator first class with a year's salary of 20,000 francs within ten years of entering the service. Within the same time an administrator in Africa would have the rank of administrator second class and would only be paid 12,000 francs a year. Jean Sore, "La Réorganisation nécessaire des cadres généraux de l'administration coloniale," *Presse coloniale*, November 15, 20, 21, 1913.
32. Joost Van Vollenhoven was the only top graduate before World War I to join the central administration in Paris.
33. A copy of this examination is contained in a scrapbook of the *Ecole Coloniale* entitled *Documents divers*, which is now available at the library of the *Institut international d'administration publique*, Paris.
34. Roberts, *History of French Colonial Policy*, I, 161.
35. M. M. Knight, "French Colonial Policy: The Decline of 'Association,' " *Journal of Modern History* V (1933), 208-224.
36. Raymond F. Betts, *Assimilation and Association in French Colonial Theory, 1890-1914* (New York, 1961); chapters iv and v are particularly instructive. See also Martin D. Lewis, "One Hundred Million Frenchmen: The Assimilationist Theory in French Colonial Policy," *Comparative Studies in Society and History* IV (January 1962), 129-153.
37. "Dix années de politiques coloniales," *Journal des débats* (October 4, 1901), p. 3. Being one of the founders of the associationist doctrine, Chailley-Bert also complained that the graduates of the school "do not always show sufficient respect toward the native chiefs who are their daily collaborators."
38. Louis Vignon, quoted in *La Libre parole*, July 27, 1894.
39. In scrapbook, *Documents divers, composition des étudiants, 1903-1908*; available at the library of the *Institut international d'administration publique*, Paris.
40. "While the European child loses his child brain when he matures, the inferior man, incapable by heredity of surpassing a certain level, stops at a certain inferior level of development." *Congrès colonial international de Paris, 1889*, p. 71.
41. Robert Delavignette, *Christianity and Colonialism*, trans. by J. R. Foster (New York, 1964), p. 33.
42. Ministère des colonies, *Organisation et fonctionnement de l'Ecole Coloniale* (Levallois-Perret, 1904), pp. 40-41.
43. Ministère des colonies, Ecole Coloniale, *Rapport à M. le président du conseil d'administration de l'Ecole Coloniale, 1908-1909* (Paris, 1909), p. 6.
44. The one who was able to put his flying to use served in AOF. In 1911 he was unfortunately involved in two accidents. In the first he broke his leg; in the second, which occurred a few months later, he fell from a height of fifty meters and broke his hip and both legs. The report of the *Ecole Coloniale* for 1911 assures its readers that "these two accidents were the only ones that occurred to M. Carles during his flight career." Ministère des colonies, Ecole Coloniale, *Rapport à M. le président du conseil d'administration de l'Ecole Coloniale, 1910-1911* (Paris, 1911), p. 7.
45. During the war, Governor-General Joost Van Vollenhoven remarked that "the *Ecole Coloniale* remains too much ignored by our university youth and it deserves to be in the same rank with the other *grandes écoles*." Comité d'initiative des amis de Vollenhoven, *Une Ame de chef: Le Gouverneur général J. Van Vollenhoven* (Paris, 1920), pp. 111-112.
46. Senate debate, quoted in *Bulletin de la Société des anciens élèves de l'Ecole Coloniale* IX (March 4, 1909), 1. (Hereafter this publication cited as *BSAEC.)*

Notes to pages 52-59

47. Charles Regismanset, *Questions coloniales (1912-1923)* (Paris, 1923), 129-130.
48. *Signal* (November 17, 1904).
49. Quoted in Albert Prévaudeau, *Joost Van Vollenhoven* (Paris, 1953), p. 16.
50. Louis Lyautey, *Paroles d'action* (Paris, 1927), p. 53; quoted in Raymond F. Betts, "The French Colonial Frontier," in Charles K. Warner, ed., *From the Ancien Régime to the Popular Front: Essays in the History of Modern France in Honor of Shepard B. Clough* (New York, 1969), p. 133.
51. Louis Bertrand, *Notre Afrique* (Paris, 1925), p. 22; quoted in Betts, "The French Colonial Frontier," p. 136.
52. *Figaro littéraire* (October 28, 1965).
53. J. F. Reste, "Grand corps et grand commis–dans la France d'outre-mer," *Revue des deux mondes* (March 15, 1959), pp. 329-330.
54. Agathon (pseud. of André Tarde and Henri Massis), *Les Jeunes gens d'aujourd'hui* (Paris, 1913), pp. 140-144.
55. *Rapport au conseil d'administration de l'Ecole Coloniale sur le concours de 1899, par M. Puaux* ([Paris],1899). None of the subsequent reports contains information regarding the social origin either of the candidates for admission or of the cadets themselves. In the 1920s, however, such information was again published.
56. *BAPAC* no. 2 (July 13, 1907), 16.
57. Commission du statut des fonctionnaires, *Rapport au conseil supérieur de statistique, rapport préliminaire* (Paris, 1908), pp. 17-18.
58. Twelve students a year were exempted from paying tuition fees, and six in the second and third year of studies were given scholarships of 1,200 francs. Decree, April 9, 1891, *J.o.: Lois et décrets,* pp. 1584-1585.
59. Answer to questionnaire, October 1965.
60. Quoted in *BSAEC* IX (March 1, 1909), 1.

Chapter IV: The Locus of Power

1. Robert Delavignette, *La Paix nazaréenne* (Paris, 1943), p. 91.
2. Albert Sarraut, former governor-general of Indochina, François Piétri, former director-general of finances in Morocco, and Théodore Steeg, former governor-general of Algeria were the only exceptions to the rule.
3. See Appendix I for the list of ministers and undersecretaries in charge of colonial affairs. For the period 1871 to 1914 the ministers and undersecretaries averaged 13 months of service; for the period 1915 to 1929, 11 months of service; and for the years 1930 to 1940, 7 months of service. Of the 74 men in charge of colonial affairs from 1871 to 1940, only 11 served more than 2 years; 5 served between 18 and 24 months, 12 served between 12 and 18 months, 15 served between 6 and 12 months, 19 served between 1 and 6 months, and 12 served a month or less.
4. Cited in Georges Hardy, *Histoire sociale de la colonisation française* (Paris, 1953), p. 47.
5. *Ibid.*
6. Adolphe Messimy, *Notre oeuvre coloniale* (Paris, 1910), p. 396.
7. Annexe procès-verbal, séance February 11, 1916, *J.o., Chambre des députés: Débats* (Paris, 1916), pp. 3-4.
8. Comité franco-britannique d'études coloniales, *Les Méthodes d'administration et de gouvernement dans les colonies anglaises et françaises* (Paris, n.d.), p. 23. A similar complaint is also voiced in Adolphe Messimy, *Mes souvenirs* (Paris, 1938), pp. 40-41.
9. Comité d'initiative, *Une Ame de chef,* pp. 53-54.
10. *J.o., Chambre des députés: Documents parlementaires,* séance January 13, 1938

(Paris, 1938), p. 49. For the best study on the colonial inspectorate see Reuben Garner, "Watchdogs of Empire: The French Colonial Inspection Service in Action, 1815-1913" (unpublished Ph.D. dissertation, Rochester University, 1970).
11. *Annales coloniales* XXXI (February 11, 1930).
12. Comité d'initiative, *Une Ame de chef,* p. 41. Even when the inspectors did file detailed reports and make recommendations, these were not always acted upon by the ministry; complaint voiced by Minister of Colonies Henri Simon, in circular, February 3, 1919; Affaires politiques, 2553/9, ANSOM.
13. Brazza to minister of colonies, August 21, 1905; Brazza Archives, ANSOM.
14. Letter from *Association des fonctionnaires civils de l'administration centrale du ministère des colonies,* to minister of colonies, Paris, March 30, 1911; in Affaires politiques, 2516/10, ANSOM.
15. Regismanset, *Questions coloniales (1912-1923),* p. 232.
16. Letter from *Association des fonctionnaires* to minister of colonies, March 30, 1911.
17. *Ibid.*
18. *Ibid.*
19. Robert Doucet, *Commentaires sur la colonisation* (Paris, 1926), p. 87.
20. Interview with former governor, February 3, 1965. This governor administered one of the colonies that was not under the authority of a governor-general; thus he dealt directly with the minister.
21. Comité d'initiative, *Une Ame de chef,* p. 47.
22. Leroy-Beaulieu, *De la colonisation chez les peuples modernes,* II, 36. For the independence of the military officers in the Sudan, see A. S. Kanya-Forstner, *The Conquest of the Western Sudan: A Study in Military Imperialism* (London, 1969).
23. EE II 308 (15), ANSOM.
24. 1 C 288, AAOF.
25. EE II 160 (2), ANSOM.
26. EE II 1206 (6), ANSOM.
27. *Gallieni au Tonkin (1892-1896): Par lui-même* (Paris, 1941), p. 56.
28. Pierre Gourou, "Gallieni," in Charles A. Julien, ed., *Techniciens de la colonisation* (Paris, 1946), p. 109.
29. Report, 4G 34, AAOF.
30. Maurice Delafosse, *Broussard, ou les états d'âme d'un colonial* (Paris, 1922), p. 136.
31. Delavignette, *Freedom and Authority in French West Africa,* pp. 6-8.
32. *Gallieni au Tonkin,* pp. 221-222.
33. *Ibid.*
34. Hubert Lyautey, *Lettres du Tonkin et de Madagascar (1894-1899)* (Paris, 1921), p. 118.
35. A long-lived myth, accepted by most French overseas officials, has it that Van Vollenhoven resigned out of protest against the excessive recruitment of black soldiers. But in fact Van Vollenhoven resigned because the appointment of the Senegalese deputy, Blaise Diagne, as commissioner of the republic in charge of recruiting black troops, required him to share his administrative powers with Diagne. The powers of the governor-general, Van Vollenhoven claimed, were indivisible. Rather than share these powers, Van Vollenhoven preferred to resign.
36. Pierre Messmer, a former governor-general and later a member of several De Gaulle cabinets, wrote of Van Vollenhoven in 1964: "His memory has always remained alive." Letter, March 20, 1964, reprinted in *Annuaire de l'Association des anciens élèves de l'Ecole nationale de la France d'outre-mer* (Paris, 1964).
37. Comité d'initiative, *Une Ame de chef,* p. 41.
38. General Mangeot, *La Vie ardente de Van Vollenhoven, gouverneur-général de*

l'AOF (Paris, 1943), p. 42.
39. Gouvernement du Soudan français, Service local, *Instructions à l'usage des commandants de régions et de cercles,* 2nd ed. (Paris, 1897), pp. 6-10.
40. M. Roux, *Manuel à l'usage des administrateurs* (Paris, 1911), p. 28.
41. Maurice Delafosse, "Les états d'âme d'un colonial," *L'Afrique française XIX* (May 1909), 163.
42. *J.o.: Lois et décrets* (Paris, 1887), p. 4453.
43. The act imposed penalties for the following offences: (1) neglect to pay taxes or perform labor service, (2) refusal to answer the administrator's summons, (3) firing of a shot during a feast, closer than 500 meters to the administrator's residence, (4) display of disrespect by word or deed against a representative of French authority, (5) hiding oneself or one's property during census, (6) giving asylum to a criminal, (7) destruction or displacement of road signs or markers, (8) failure to dispose of dead animals, (9) burial outside regulated areas and regulated depths, (10) the making of speeches in public tending to weaken respect for French authority, (11) refusal to give statistical information, or the willful giving of misleading information, (12) failure to appear before an administrator making a judicial inquest, (13) failure or neglect to help in case of emergency, (14) failure in case of epidemics to execute sanitary regulations ordered by the administrator, (15) usurpation of the functions of village or *canton* chief, (16) keeping vagrant animals and the refusal to return them. *Arrêté,* October 12, 1888, *Bulletin administratif du Sénégal* (Gorée, 1888), pp. 267-268.
44. Circular of governor-general to the *commandants de cercles,* May 24, 1912, in 7G 63 AAOF.
45. "Instruction sur l'application du décret du 10 novembre 1903," reprinted in Georges François, *L'Afrique occidentale française* (Paris, 1907), pp. 158-159.
46. *Ibid.,* p. 163.
47. Circular of governor-general to *commandants de cercles,* May 24, 1912, in 7G 63 AAOF.
48. William Ponty, "Instructions remises à M. le Gouverneur Angoulvant, lieutenant-gouverneur de la Côte d'Ivoire," August 29, 1914, Affaires politiques, 556, 1, ANSOM.
49. Quoted in P. F. Gonidec, *Droit d'outre-mer* (Paris, 1959), I, 185.
50. Messimy, *Notre oeuvre coloniale,* p. 60.
51. Minister of colonies to governor-general of AOF, Paris, October 29, 1902; AOF, I, 9, ANSOM.
52. 4G 21, AAOF. "Prestations" was a form of forced labor mainly employed to build roads; the system of "portages" permitted the recruitment of porters.
53. Hubert Deschamps and Paul Chauvet, eds., *Gallieni, pacificateur: Ecrits coloniaux de Gallieni* (Paris, 1949), p. 364. In German East Africa taxes were imposed in 1897 for their supposed educational benefits, rather than revenue purposes. Austen, *Northwest Tanzania,* p. 54.
54. "Commission pour l'organisation du Cameroun et de l'AEF," in Affaires politiques, 649/17, ANSOM.
55. Telegram, Brazza to minister of colonies, July 26, 1905; Brazza Archives, ANSOM.
56. Challaye, *Souvenirs sur la colonisation,* pp. 86-87.
57. Brazza to minister of colonies, August 21, 1905; Brazza Archives, ANSOM.
58. Often used by Ponty; see his "Discours prononcés par M. Ponty, gouverneur-général de l'Afrique occidentale française, 1909" (Gorée, 1909), p. 12; circular of April 1, 1913, in 17G 38, AAOF.
59. Quoted by Lyautey, *Lettres du Tonkin,* p. 71. For some earlier advocates of a similar view see Osborne, *The French Presence,* pp. 44-46.
60. Rémi Clignet, "The Legacy of Assimilation in West African Educational Systems," *Comparative Educational Review* (February 1968), pp. 65-66.

Notes to pages 73-78

61. Ronald Robinson and John Gallagher, *Africa and the Victorians* (London, 1963); Henri Brunschwig, *Mythes et réalités de l'impérialisme colonial français, 1871-1914* (Paris, 1960).
62. Debate, February 13, 1888, *J.o., Chambre des députés: Débats* (Paris, 1888), p. 394.
63. Among the 83 members of the Sudan Political Service recruited from 1899 to 1914, for example, 36 were graduates of Oxford, 20 of Cambridge, 9 of Sandhurst, and 6 of Trinity College, Dublin. Prosser Gifford, "Indirect Rule: Touchstone or Tombstone for Colonial Policy," in Prosser Gifford and William Roger Louis, eds., *Britain and Germany in Africa* (New Haven, Conn., 1967), p. 356.
64. *Ibid.,* p. 357.
65. Robert Delavignette, *Service africain* (Paris, 1946), p. 38. I am using the French edition since this passage is significantly abbreviated in the English translation.
66. Interview, Paris, March 23, 1965.
67. Henri Labouret, Robert Delavignette, and Albert Charton, "L'Afrique occidentale française, aujourd'hui–demain," *Le Monde colonial illustré* CXXIV (1933), 188.
68. Quoted by *Afrique française* XX (July 1910), 215; also in Jean Suret-Canale, *Afrique noire, occidentale et centrale:* vol. II, *L'Ere coloniale, 1900-1945* (Paris, 1964), p. 103.
69. Jacques Lombard, *Autorités traditionnelles et pouvoirs européens en Afrique noire* (Paris, 1967), p. 106.
70. Quoted in Neton, *Delcassé,* p. 128.
71. Circular, January 30, 1914, 17G 38, AAOF.
72. *Commandant de cercle* of Ségou in marginal notes answering observations made by Inspector-General Méray, in his report to the minister of colonies on the Sudan in 1910; 4G 10, AAOF.
73. Quoted in Jean Suret-Canale, "La Fin de la chefferie en Guinée," *Journal of African History* VII (1966), 467.
74. Henri Labouret, *A la recherche d'une politique indigène dans l'Ouest africain* (Paris, 1931), p. 38.
75. Louis Binger, *Du Niger au golfe de Guinée par le pays Kong et les Mossi, 1887-1889* (Paris, 1892), I, 467; quoted in Elliot P. Skinner, *The Mossi of the Upper Volta* (Stanford, Calif., 1964), p. 143.
76. Messimy, *Notre oeuvre coloniale,* pp. 42-50.
77. *Ibid.,* p. 3.
78. Comité d'initiative, *Une Ame de chef,* p. 203.
79. One example is an administrator who served in Oubangui-Chari in 1911; 1C 797 AAOF.
80. Interview with administrator who served during the interwar years, Paris, February 2, 1965.
81. Martin A. Klein, *Islam and Imperialism in Senegal: Sine Saloum, 1847-1914* (Stanford, Calif., 1968), p. 170 and *passim.* For a spirited debate on French rule see Hubert Deschamps, "Et maintenant, Lord Lugard?" *Africa* XXXIII, no. 4 (October 1963), 293-306; and Michael Crowder, "Indirect Rule–French and British Style," *Africa* XXXIV, no. 3 (July 1964), 197-205. Basing his argument on British administration in East Africa, M. Semakula Kiwanuka argues that there never was a difference between the British and French systems of colonial administration. "Colonial Policies and Administrations in Africa: The Myths of the Contrasts," *African Historical Studies* III, no. 2 (1970), 295-315.
82. Brian Weinstein, "Félix Eboué and the Chiefs: Perceptions of Power in Early Oubangui-Chari," *Journal of African History* XI (January 1970), 107-126.
83. *Ibid.*
84. In 1910 in AOF there was one administrator for 5,457 square kilometers, in Madagascar one per 1,901 square kilometers, in the Congo region one per 8,102

Notes to pages 78-87

square kilometers. In relation to population, there was one per 12,290 inhabitants for AOF, one per 8,769 for Madagascar, and one per 37,383 inhabitants for the Congo region. Messimy, *Notre oeuvre coloniale*, p. 322.
85. A. Demougeot, *Notes sur l'organisation politique et administrative du Labé* (Dakar, 1944), p. 50.
86. Deschamps and Chauvet, *Gallieni, pacificateur*, p. 246.
87. Comité d'initiative, *Une Ame de chef*, p. 208.
88. "Etats d'âme d'un colonial," *L'Afrique française* XIX (May 1909), 164; also quoted by Suret-Canale, *Afrique noire, occidentale et centrale*, pp. 404-405.
89. Report of inspector-general to minister of colonies, Dakar, May 22, 1919; 4G 21, AAOF.
90. 1C 949, AAOF.
91. Angoulvant to governor-general of AOF, Bingerville, February 17, 1919, in 1C 43, AAOF.
92. EE II 140 (1), ANSOM.
93. 1C 612, AAOF.
94. 1C 694, AAOF.
95. 1C 267, AAOF.
96. 1C 248, AAOF.
97. 1C 56, AAOF.
98. 1C 368, AAOF.
99. For the drug addict, see EE II 308 (14), ANSOM. Several files of alcoholics transferred to the Congo can be cited: EE II 140 (1), EE II 308 (14), EE II 1158 (4), ANSOM; 1C 598, AAOF.
100. Letter, December 17, 1915, in 1C 106, AAOF. Writing of the leniency with which acts of maladministration were treated, Van Vollenhoven noted that a habit had developed of "giving a thousand excuses to explain, to attenuate, and let us say the word, because I must speak frankly, to hide the facts." Circular of July 12, 1917, *BAPAC* XXXIX (August 31, 1917), 38.
101. EE II 1002 (3), ANSOM.
102. Brazza to Desruisseaux, May 13, 1905; Brazza Archives, ANSOM.
103. Richard Hill, "Government and Christian Missions in the Anglo-Egyptian Sudan, 1899-1914," *Middle Eastern Studies* I (1965), 115, quoted in Gifford, "Indirect Rule," p. 356.
104. 1C 28, AAOF.
105. 1C 308, AAOF.
106. 1C 521, AAOF.
107. 1C 367, AAOF.
108. EE II 1158 (2), ANSOM.

Chapter V: The Colonial School and the New Generation

1. Citation of October 8, 1926; reprinted in *Annuaire de l'Association des anciens élèves de l'Ecole nationale de la France d'outre-mer* (Paris, 1964).
2. In 1921, for instance, 45 candidates competed for 21 posts. Ministère des colonies, Ecole Coloniale, *Rapport à M. le président du conseil de l'administration de l'Ecole Coloniale, année 1921-1922* (Paris, 1922), p. 6.
3. Letter reprinted in *BAPAC* 54 (July 31, 1922), 233.
4. François Mury, "Nos administrateurs coloniaux en Afrique," *Le Courrier colonial* (March 22, 1929).
5. Marie Roustan, "Pour nos administrateurs coloniaux," *Annales coloniales* (September 1, 1928).
6. Sharp, *The French Civil Service*, p. 25.
7. XXX (pseud.), *Réalités coloniales* (Paris, 1934), p. 255.
8. Letter from Georges Hardy to author; Jaulgonne, August 14, 1968.

9. Théodore Zeldin, "Higher Education in France, 1848-1940," *Journal of Contemporary History* II (1967), pp. 69-80.
10. Ministère des colonies, Ecole Coloniale, *Rapport à M. le président du conseil de l'administration de l'Ecole Coloniale, année 1934-1935* (Paris, 1936), pp. 1-2.
11. R. S. (pseud.), "Evolution du concours d'entrée," *BSAEC* XLIV (1944), 27.
12. *Ibid.*, p. 29.
13. Pierre Lalumière, *L'Inspection des finances* (Paris, 1959), pp. 29-49; cited in Alain Girard, *La Réussite sociale en France* (Paris, 1961), p. 311.
14. These statistics are based on the yearly reports of the *Ecole Coloniale*. Basing his work on the same documents and using the same categories, Roy Jumper, "The Recruitment and Training of Civil Administrators for Overseas France: A Case Study in French Bureaucracy" (unpublished Ph.D. dissertation, Duke University, 1955), p. 165, arrives at somewhat different figures. As a rule, however, we differ only by a few percentage points. The difference stems from the divergence in interpretation on classifying certain professions. Note that high administration is not the same as "haute administration," a term which the French reserve for the highest echelons of the administration.
15. Interview with a former governor-general of Indochina; Paris, June 24, 1965.
16. Heussler, *Yesterday's Rulers, passim.*
17. Armand Rio, "A l'Ecole Coloniale: L'Expansion de l'énergie française," *Je sais tout,* 257 (May 1927), 124-127.
18. Georges Hardy, "Histoire coloniale et psychologie ethnique," *Revue de l'histoire des colonies françaises* XVIII (1925), 172.
19. Hardy, *Ergaste,* p. 101.
20. Georges Hardy, "La France d'aujourd'hui et le problème colonial," *La Nouvelle revue des jeunes* III (July 15, 1931), 30-31.
21. Quoted in Rio, "A l'Ecole Coloniale."
22. Answer to questionnaire.
23. 1C 861, AAOF.
24. *Ibid.*
25. Of the sixty-nine men attending the school under Hardy's directorship and answering the questionnaire, twenty-two pointed to Hardy as the single most important influence.
26. Answer to questionnaire.
27. Ernest Roume, speech of November 11, 1929; quoted in *BSAEC* XXIX (February 1930).
28. Letter from Hardy to author; Jaulgonne, August 14, 1968.
29. "Eloge de Charles Robéquin et Henri Labouret, séance du 5 fevrier 1965, réception de M. Robert Cornevin," *Comptes rendus, Académie des sciences d'outre-mer* (Paris, 1965), pp. 24-25.
30. *Ibid.*
31. Roberts, *History of French Colonial Policy,* I, 166.
32. Quoted in *BSAEC* XXIX (February 1930), 5.
33. According to Hardy in *BSAEC* XXX (February 1931), 8.
34. Raymond Leslie Buell, *The Native Problem in Africa* (New York, 1928), I, 985.
35. Decree, May 7, 1938, *Bulletin officiel des colonies* LII (Paris, 1938), 482-483.
36. 1C 1143, AAOF.
37. Gaston Roupnel, *Histoire de la campagne française* (Paris, n.d.), p. 305.
38. Michel Frochot, "Que ma joie demeure," *L'Observatoire colonial,* New Series, XII (June 1938), 4. The school paper, which came out at different times under different titles, usually appeared in mimeographed form. The most complete set is available at the *Institut international d'administration publique,* Paris.
39. Robert Delavignette, "Connaissances des mentalités indigènes en AOF," *Congrès international et intercolonial de la société indigène* I (Paris, 1931), 564.
40. Robert Delavignette, "La Formation professionnelle de l'administrateur colonial," in René Maunier et al., *L'Empire français et ses ressources* (Paris,

1942), pp. 30-31.
41. Interview with Delavignette, Paris, April 1, 1965.
42. "L'Ecole Coloniale," in *De Vorming van den bestuursamtenaar voor overzeesche gewesten in Nederland, Engeland, Frankrijk, Belgie en Italie* (Leiden, 1937), p. 106. Thirty years later Delavignette described the school's role in a similar vein; interview, April 1, 1965.
43. *L'Observatoire colonial* (March-April 1945), p. 8.
44. Anon., *Guide des carrières: Les Carrières dans le corps des administrateurs coloniaux* (Paris, 1931), p. 4.
45. Delavignette, *Freedom and Authority*, p. 28.
46. Answers to questionnaire; if no reference is given to the motives, they come from the questionnaire.
47. R. S. (pseud.), "Evolution du concours d'entrée," p. 29.
48. Hubert Deschamps, "La vocation coloniale et métier d'administrateur," *Afrique française*, supplement, XLI (September 1931), 499.
49. Patrick O'Reilly, *Mon ami Gilbert l'africain* (Dijon, 1942), p. 85.
50. E. Mournat, "Comment on cherche et on trouve une place aux colonies," (mimeographed copy, 1937); available at the *Bibliothèque nationale*.
51. Anon., *Quatre anciens de Colo* (Paris, 1935).
52. *Ibid.*
53. Buell, *The Native Problem in Africa*, I, 985.
54. J. Wilbois, *Le Cameroun* (Paris, 1934), p. 201.

Chapter VI: The Era of Lost Opportunities

1. 1C 1102 *bis*, AAOF.
2. 1C 979, AAOF.
3. 1C 194, AAOF. An unprecedented proportion of administrators entering the Corps in the interwar period were considered good functionaries by their superiors. Of 345 files belonging to men joining the service in this period, 75 percent (262) belonged to satisfactory functionaries, only 17 percent (61) to men considered brutal, or otherwise ineffective; 22 files, or 8 percent, contained insufficient information for coding.
4. Hubert Deschamps, "Les Empires coloniaux et les nationalités d'outre-mer" (mimeographed copy of course given at the Sorbonne in 1947-1948), p. 45.
5. Hubert Deschamps, "La France d'outre-mer et la Communauté" (mimeographed copy of lectures given at the *Institut d'etudes politiques* in 1958-1959), p. 60.
6. *Gallieni au Tonkin*, pp. 215-216.
7. Deschamps and Paul Chauvet, *Gallieni, pacificateur*, p. 26.
8. Jacques Chastenet, *Les Années d'illusions, 1919-1931* (Paris, 1960), p. 300; H. Hauser, "Colonies et Métropole," *Revue d'économie politique* LIII (1939), 491.
9. The proposal was separately published as *La Mise en valeur des colonies françaises* (Paris, 1923).
10. *Ibid.*, pp. 24-25.
11. *Ibid.*, pp. 60-63.
12. "Commission pour l'organisation du Cameroun et de l'AEF, séance 15 mars 1920," in Affaires politiques, carton 649, file 17, in ANSOM.
13. Quoted in *J.o. de la Fédération des associations amicales et professionnelles des fonctionnaires et agents coloniaux* (December 1922).
14. Henri Cosnier, *L'Ouest africain français* (Paris, 1921), p. xix.
15. Sarraut, *La Mise en valeur*, p. 22.
16. *Afrique française* XLVII (June 1937), 333.
17. *Annales coloniales* XXXII (July 23, 1931).
18. Quoted in Buell, *The Native Problem in Africa*, I, 939.

19. *Annales coloniales* XXXII (July 23, 1931).
20. André Gide, *Travels in the Congo [and] Return from Chad,* trans. by Dorothy Bussy (New York, 1937), p. 27.
21. Buell, *The Native Problem in Africa,* I, 941.
22. Henri Labouret, *Colonialisation, colonialisme, et décolonisation* (Paris, 1952), p. 176.
23. 1934 report of inspector, in 1C 704, AAOF.
24. Marcel Olivier, *Six ans de politique sociale à Madagascar* (Paris, 1931), p. 42.
25. Lucien Hubert, "La Politique coloniale de la France," in Henri Brenier *et al., La Politique coloniale de la France* (Paris, 1924), p. 274.
26. Olivier, *Six ans de politique sociale à Madagascar,* p. 42.
27. For a British example in Southeast Tanzania, see Gus Liebenow, "The Dilemmas of Development: Makonde" (unpublished manuscript). I am grateful to Professor Liebenow for letting me read his study which is currently in press.
28. 1C 1029, AAOF.
29. Robert Delavignette, "Pour le paysan noir, pour l'esprit africain," *Esprit* IV (1935), p. 384.
30. Henri Labouret, "A la recherche d'une politique coloniale," *Le Monde coloniale illustré* LXXXII (1930), 133.
31. Deschamps, "La France d'outre-mer," p. 76.
32. "Rapport politique, 4ème semestre de 1919, par le gouverneur de Dahomey," Affaires politiques, carton 574, file 5, in AAOF.
33. Lombard, *Autorités traditionnelles,* p. 152.
34. Comité d'initiative, *Une Ame de chef,* p. 48.
35. *Ibid.,* pp. 48-50.
36. "Rapport politique," November 1921, in 17G 40, AAOF.
37. Henri Labouret, "Le Noir et l'homme blanc en Afrique," *Le Monde colonial illustré* LIV (July 1928), pp. 147-148. Later Labouret rejected both direct and indirect rule. "Politique indigène en Afrique tropicale," *Afrique française* XLVIII (May 1938), 203-207; (June 1938), 267-270.
38. Ministerial circular, October 9, 1929, in *Bulletin officiel des colonies* (Paris, 1929), pp. 1668-1670.
39. Quoted in *Annales coloniales* (January 26, 1931).
40. Circular, December 10, 1931; 18G 55, AAOF.
41. Governor-general to minister of colonies, August 30, 1927; quoted in James S. Spiegler, "Aspects of Nationalist Thought among French-Speaking Africans, 1921-1939" (unpublished dissertation, Nuffield College, 1968), p. 230. I wish to express my thanks to Dr. Spiegler for letting me read his study.
42. Delavignette, *Christianity and Colonialism,* p. 30.
43. Robert Randau (pseud. of Robert Arnaud), *Les Meneurs d'hommes* (Paris, 1931), p. 55.
44. Quoted in Anon., "Les Administrateurs de la France d'outre-mer," *L'Economie* 451 (July 1, 1954), 17.
45. Circular, August 18, 1932; quoted in Lombard, *Autorités traditionnelles,* p. 103, fn. 15.
46. Pierre Hugot, *Le Tchad* (Paris, 1965), pp. 65-66.
47. Quoted in Suret-Canale, "La Fin de la chefferie en Guinée," p. 476.
48. *Ibid.,* p. 488.
49. Olivier, *Six ans de politique sociale à Madagascar,* p. 237. Olivier's italics.
50. *Ibid.*
51. "Rapport sur le commandement indigène pour 1930," governor of Senegal to governor-general of AOF, Saint Louis, May 18, 1931; in 2G 30, AAOF.
52. "AOF, affaires politiques, rapport politique du gouverneur général, 1937," pp. 81-82; unnumbered file, AAOF.
53. Decree, November 15, 1924, in *AOF, Journal officiel* (Dakar, 1924), pp. 575-578.
54. "Soudan, Rapport politique annuel, 1935," 2G 35/9, AAOF.
55. "Sénégal, Rapport politique annuel, 1934," 2G 34/5, AAOF.
56. Interview with administrator who served in Senegal in the 1930s; Dakar, March 15, 1966.
57. Deschamps, "La France d'outre-mer," p. 60.

58. Undated letter, written in 1928; 18G 138, AAOF.
59. *BAPAC* XXVIII (February 1, 1935), 35.
60. Delavignette, *Freedom and Authority*, p. 22.
61. *Ibid.*, p. 11.
62. Letter, governor-general to minister of colonies, January 2, 1931; 18G 63/17, AAOF.
63. Quoted in Marc Simon, *Souvenirs de brousse, 1910-1912* (Rennes, 1962), p. 41.
64. Circular, February 15, 1932; 18G 55, AAOF.
65. Governor Fousset, quoted in Robert Delavignette, *Soudan, Paris, Bourgogne* (Paris, 1935), p. 91.
66. Letter, lieutenant-governor of Dahomey to governor-general, Porto Novo, May 29, 1933; 18G 67/17, AAOF.
67. Suret-Canale, *Afrique noire, occidentale et centrale*, p. 392; *Discours par M. Antonetti à la séance de l'ouverture du conseil du gouvernement, session ordinaire, 1928* (Brazzaville, 1928), p. 33.
68. Letter, governor-general to minister of colonies; Dakar, June 2, 1931; 18G 63/17, AAOF.
69. *Ibid.*
70. P. Blondiaux, "Cinquante années d'administration française à Melfi (1903-1952)" (unpublished mémoire, *Centre de hautes études administratives sur l'Afrique et l'Asie modernes*, 1953), pp. 19-20.
71. Cosnier, *L'Ouest africain français*, viii.
72. Information kindly provided by Professor Brian Weinstein, Howard University.
73. Appendix III.
74. Liebenow, "The Dilemmas of Development: Makonde."
75. André Davesne, *Croquis de brousse* (Paris, 1946), p. 334.
76. 1C 1030, AAOF.
77. René Grivot, "Problèmes d'Afrique noire: Le Beau métier d'administrateur colonial; Essai de psychologie du commandement en brousse" (mimeographed copy, n.d.), p. 11.
78. Jacques Kuoh Moukouri, *Doigts noirs: Je fus écrivain-interprète au Cameroun* (Montreal, 1963), pp. 28-30. I am grateful to Mrs. Dorothy White for bringing this passage to my attention.
79. Documents relating to these proposals in 17G 43, AAOF.
80. *J.o. de la Fédération nationale des associations et syndicats de fonctionnaires et agents coloniaux* XV (February 3, 1933).
81. Gourou, "Gallieni," p. 105.
82. XXX (pseud.), *Réalités coloniales* (Paris, 1934), p. 232.
83. Geoffrey Gorer, *Africa Dances* (London, 1935), p. 117.
84. Letter, Edward Guyenga to minister of colonies; Balang, January 30, 1909; in Dahomey, carton 7, file 8, ANSOM.
85. Brévié's marginal notation in pencil on an article on this problem in *Le Courrier colonial* (September 27, 1935), 18G 98, AAOF.
86. Delavignette, "Connaissances des mentalités indigènes en AOF," p. 561.
87. Jean Claude Froelich, "De quelques anciens élèves de l'Ecole qui se sont illustrés dans les sciences humaines," *Latitudes* (1963), p. 10.
88. Robert Delavignette, "Colo et chercheur," *Latitudes* (1963), p. 8.
89. J. C. Froelich, "Delavignette et le Service africain," *Revue française d'histoire d'outre-mer* LIV (1967), 50.
90. The Vichy regime also abrogated this decree.
91. Gorer, *Africa Dances*, p. 117.
92. W. R. Crocker, *On Governing Colonies* (London, 1947), p. 76.
93. Circular, October 27, 1937; unnumbered file, AAOF.
94. Delavignette, "Connaissances des mentalités indigènes en AOF," p. 561.
95. Cosnier, *L'Ouest africain français*, p. 163.
96. Circular, May 1, 1918, *J.o. AOF*; quoted in Dov Ronen, "Political Development

in a West African Country: The Case of Dahomey" (unpublished Ph.D. dissertation, Indiana University, 1969), p. 107. I wish to thank Dr. Ronen for allowing me to read his study.
97. Sarraut, *La mise en valeur,* pp. 104-105.
98. *Ibid.,* p. 115.
99. *Ibid.,* pp. 117-120.
100. Project of May 30, 1922; reprinted in *Congrès colonial national, Congrès de l'organisation coloniale, comptes rendus et rapports,* vol. I (Marseilles, 1923), 145.
101. *Ibid.,* p. 166.
102. Olivier, *Six ans de politique sociale à Madagascar,* p. 226.
103. Hugot, *Le Tchad,* p. 58.
104. "Rapports d'ensemble, AOF, 1931, section B," p. 27; 2G 31/18, AAOF.
105. For his defense, see letter, governor-general to minister of colonies; Dakar, June 13, 1934; 18G 66 (17), AAOF.
106. Austen, *Northwest Tanzania,* p. 154.
107. Circular of August 23, 1932; reprinted in *Circulaires de M. le Gouverneur général J. Brévié sur la politique indigène et l'administration indigène en Afrique occidentale française* (Gorée, 1935), pp. 22-23.
108. Letter, de Coppet to governor-general; Porto Novo, March 26, 1934; quoted in "AOF, Rapport politique annuel, 1934," 2G 34/12, AAOF. In the nineteenth century the inhabitants of four communes in Senegal—Gorée, Dakar, Saint Louis, and Rufisque—had been made citizens.
109. "AOF, Rapport politique annuel, 1934."
110. Circular, June 10, 1930, *Bulletin officiel des colonies* (Paris, 1930), pp. 907-910.
111. Governor-general to minister of colonies, April 3, 1939; quoted in J. S. Spiegler, "Aspects of Nationalist Thought," p. 273.
112. Camille Guy, "La Politique coloniale de la France," in Henri Brenier *et al., La Politique coloniale de la France* (Paris, 1924), p. 267.
113. Manuela Semidei, "De l'Empire à la décolonisation, à travers les manuels scolaires français," *Revue française de science politique* XVI (February 1966), 71.
114. Copy of this report in 17G 59, AAOF. Among the members of the council were prominent experts on colonial law such as Arthur Girault and Paul Dislère, and the director of political affairs of the ministry of colonies, André Duchêne.
115. Quoted in Deschamps, "La France d'outre-mer," p. 57.
116. Henri Labouret, "L'Accession des indigènes à la cityoenneté française," *Afrique française* (1935), p. 721; quoted in Rudolf von Albertini, *Dekolonisation* (Cologne, 1966), pp. 392-393.
117. Deschamps, "La France d'outre-mer," p. 69.
118. XXX, *Réalités coloniales,* pp. 112-114.
119. *Ibid.,* p. 116.
120. Copy of governors-general's conference, in 17G 86, AAOF.
121. Decree, April 26, 1938, *Bulletin officiel des colonies* LII (1938), p. 423.
122. Delavignette, *Christianity and Colonialism,* p. 33.
123. Lucien Hiquily, *La Politique impériale et la conférence coloniale de 1935* (Lyon, 1937), p. 34.
124. All French officials serving overseas were paid a "basic salary" plus a "colonial supplement" which was 70-100 percent of the basic salary. The Africans would have been paid only the basic salary.
125. Naturalized Africans had, of course, always been able to enter the service.
126. Olivier, *Six ans de politique sociale à Madagascar,* pp. 269-270.
127. *Ibid.*
128. "Procès verbal de la séance inaugurale, tenue jeudi 8 juillet [1937] à 15 heures au ministère des colonies," 7G 252, AAOF.

129. *Ibid.*; the last part of the phrase, beginning with the words "take care" was underlined by de Coppet in his copy of the speech. Was the liberal official comforted or irritated by Moutet's cautiousness?
130. Interview with Robert Delavignette; Paris, April 16, 1966.
131. Deschamps, "La France d'outre-mer," p. 58.
132. Inspection tour by Inspector-General Bourgeois-Gavardin in Dahomey, 1940-1941; 17G 111, AAOF. The report written on administration in the Sudan came to similar conclusions.
133. *Race nègre* (February 1932); quoted in Spiegler, "Aspects of Nationalist Thought," p. 230.
134. *La Presse Porto Novienne*, July 1933; quoted in Ronen, "Political Development in a West African Country," p. 127.
135. *Le Phare du Dahomey*, August 1933, quoted in Ronen, "Political Development in a West African Country," p. 137.
136. Quoted in Spiegler, "Aspects of National Thought," p. 69.
137. *Circulaire no. 517c, L'Esprit nouveau, 11 juillet 1941* (Dakar, 1941), p. 1.
138. Gifford, "Indirect Rule," pp. 351-391.
139. Lord Hailey, *Native Administration and Political Development in British Tropical Africa* (London, 1942), p. 22; quoted in Austen, *Northwest Tanzania*, pp. 214-215.
140. Froelich, "Delavignette et le Service africain," p. 45.
141. Henri Baudet, *Paradise on Earth*, trans. by Elizabeth Wentholt (New Haven, Conn., 1965).
142. Delavignette, *Freedom and Authority*, pp. 147-148.
143. P. O. Lapie, *My Travels through Chad*, trans. by Leslie Bull (London, 1943), pp. 186, 188.

Chapter VII: The ENFOM, 1940-1959

1. Jumper, "The Recruitment and Training of Civil Administrators," p. 141.
2. Robert Delavignette, "La Formation professionnelle de l'administrateur," in Maunier *et al., L'Empire français et ses ressources*, p. 29.
3. *Ibid.*, p. 30. Delavignette's italics.
4. Decree, August 6, 1941, *Bulletin officiel des Colonies* LV (Paris, 1941), 271-272. (Henceforth this publication will be cited as *BOC*.)
5. *Arrêté*, February 5, 1944, *BOC* LVIII (Paris, 1944), pt. I, 49.
6. Robert Delavignette, quoted in *Colo* 46 (January 1946), 6; Jumper, "The Recruitment and Training of Civil Administrators," p. 142.
7. Jumper, "The Recruitment and Training of Civil Administrators," p. 142.
8. His stepson Jean Mairey played an important part in the liberation of Dijon and was after the war a *Commissaire de la République*; Delavignette's wife also played a role in the resistance.
9. Interview with Robert Delavignette; Montbard, September 9, 1965.
10. Answers to questionnaire.
11. Ministère des colonies, Agence économique des colonies, *Vous voulez aller aux colonies* (Paris, 1943).
12. Jumper, "The Recruitment and Training of Civil Administrators," p. 142.
13. In 1950, there were still 75 officials in the Corps who had gained entrance to it as a result of their resistance activities. Their educational level was as follows: 18 percent had less than secondary school education, 42 percent had only a secondary education, 18 percent had a *licence* in law, 9 percent had a *licence* in letters, 4 percent had a doctorate in law, 3 percent had diplomas from Saint Cyr, 4 percent had degrees from the *Institut d'étude politique*, 1 percent were doctors in medicine, and 1 percent had a *licence* in science.
14. Speech by Robert Delavignette, March 15, 1945; quoted in *L'Observatoire colonial* (March-April 1945), p. 12.

Notes to pages 147-154

15. Anon., *Centre de hautes études administratives sur l'Afrique et l'Asie modernes* (Paris, 1959); I wish to thank M. J. C. Froelich, director of curriculum at CHEAM, for information about the center in interviews with him in Paris, October 1965.
16. A motto frequently used by Delavignette; for instance, see his "L'Administrateur territorial en Afrique noire française," *Revue des travaux de l'Académie des sciences morales et politiques* CXVIII (1965), 88.
17. Ministère des colonies, *Bulletin hebdomadaire d'information*, November 27, 1944.
18. Mus was one of the few Frenchmen whom Ho Chi Minh had trusted and through whom he had negotiated with the French government. In 1954 Mus expressed his liberal views on overseas policy in his book, *Le Destin de l'Union Française, de l'Indochine à l'Afrique* (Paris, 1954). Mus is currently professor of Asian studies at Yale University and a leading authority on Vietnam in the United States.
19. Interviews with a number of former officials of the ENFOM and with some of Mus's former students.
20. Quoted in P. Laubriet, "A la conquête des coeurs, par l'Ecole nationale de la France d'outre-mer," *Mer-Outre-Mer* I (June-July 1947), 9.
21. This essay is now available in the library of the *Institut international d'administration publique*, Paris.
22. Interview with former administrator; Paris, October 18, 1965.
23. Decree of October 30, 1950, in *J.o.: Lois et décrets* (Paris, 1950), pp. 11189-11198, amended and corrected in *J.o.: Lois et décrets* (Paris, 1950), p. 12563. On the reforms of 1950, see Jumper, "The Recruitment and Training of Civil Administrators," pp. 180-181; Paul Bouteille, 'L'Ecole nationale de la France d'outre-mer," *Revue économique française* LXVIII (May 1955), 2-5; Pierre Hugot, "L'Ecole nationale de la France d'outre-mer," *La Nouvelle revue française d'outre-mer* IL (July 1957), 391-394.
24. Quoted in Jumper, "The Recruitment and Training of Civil Administrators," p. 180.
25. These essays varied in quality, but some of them are still a useful source of information on French Africa. The essays are stored in the library of the *Institut international d'administration publique*, Paris.
26. Jumper, "The Recruitment and Training of Civil Administrators," p. 183.
27. *Ibid.*, pp. 177-178.
28. *Ibid.*, p. 164, fn. 4.
29. Paul Mus, "La Formation des cadres administratifs d'outre-mer: ENFOM ou ENA?" *La Revue administrative* 2 (March-April 1948), pp. 16-23; Jumper, "The Recruitment and Training of Civil Administrators," pp. 155-157.
30. Jumper, "The Recruitment and Training of Civil Administrators," pp. 232-233.
31. Source: *Ibid.*, pp. 165, 195. Note that the figures for the ENFOM refer to all students entering the school, not only to those in the administrative section.
32. Ministère de la France d'outre-mer, *ENFOM* (Paris, 1956), pp. 37-40.
33. *Ibid.*, p. 56.
34. Anon., "Africanisation," *Le Bleu d'outre-mer* (April 1956).
35. Anon., "Suggestions," *Le Bleu d'outre-mer* (April 1956).
36. Among those signing the manifesto were 29 out of 34 students in their first year of studies, 24 out of 29 students in their second year of studies, and 18 out of the 34 students in their third year.
37. Quoted in *Le Monde* XIII (February 12-13, 1956), p. 2.
38. Interviews with former staff members of the ENFOM, and with one of the sponsors of the manifesto, Jean Bugnicourt; Dakar, April 9, 1966.
39. The definite break with traditional overseas policy inherent in the spirit of the manifesto was also reflected in the actions of the Socialist student movement which that year was expelled from the Socialist Party after inviting Algerian

Notes to pages 155-166

FLN representatives to a conference on decolonization held on the Côte d'Azur.
40. Interview with Jean Bugnicourt; Dakar, April 9, 1966.
41. In December of that year the student newspaper of the ENFOM reprinted strongly worded anticolonial extracts from Jacques Rabemananjara, *Témoignage malgache et colonialisme* (Paris, 1956), in *Bleu d'outre-mer* (December 1956).
42. Hubert Deschamps, "Les Assemblées locales dans les territoires d'outre-mer," *Politique étrangère* XIX (August-October 1954), 427-436.
43. Anon., "Africanisation," *Le Bleu d'outre-mer* (April 1956).
44. See Chapter VIII for discussion of the Defferre laws.
45. The decrees gave increased access to the populations of all the overseas territories; localization, rather than Africanization, would be a more apt term. On the other hand, most of the overseas territories were African; the rest were small and insignificant areas in the Pacific such as New Caledonia or Tahiti.
46. Delavignette, "L'Administrateur en Afrique noire française," p. 96.
47. Among these the single largest contingent of students came from Madagascar with 174 students; the second largest number came from Congo, Leopoldville, with 100 students. The rest came from the French successor states, with the exception of one student from Nigeria. Anon., "L'Institut de hautes études d'outre-mer à l'honneur," *Marchés tropicaux et méditerranéens* XIX (February 16, 1963), 313.
48. In 1966 the administration removed the Buddhas thinking that their presence might hurt some students' sensibilities.

Chapter VIII: The Corps in an Era of Change

1. Albert Tevoedjre, *L'Afrique révoltée* (Paris, 1958), p. 33; quoted in Claude Wauthier, *L'Afrique des africains* (Paris, 1964), p. 119.
2. Between 1933 and 1946, Upper Volta, because of economy measures, was administered by an "administrateur supérieur" instead of a governor.
3. For the entire story of his resistance activities, see Emile Louveau, *Au bagne entre les griffes de Vichy et de la milice* (Bamako, 1947).
4. Suret-Canale, *Afrique noire, occidentale et centrale*, p. 570.
5. Jacques Soustelle, *Envers et contre tout* (Paris, 1947), I, 172.
6. Quoted in Hubert Deschamps, *Méthodes et doctrines coloniales de la France du XIVe. siècle à nos jours* (Paris, 1953), p. 177.
7. Suret-Canale, *Afrique noire, occidentale et centrale*, p. 570.
8. See, for instance, circular of Governor-General Boisson to his governors, June 26, 1941; in 17G 119, AAOF.
9. *Circulaire no. 517c, L'esprit nouveau, 11 juillet 1941*, p. 1.
10. 1C 1047, 1C 1095, 1C 1032, AAOF.
11. Meeting of June 17, 1942, in *Comptes rendus de l'Académie des sciences coloniales* (1942), p. 408.
12. *Ibid.*
13. Meeting of May 1942, in *ibid.*, pp. 307-309.
14. Robert W. July, *The Origins of Modern African Thought* (New York, 1967), p. 237.
15. Félix Eboué, *La Nouvelle politique indigène pour l'Afrique équatoriale française* (Brazzaville, 1941), p. 15.
16. *Ibid.*, pp. 24-25.
17. Von Albertini, *Dekolonisation*, p. 418.
18. Charles de Gaulle, *Mémoires de guerre*, vol. II (Paris, 1956), pp. 223-225.
19. "Programme de la conférence inpériale de Brazzaville, rapport préliminaire" (mimeographed copy, undated).
20. *Ibid.*

21. De Gaulle, *Mémoires de guerre,* II, 478.
22. It has been argued that the conference reflected the opinions of the younger members of the colonial service. This point is made, for instance, by Kenneth Robinson, "The Public Law of Overseas France since the War," *Journal of Comparative Legislation* 32 (1952), 42. Most of the delegates, however, were older officials. One could make a stronger point in arguing that the recommendations of the conference closely reflected those of Commissioner of Colonies René Pleven.
23. Quoted in Winston S. Churchill, *The Second World War,* vol. III (Boston, 1950), p. 443.
24. Ministère des colonies, *Conférence africaine française–Brazzaville* (Paris, 1945), p. 22.
25. *Ibid.,* p. 32.
26. *Ibid.,* p. 39.
27. *Ibid.*
28. *Ibid.,* p. 37.
29. *Ibid.,* p. 61.
30. Anon., "L'Epuration," *Défense de l'occident* (January-February 1957), pp. 78-85.
31. In 1943-1944 the Gaullist governor-general of AOF recommended the promotion of six out of thirty-six officials whom he considered to have been "politically unreliable."
32. Peter Novick, *The Resistance versus Vichy: The Purge of Collaborators in Liberated France* (New York, 1968), p. 90. The ministry of foreign affairs, for instance, was hardly purged, keeping most of its former officials. The ministry of interior and the prefectoral corps seem to have been among the few organizations which were purged. See Raymond Aron, "Social Structure and the Ruling Class," *British Journal of Sociology* I, no. 2 (1950), 127.
33. The designation "territory" was given to all the areas formerly dependent upon the ministry of colonies, except for the "old colonies" which had become departments, and the mandated areas and Indochina.
34. Debate, August 27, 1946, *J.o., Assemblée nationale: Débats* (Paris, 1946), p. 334.
35. Herbert Luethy, "La République continue," *Preuves* 89 (July 1958), 14.
36. Robert Delavignette, "L'Union Française à l'échelle du monde, à la mesure de l'homme," *Espoir* (July 8, 1945); quoted in Ministère des colonies, *Bulletin hebdomadaire d'information* (September 17, 1945), p. 22.
37. Answer to 1965 questionnaire.
38. Anon., "Faillite de la colonisation? " *Colo* (December 1947), p. 7.
39. All French political groups favored the continuation of close bonds between France and her overseas territories. Only the Communist Party at times was sympathetic to independence movements.
40. Ministère de la France d'outre-mer, *Bulletin d'information* (September 8, 1947), annex, p. 5.
41. Marius Moutet, "The French Colonial Empire," in *General Directory of Exportation and of the World Commercial Fairs* (Paris, 1948), p. 186.
42. There had always been an overseas magistrature, but before the war it had served primarily in courts dealing with French civil law.
43. Letter to author; Paris, October 12, 1965.
44. Answers to questionnaire. For a bemused description of a young overseas judge's efforts to put his ideals into action, see Théophile Crouzat, *Azizah de Niamkoko* (Paris, 1959).
45. Maurice Méker, "Cinq années d'évolution d'un cercle soudanais, Bougouni," *Colo* LII (April 1952), 16.
46. *Ibid.,* pp. 16-21.
47. Africanus (pseud.), *L'Afrique noire devant l'indépendance* (Paris, 1958), p. 67.

48. Ruth Schachter Morgenthau, *Political Parties in French-Speaking West Africa* (New York, 1965), p. 123. A French legal expert wrote in 1959: "The administrator...cannot afford to contradict the elected representative of his region; sometimes he gets on so well with him that if the elected representative changes, then the administrator also has to be changed." François Luchaire, "Les Grandes tendances de l'Afrique noire," *Revue française de science politique* IX, no. 3 (September 1959), 592.
49. Circular, April 14, 1949, *Bulletin officiel de la France d'outre-mer* (1949).
50. Morgenthau, *Political Parties in French-Speaking West Africa*, p. 203.
51. Interview; Paris, October 18, 1965.
52. *Ibid.*
53. Circular, April 14, 1949, *loc. cit.*
54. Raymond Gauthereau, *Passage du feu* (Paris, 1958), p. 69.
55. De Kat Angelino, *Colonial Policy*, I, 507.
56. *Ibid.*, I, 508.
57. Answer to questionnaire.
58. Answer to questionnaire. Henri Saurin, inspector-general in the Corps of Overseas Inspectors, reflected the opinion of some of the older members of the colonial administration when in 1948 he complained that it was absurd to grant "French citizenship to the peasant of the Red River or of the Congo." The seating of "deputies of all colors in our National Assembly" he found to be "a parody of the democratic regime [which] tends to do nothing but disorganize [and] to deliver the working masses into the hands of bad chiefs." Speech to *Académie des sciences coloniales*, meeting January 16, 1948; in *Comptes rendus de l'Académie des sciences coloniales* (1948), p. 4.
59. Answers to questionnaire.
60. Mimeographed memorandum by the secretary-general of AOF, Dakar, 1945, AAOF.
61. *Ibid.*
62. Circular, May 1946, reprinted in Ministère des colonies, *Bulletin d'Information* (June 17, 1946).
63. Crozier, *The Bureaucratic Phenomenon*, pp. 195-199.
64. Anon., "L'Avenir du corps des administrateurs de la France d'outre-mer," *Latitudes* 2 (1957), 21.
65. Quoted in Paul Alduy, *L'Union Française* (Paris, 1948), p. 66.
66. Interview with administrators who had served in Chad and Sudan; Paris, October 18, 1965. In Guinea, both the *indigénat* code and forced labor seem to have continued in some regions. Suret-Canale, "La Fin de la chefferie en Guinée," pp. 482-483.
67. Jacques Le Cornec, *Histoire politique du Tchad de 1900 à 1962* (Paris, 1963), p. 69.
68. Answer to questionnaire in reference to the Defferre decrees.
69. These men played the role which Crozier has called "authoritarian reform figures." Like the castes of higher civil servants making up the *grands corps*, the political appointees overseas tended to "minimize the authoritarian aspects of their own role by their impartiality and the prestige they enjoy because of their elite situation." Crozier, *The Bureaucratic Phenomenon*, pp. 197-198.
70. *Discours prononcé par le haut commissaire de la République Française devant le grand conseil de l'AOF à l'ouverture de la session; 3 septembre 1949* (Dakar, 1949), pp. 5-6.
71. In 1944 in Senegal 12 out of 37 administrators occupied desk jobs, in Mauritania 3 out of 13, in Niger 6 out of 24, in Sudan 11 out of 45. In 1950 the proportions were quite similar; in Dahomey, for instance, 12 out of 41 administrators were in desk posts.
72. Méker, "Cinq années d'évolution," p. 16.
73. M. Hervé, "Le District de Kouango," unpublished mémoire, *Centre de hautes*

etudes administratives sur l'Afrique et l'Asie modernes (1950), p. 66.
74. Circular, April 14, 1949, *loc. cit.*, p. 313.
75. Ministère des colonies, *Conférence africaine française*, p. 83.
76. Speech by Laurentie, June 4, 1945; reprinted in Ministère des colonies, *Bulletin hebdomadaire d'information* (June 11, 1945), pp. 7-8.
77. Pierre Alexandre, "L'Organisation politique des Kotokoli du Nord Togo," *Cahiers d'études africaines* VI (1963), 269, fn. 3.
78. P. Garreau, "Evolution administrative d'un cercle voltaïque" (unpublished mémoire, *Centre de hautes études administratives sur l'Afrique et l'Asie modèrnes*, 1956, p. 12.
79. Territoire de la Guinée française, *Conférence des commandants de cercles Conakry, 25, 26, et 27 juillet 1957* (Conakry, 1957), p. 23.
80. *Ibid.*, p. 9.
81. Quoted in Ministère des colonies, *Bulletin d'information* (August 26, 1946), p. 7.
82. Quoted in Ministère de la France d'outre-mer, *Bulletin d'information* (October 1950), p. 3.
83. François Mitterrand, *Présence française et abandon* (Paris, 1957), pp. 186-187.
84. *Ibid.*, p. 199.
85. Answer to questionnaire.
86. Speech, February 1957, quoted in Pierre Gentil, "Le Tchad: Décolonisation et indépendance," *Comptes rendus, Académie des sciences d'outre-mer, séances des 3 et 17 janvier 1969* XXIX (January 1969), p. 2.
87. A good example of this type was Pierre Gentil, who as administrator in Indochina had written a critical account of French rule; see his *Sursaut de l'Asie, remous du Mékong* (Paris, 1951). Once in Africa, he was to favor reform. In the answers to the questionnaire a larger proportion of administrators with former service in Indochina indicated support of the reforms of 1946 and of 1956-1957 than those who had served only in Africa.
88. *Chroniques d'outre-mer* (May 1955), p. 37.
89. Quoted in Ministère de la France d'outre-mer, "Pour un meilleur destin dan les territoires d'outre-mer, bilan d'un gouvernement, février 1955-janvier 1956" (Paris, 1956), p. 4.
90. *Ibid.*, p. 7.
91. *Ibid.*, p. 19.
92. Speech, November 10, 1955; in *Chroniques d'outre-mer* (December 1955), p. 24.
93. *Ibid.*, p. 25.
94. "It is beyond doubt that the parliament violated the constitution," writes one of the foremost French legal experts, P. F. Gonidec, *Droit d'outre-mer* I, 466.
95. *Ibid.*, I, 472-473.
96. Interview, Paris, October 19, 1965, with four former administrators who in 1956 had been in such diverse areas as Chad, Sudan, Dahomey, and Senegal.
97. Georges Rey, "Réformes en Afrique noire," *Encyclopédie mensuelle d'outre-mer* 78 (February 1957), p. 49.
98. Jean Coste, "Problèmes et perspectives de l'administration du Sénégal" (unpublished dissertation, Université de Bordeaux, Faculté de droit et des sciences économiques, 1965), p. 68.
99. Gentil, "Le Tchad," p. 6.
100. Pierre Paraf, *L'Ascension des peuples noirs* (Paris, 1958), pp. 44-45.
101. *Ibid.*
102. Anon., "L'Africanisation des cadres en Côte d'Ivoire," *Encyclopédie mensuelle d'outre-mer* 70 (June 1956), p. 250.
103. Territoire de la Guinée française, *Conférence des commandants*, p. 74.
104. Robert Cornevin in speech to *Académie des sciences d'outre-mer*, meeting February 15, 1957, in *Comptes rendus de l'Académie des sciences d'outre-mer*

(1957), p. 69.
105. Information provided by Professor David Muffett, a former British official in Northern Nigeria; Bloomington, Indiana, December 13, 1967.
106. Quoted in Michael Crowder, "Independence as a Goal in French West African Politics, 1944-1960," in William H. Lewis, ed., *French-Speaking Africa* (New York, 1965), p. 29.
107. Answer to questionnaire.
108. Crowder, "Independence as a Goal," pp. 15-41.
109. Speech, January 29, 1957; *J.o., Assemblée nationale* (Paris, 1957), p. 373.
110. François Mitterrand, *Présence française et abandon*.
111. Independence within the Community was not permitted by the Constitution, but de Gaulle conveniently ignored it.
112. Visiting the ministry of overseas France in the summer of 1958, Professor John H. Morrow discovered that "it was clear that any idea of independence in the foreseeable future was far from the minds of those in charge." John H. Morrow, *First American Ambassador to Guinea* (New Brunswick, N.J., 1968), p. xi.
113. Answer to questionnaire.
114. The works of disillusioned leftists, such as that of René Dumont, *L'Afrique noire est mal partie* (Paris, 1962), can also lead to such conclusions.
115. Answer to questionnaire.
116. Robert Cornevin claims that the bush administrators remained quite ignorant of the political evolution of the territories. "They still thought the situation could be saved." Interview with Robert Cornevin; Paris, June 1, 1965.

Chapter IX: The Legacy

1. Speech by Ibrahima Sow, March 19, 1960; *Sénégal magazine* 3-4 (April-May 1960).
2. Speech by Ibrahima Sar, minister of labor and public works, March 19, 1960; *ibid*.
3. Theresa Hayter, *French Aid* (London, 1966), pp. 160-161.
4. Interview with former administrator; October 18, 1965.
5. A short comparison of the process of Africanization, or rather "localization," of the civil services in the former colonies and of the role of the colonial administrations after independence may be found in Richard Symonds, *The British and Their Successors* (London, 1966).
6. Among those who have expressed their admiration for the French method of granting administrative aid after independence are Richard Symonds, a former British official in India (*ibid.*, pp. 216-217), and a high Ghanian civil servant, A. L. Adu (*The Civil Service in Africa* [London, 1965], p. 85).
7. Adding the number of former administrators who were not members of the alumni association, one would reach a figure of approximately 220 former administrators serving overseas under the French technical assistance program. The alumni association listed the distribution of its members in the technical assistance program as follows: 16 officials were in the Cameroons, 12 in the Central African Republic, 4 in the Congo (Brazzaville), 34 in the Ivory Coast, 7 in Dahomey, 7 in Upper Volta, 40 in Madagascar, 13 in Niger, 14 in Senegal, 12 in Chad, and 5 in Togo.
8. Charles F. Darlington and Alice B. Darlington, *African Betrayal* (New York, 1968), p. 40.
9. François Zucarelli, "Du canton à l'arrondissement sénégalais" (unpublished mémoire for the Diplôme d'études supérieures de droit public, Dakar, 1965), pp. 56-57. He examined 73 out of 86 files belonging to *chefs d'arrondissements* and found that only 37 out of 73 belonged to chiefs who had formerly been *chefs de cantons*.

10. "Communication du ministère de l'intérieur sur la réforme administrative" (St. Louis, 1960), p. 8.
11. For the development of local government in the French-speaking world, see the special issue of *Revue juridique et politique de l'indépendance et coopération* XXII (April-June 1968). A summary of the African experience is given by Pierre Lampué, "Le Régime municipal dans les états francophones," *ibid.*, pp. 463-484.
12. Ladipo Adamoleku, "Politics and Administration in West Africa: The Guinean Model," *Journal of Administration Overseas,* VIIII (October 1969), 238.
13. Interview, February 1966.
14. See, for instance, the thoughtful discussion by Robert Delavignette, "L'Administrateur territorial en Afrique noire française," *Revue des travaux de l'Académie des sciences morales et politiques* XCVIII (1965), 83-96.
15. Numerous interviewees and answers to the questionnaire.
16. James Coleman, "The Legal Aspects of Staff Problems in Tropical and Sub-tropical Countries," working paper for the 32nd study session of the International Institute of Differing Civilizations, Munich, 1960, General Report, I, p. 15. See also Fred G. Burke, "Public Administration in Africa: The Legacy of Inherited Colonial Institutions," *Journal of Comparative Administration* I (November 1969), 345-378.
17. To some French-speaking Africans the political neutrality of the administration seems to be one of the hallmarks of their English-speaking neighbors. The governor of the Casamance region visited Nigeria in 1965. He found the political neutrality of the administration to be one of the most striking features of Nigerian administration. Interview, Ziguinchor, February 1966.
18. For a general survey of these schools see A. Bernard, "Les écoles nationales d'administration en Afrique noire," *Coopération et développement,* no. 2 (August 1964), pp. 28-35. For a pessimistic evaluation of the school in Senegal, which is probably one of the best in French-speaking Africa, see Philippe Georges, "L'Ecole nationale d'administration du Sénégal," *Penant* LXXIV (1964), 523-534. For evaluations of other national schools of administration see A. H. Marchand, "La Formation des cadres supérieurs de l'administration ivoirienne," *Penant* LXXIX (April-June 1969), 171-208; (July-September 1969), 333-361; (October-December 1969), 443-529; Paul Torrès, "La Formation des cadres de l'administration régionale en Afrique centrale," *International Review of Administrative Sciences* XXXV, no. 4 (1969), 302-314.
19. Anon., "Sénégal, du contrôle des administrations," *Afrique nouvelle* (November 9-16, 1967).
20. *Ibid.*
21. Michel Legris, "Esquisses contrafricaines," *Le Monde* XXIII (January 4, 1966), 4.
22. Gilbert Comte, "Les Difficultés de l'Afrique noire. Un example: Le Niger," *Europe-France-Outre-mer* (May 1964), quoted in Pierre de Briey, "The Administrations of the New States," *Civilisations* XIV (1964), 7.
23. François Zucarelli, "Le Département sénégalais," *Revue juridique et politique d'indépendance et coopération* XXII (July-September 1968), 873, fn. 35.
24. This point is argued rather persuasively by Jean Merlo, "Les Fonctionnaires africains et le mécontentement des masses rurales," *Le Mois en Afrique* 2 (February 1966), 60-68.
25. A free car, free housing, and two paid servants also added to the opulence of the regional administrators.
26. Anon., "Salaires, soldes et traitements au Sénégal," *Afrique documents* no. 104 (1969), 249.
27. *Agence France presse, spécial outre-mer,* February 23, 1965.
28. République du Sénégal, Ministère du plan et du développement, *Carte pour servir à l'aménagement du territoire* (Dakar, 1965), p. 35.

29. Zucarelli, "Le Département sénégalais," p. 872, fn. 3.
30. Delavignette, "L'Administrateur territorial en Afrique noire française," p. 96.
31. J. P. N'Diaye, *Enquête sur les étudiants noirs* (Paris, 1962), p. 231.
32. N'Diaye (*ibid.*, p. 232) found that the motives for entering public service could be divided into the following categories:

1.	To serve the State, Africa, my people	52.6 percent
2.	Gratitude toward my people, because I am a scholarship student	16.5 percent
3.	By vocation, choice of studies	10.3 percent
4.	Socialist ideal for the country	8.5 percent
5.	Security	5.5 percent
6.	Other	3.8 percent
7.	No explanation	2.8 percent

33. Interview with Pierre Alexandre; Paris, October 15, 1965.
34. N'Diaye, *Enquête sur les étudiants noirs*, p. 200.
35. In 1965 Congo, Leopoldville, a Belgian successor state, also gained admission to the organization.
36. Quoted in Robert Delavignette, "Tiers monde, tiers état?" *La Revue de Paris* LXXII (December 1965), 86.
37. For a review of the "francophone" movement see Jean Louis Goelan, "L'Afrique d'expression française et la francophonie," *Penant*, LXXIX (January-March 1969), 1-32; (April-June 1969), 209-242.
38. Hayter, *French Aid*, p. 9.
39. Quoted in *ibid.*, pp. 10-11. Foreign Minister Couve de Murville told the French National Assembly that "the mission of France is to teach our language and make known our culture." *J.o. Assemblée nationale* (November 4, 1966), p. 4191.
40. Delavignette, "Tiers monde, tiers état?" p. 90.
41. M. Dannaud in a speech to the *Académie des sciences morales et politiques*, March 1965, quoted by Delavignette in *ibid.*
42. Charles de Gaulle, *Mémoires d'espoir*, vol. I (Paris, 1970), 43.
43. Eighty-two percent answered negatively. N'Diaye, *Enquête sur les étudiants noirs*, p. 291.
44. *Ibid.*, pp. 295, 297.
45. Of the students interviewed 87 percent desired continued economic, political, and cultural ties. In cultural affairs, an even higher proportion, 95 percent, desired continued relations. *Ibid.*, pp. 303-304.
46. Delavignette, "Tiers monde, tiers état?" pp. 88-89.
47. Since 1959, the successor states have substantially increased their own tax receipts. Miss Hayter gives the following figures for the increase in tax receipts between 1959 and 1965: for the Ivory Coast 34 percent, Upper Volta 130 percent, Mali 87 percent, Congo 102 percent, Gabon 87 percent, Senegal 59 percent, Central African Republic 75 percent, Chad 80 percent, Mauritania 190 percent. Hayter, *French Aid*, p. 162.

Bibliography

Note on Archives

Archives de l'Afrique occidentale française, Dakar. Correspondence between governor-general and governors and vice versa on administrative and personnel problems, 1904-1940. Administrators' personnel files (series 1C), 1887-1940.

Archives de l'Ecole nationale de la France d'outre-mer. Located at the present *Institut international de l'administration publique,* Paris. Includes essays of former ENFOM students, scrapbook recording the institution's history, mimeographed reports of the school's activities and the only full-run of the school's paper. 1889-1959.

Archives nationales, Senegal, Dakar. Correspondence regarding administrative and personnel problems. This includes letters to Paris and correspondence between regional administrators and the governor of Senegal, 1840-1940.

Archives nationales, France, Section outre-mer. (Archives of the former ministry of colonies.) Correspondence with governors-general and governors on administrative and personnel problems, 1840-1920. Administrators' personnel files (series EE II), 1887-1914.

Memoirs and Secondary Sources

Adloff, Richard. *West Africa: The French-Speaking Nations, Yesterday and Today.* New York, 1964.

Adu, A. L. *The Civil Service in Africa.* London, 1965.

"Africanus." *L'Afrique noire devant l'indépendance.* Paris, 1958.

Albertini, Rudolf von. *Dekolonisation.* Cologne, 1966.

Alduy, Paul. *L'Union Française: Mission de la France.* Paris, 1948.

Ananké, Paul Tisseyre. *L'Assiette au beurre coloniale.* Paris, 1911.

Annet, Armand. *Je suis gouverneur d'outre-mer.* Paris, 1957.

Anon. *A la jeunesse française: L'Appel de la France extérieure.* Paris, n.d.

_____. *Les Carrières coloniales.* Paris, 1946.

_____. *Centre de hautes études administratives sur l'Afrique et l'Asie modernes.* Paris. 1959.

_____. *L'Ecole Coloniale.* Paris, 1906.

——————. *Les Fonctionnaires.* Paris, 1911.

——————. *Les Fonctionnaires des colonies en avant, par un voyageur.* Paris, 1884.

——————. *Guide des carrières: Les Carrières dans le corps des administrateurs coloniaux.* Paris, 1931.

——————. *Marine et colonies, opinion d'un marin, ancien gouverneur des colonies.* Paris, 1886.

——————.*Quatre anciens de Colo.* Paris, 1935.

——————. *Renseignements complets sur toutes les études, toutes les écoles, ainsi que sur toutes les carrières.* Paris, 1930.

——————. *La Vie lucide et passionnée de Joost Van Vollenhoven: Grand administrateur colonial, soldat héroïque.* Lyon, 1942.

Archimbaud, Léon. *La Plus grande France.* Paris, 1928.

Association des anciens élèves de l'ENFOM. *Annuaire, 1964.* Paris, 1964.

——————. *Annuaire, 1967.* Paris, 1967.

Atger, Paul. *La France en Côte d'Ivoire de 1843 à 1893.* Dakar, Senegal, 1962.

Augagneur, Victor. *Erreurs et brutalités coloniales.* Paris, 1927.

Austen, Ralph A. *Northwest Tanzania under German and British Rule.* New Haven, Conn., 1968.

Barot, Dr. *Guide pratique de l'européen dans l'Afrique occidentale.* Paris, 1902.

Bastien, Paul. *Les Carrières coloniales.* Paris, 1904.

Baudet, Henri. *Paradise on Earth.* Trans. by Elizabeth Wentholt. New Haven, Conn., 1965.

Benilan, Jean. *Le Statut des administrateurs des colonies.* Paris, 1932.

Bettencourt, Victor. *Du choix d'une carrière indépendante.* Paris, 1903.

Betts, Raymond F. *Assimilation and Association in French Colonial Theory, 1890-1914.* New York, 1961.

Blancsubé, Jean. *Projet d'organisation d'un ministère des colonies.* Paris, 1883.

Bobichon, Henri. *La Politique indigène.* Paris, 1912.

Bonifacio, Sylvestre. *Souvenirs de Madagascar et de la grande guerre de 1900 à 1929.* Paris, 1931.

Borella, François. *L'Evolution politique et juridique de l'Union Française depuis 1945.* Paris, 1958.

Boutmy, Emile. *Le Recrutement des administrateurs coloniaux.* Paris, 1895.

Brenier, Henri, et al. *La Politique coloniale de la France.* Paris, 1924.

Brévié, Jules. *Islamisme contre naturalisme au Soudan français.* Paris, 1923.

Brook, Ian. *The One-Eyed Man Is King.* New York, 1966.

Brunel, I. M. *Le Général Faidherbe.* Paris, 1890.

Brunschwig, Henri. *L'Avènement de l'Afrique noire.* Paris, 1963.

———. *Mythes et réalités de l'impérialisme colonial français, 1871-1914.* Paris, 1960.

Buell, Raymond L. *The Native Problem in Africa.* New York, 1928. 2 vols.

Canu, A. H. *La Pétaudière coloniale.* Paris, 1894.

Carrère, Frédéric, and Paul Holle. *De la Sénégambie française.* Paris, 1855.

Chailley-Bert, Joseph. *Colonisation de l'Indochine: L'Expérience anglaise.* Paris, 1891.

———. *La Hollande et les fonctionnaires des Indes Néerlandaises.* Paris, 1902.

Challaye, Félicien. *Souvenirs sur la colonisation.* Paris, 1935.

Chastenet, Jacques. *Histoire de la Troisième République.* Paris, 1952-1963. 7 vols.

Churchill, Winston S. *The Second World War.* Boston, 1948-1953. 6 vols.

Clozel, F. J. *Dix ans à la Côte d'Ivoire.* Paris, 1906.

Comité d'initiative des amis de Vollenhoven. *Une Ame de chef: Le Gouverneur général J. Van Vollenhoven.* Paris, 1920.

Comité franco-britannique d'études coloniales. *Les Méthodes d'administration et de gouvernement dans les colonies anglaises et françaises.* Paris, n.d.

Comyn, D. C. E. *Service and Sport in the Sudan.* London, 1911.

Congrès colonial national. *Recueils des délibérations du congrès colonial national, Paris, 1889-1890.* Paris, 1890.

———. *Comptes rendus et rapports.* Vol. I. Marseilles, 1923.

Cosnier, Henri. *L'Ouest africain français: Ses ressources agricoles, son organisation économique.* Paris, 1921.

Crocker, W. R. *On Governing Colonies.* London, 1947.

Cros, Charles. *La Parole est à M. Blaise Diagne: Premier homme d'état africain.* Paris, 1964.

Crowder, Michael. *Senegal: A Study in French Assimilation Policy.* London, 1962.

———. *West Africa under Colonial Rule.* Evanston, Ill., 1968.

Crozier, Michel. *The Bureaucratic Phenomenon.* Chicago, 1964.

Cultru, P. *Histoire du Sénégal du XVe. siècle à 1870.* Paris, 1910.

Darlington, Charles F., and Alice B. Darlington. *African Betrayal.* New York, 1968.

Davesne, André. *Croquis de brousse.* Paris, 1946.

Deherme, Georges. *L'AOF: Action politique, action économique, action sociale.* Paris, 1908.

Delafosse, Maurice. *Broussard, ou les états d'âme d'un colonial.* Paris, 1922.

Delavignette, Robert. *Afrique équatoriale française.* Paris, 1957.

———. *L'Afrique noire française et son destin.* Paris, 1962.

———. *Afrique occidentale française.* Paris, 1931.

———. *Birama.* Paris, 1955.

———. *Christianity and Colonialism.* Trans. by J. R. Forster. New York, 1964.

———. *Freedom and Authority in French West Africa.* London, 1950.

———. *Soudan, Paris, Bourgogne.* Paris, 1935.

———, and Charles André Julien. *Les Constructeurs de la France d'outre-mer.* Paris, 1946.

Demougeot, A. *Notes sur l'organisation politique et administrative du Labé avant et depuis l'occupation française.* Paris, 1944.

Desanti, H. *Du Dahomey au Benin-Niger.* Paris, 1945.

Deschamps, Hubert. *La Fin des empires coloniaux.* Paris, 1959.

———. *The French Union.* Paris, 1956.

———. *Les Méthodes et doctrines coloniales de la France du XVIe. siècle à nos jours.* Paris, 1953.

———, and Paul Chauvet, eds. *Gallieni, pacificateur: Ecrits coloniaux de Gallieni.* Paris, 1949.

Dessarre, Eve. *Quel sera le destin de l'Afrique?* Paris, 1961.

Dislère, Paul. *Notes sur l'organisation des colonies.* Paris, 1888.

Doucet, Robert. *Commentaires sur la colonisation.* Paris, 1926.

Dubois, Marcel, and Auguste Terrier. *Les Colonies françaises: Un Siècle d'expansion coloniale.* Paris, 1902.

Duchêne, Albert. *Histoire des finances coloniales de la France.* Paris, 1938.

———. *La Politique coloniale de la France.* Paris, 1928.

Dumont, René. *L'Afrique noire est mal partie.* Paris, 1962.

Eboué, Félix. *La Nouvelle politique indigène pour l'Afrique équatoriale française.* Brazzaville, 1941.

Elgey, Georgette. *La République des illusions, 1945-1951.* Paris, 1965.

Epting, Karl. *Das Französische Sendungsbewusstsein in 19. und 20. Jahrhundert.* Heidelberg, 1952.

Favrod, Charles Henri. *L'Afrique seule.* Paris, 1961.

Ferrandi, Jean. *L'Officier colonial.* Paris, 1930.

Fonssagrives, Jean. *Notice sur le Dahomey.* Paris, 1900.

Fournier, François. *Aspects politiques du problème des chefferies au Soudan présahelien.* Paris, 1955.

François, Georges. *L'Afrique occidentale française.* Paris, 1907.

———. *Le Guide des carrières coloniales.* Paris, 1908.

———, and H. Mariol. *Législation coloniale.* Paris, 1929.

Gallieni, Joseph. *Gallieni au Tonkin (1892-1896): Par lui-même.* Paris, 1941.

──────────. *Instructions à MM. les commandants de Morondava et de Maintiriano, sur le remaniement des cercles de Morondava et de Maintiriano et l'organisation des protectorats intérieurs de Menabé.* Tananarive, 1904.

──────────. *Lettres de Madagascar, 1896-1905.* Paris, 1928.

Gandolfi, Alain. *L'Administration territoriale en Afrique noire de langue française.* Aix-en-Provence, France, 1959.

Gann, Lewis, and Peter Duignan. *Burden of Empire.* New York, 1967.

──────────, eds. *Colonialism in Africa.* Vol. I. Cambridge, Eng., 1969.

Gaulle, Charles de. *Mémoires de guerre.* Paris, 1954-1959. 3 vols.

──────────. *Mémoires d'espoir.* Vol. I. Paris, 1970.

Geertz, Clifford, ed. *Old Societies and New States: The Quest for Modernity in Asia and Africa.* Glencoe, Ill., 1963.

Gentil, Pierre. *Confins Libyens, Lac Tchad, Fleuve Niger.* Paris, 1946.

──────────. *Sur les sentiers malgaches.* Paris, 1956.

──────────. *Sursaut de l'Asie, remous du Mékong.* Paris, 1951.

Germain, Roger. *La Politique indigène de Bugeaud.* Paris, 1955.

Gide, André. *Travels in the Congo [and] Return from Chad.* Trans. by Dorothy Bussy. New York, 1937.

Girard, Alain. *La Réussite sociale en France.* Paris, 1961.

Girardet, Raoul. *La Société militaire dans la France contemporaine, 1815-1939.* Paris, 1953.

Girault, Arthur. *Principes de colonisation et de législation coloniale.* 3rd ed. Paris, 1907. 3 vols.

Goblot, Edmond. *La Barrière et le niveau: Etude sociologique sur la bourgeoisie française moderne.* Paris, 1925.

Godineau, Henri. *L'Union Française et la disparition du système colonial.* Bordeaux, 1949.

Gonidec, P. F. *Droit d'outre-mer.* Paris, 1959-1960. 2 vols.

Gorer, Geoffrey. *Africa Dances.* London, 1935.

Goujon, Joseph (under pseudonym of René Saint-Clair). *L'Administrateur colonial: Son rôle social et moral.* Niort, France, 1909.

Gournay, Bernard, ed. *L'Administration française: Administrations centrales. Bibliographie.* Paris, 1961.

Gousset, Marcel. *En brousse, AEF.* Paris, 1943.

Grandidier, G., and E. Joucla. *Bibliographie générale des colonies françaises.* Paris, 1937.

Greslé, I. P. *Essai de politique indigène.* Paris, 1919.

Grivot, René. *Réactions dahoméennes.* Paris, 1954.

Grosser, Alfred. *La Politique extérieure de la Ve. République.* Paris, 1965.

——————. *La Quatrième République et sa politique extérieure.* Paris, 1961.

Gueye, Lamine. *Etapes et perspectives de l'Union Française.* Paris, 1955.

Guy, Camille. *L'Afrique occidentale française.* Paris, 1929.

——————. *Itinéraire africain.* Paris, 1966.

Hanna, A. J. *European Rule in Africa.* London, 1961. [Pamphlet of the Historical Association, no. 46.]

Hanotaux, Gabriel and Alfred Martineau, eds. *Histoire des colonies françaises et de l'expansion de la France dans le monde.* Vol. IV. Paris, 1931.

Hardy, Georges. *Ergaste, ou la vocation coloniale.* Paris, 1929.

——————. *Faidherbe.* Paris, 1947.

——————. *Histoire de la colonisation française.* 5th ed. Paris, 1947.

——————. *Histoire sociale de la colonisation française.* Paris, 1953.

——————. *Nos grands problèmes coloniaux.* Paris, 1929.

——————. *La Politique coloniale et le partage de la terre aux XIXe et XXe siècles.* Paris, 1937.

Harmand, Jules. *Colonisation et domination.* Paris, 1910.

Hayter, Theresa. *French Aid.* London, 1966.

Heussler, Robert. *Yesterday's Rulers.* Syracuse, N.Y., 1963.

Hiquily, Lucien. *La Politique impériale et la conférence coloniale de 1935.* Lyon, 1937.

Howe, Susan. *Novels of Empire.* New York, 1940.

Hubert, Lucien. *L'Eveil d'un monde: L'Oeuvre de la France en Afrique occidentale.* Paris, 1909.

Hugonnet, F. *Souvenirs d'un chef de bureau arabe.* Paris, 1858.

Hugot, Pierre. *Le Tchad.* Paris, 1965.

Institut colonial international. *Les Fonctionnaires coloniaux: Documents officiels.* Vol. I. Paris, 1897.

Joseph, Gaston, et al. *L'Ame d'un empire.* Paris, 1944.

Julien, Charles André. *Histoire de l'Algérie contemporaine.* Vol. I. Paris, 1964.

July, Robert W. *The Origins of Modern African Thought.* New York, 1967.

Kalck, Pierre. *Réalités oubanguiennes.* Paris, 1959.

Kanya-Forstner, A. S. *The Conquest of the Western Sudan: A Study in Military Imperialism.* London, 1969.

Kat Angelino, A. D. A. de. *Colonial Policy.* The Hague, 1931. 2 vols.

Klein, Martin A. *Islam and Imperialism in Senegal: Sine-Saloum, 1847-1914.* Stanford, Calif., 1968.

Labouret, Henri. *A la recherche d'une politique indigène dans l'Ouest africain.* Paris, 1931.

——————. *Colonisation, colonialisme, et décolonisation.* Paris, 1952.

Lalumière, Pierre. *L'Inspection des finances.* Paris, 1959.

Lapalud, Maurice. *L'Administrateur colonial à Madagascar.* Paris, 1903.

Lapie, P. O. *My Travels through Chad.* Trans. by Leslie Bull. London, 1943.

Lartéguy, Jean. *Les Clefs de l'Afrique: Femmes, confréries et fétiches.* Paris, 1957.

Le Cornec, Jacques. *Histoire politique du Tchad, de 1900 à 1962.* Paris, 1963.

Lefas, Alexandre. *L'Etat et les fonctionnaires.* Paris, 1913.

Leroy-Beaulieu, Paul. *De la colonisation chez les peuples modernes.* Rev. 5th ed. Paris, 1902. 2 vols.

Lewis, William H., ed. *French-Speaking Africa.* New York, 1965.

Lombard, Jacques. *Autorités traditionnelles et pouvoirs européens en Afrique noire.* Paris, 1967.

Louveau, Emile. *Au bagne: Entre les griffes de Vichy et de la milice.* Bamako, 1947.

Lowell, A. Lawrence. *Colonial Civil Service.* New York, 1900.

Lyautey, Hubert. *Lettres du sud de Madagascar, 1900-1902.* Paris, 1935.

——————. *Lettres du Tonkin et de Madagascar (1894-1899).* 2nd ed. Paris, 1921.

Ma, Pierre. *Organisation du ministère des colonies.* Paris, 1910.

Mager, Henri. *Vingt cinq années de politique coloniale.* Paris, n.d.

Mangeot, General. *La Vie ardente de Van Vollenhoven, gouverneur général de l'AOF.* Paris, 1943.

Mannoni, O. *Prospero and Caliban: The Psychology of Colonisation.* Trans. by Pamela Powesland. London, 1956.

Mariol, H. *Abrégé de législation coloniale.* Paris, 1937.

Martin du Gard, Maurice. *Pour l'empire.* Paris, 1937.

Mason, Philip (under pseudonym of Philip Woodruff). *The Men Who Ruled India.* London, 1954. 2 vols.

——————. *Prospero's Magic.* London, 1962.

Maunier, René. *The Sociology of Colonies: An Introduction to the Study of Race Contact.* Ed. and trans. by E. O. Lorimer. London, 1949. 2 vols.

——————, et al. *L'Empire français et ses ressources.* Paris, 1942.

McCloy, Shelby T. *The Negro in France.* Lexington, Ky., 1961.

Memmi, Albert. *Portrait du colonisé précédé du portrait du colonisateur.* Paris, 1957.

Mérat, Louis. *Fictions et réalités coloniales.* 2nd ed. Paris, 1947.

Messimy, Adolphe. *Mes souvenirs.* Paris, 1937.

───────. *Notre oeuvre coloniale.* Paris, 1910.

Mitterrand, François. *Présence française et abandon.* Paris, 1957.

Monnerville, Gaston, ed. *Où va l'Union Française?* Paris, 1955.

Morgenthau, Ruth Schachter. *Political Parties in French-Speaking West Africa.* New York, 1965.

Morrow, John H. *First American Ambassador to Guinea.* New Brunswick, N.J., 1968.

Mouëzy, Henri. *Assinie et le royaume de Krinjabo.* Paris, 1953.

Moukouri, Jacques Kuoh. *Doigts noirs: Je fus écrivain-interprète au Cameroun.* Montreal, 1963.

Moulin and Clabaux, eds. *Annuaire et livre d'or des administrateurs coloniaux, 1902.* Paris, 1902.

Mus, Paul. *Le Destin de l'Union Française: De l'Indochine à l'Afrique.* Paris, 1954.

N'Diaye, Jean Paul. *Enquête sur les étudiants noirs.* Paris, 1962.

Neres, Philip. *French-Speaking West Africa: From Colonial Status to Independence.* London, 1962.

Neton, Albéric. *Delcassé.* Paris, 1952.

Novick, Peter. *The Resistance versus Vichy: The Purge of Collaborators in Liberated France.* New York, 1968.

Olivier, Marcel. *Le Sénégal.* Paris, 1907.

───────. *Six ans de politique sociale à Madagascar.* Paris, 1931.

O'Reilly, Patrick. *Mon ami Gilbert l'africain.* Dijon, 1942.

Osborne, Milton E. *The French Presence in Cochinchina and Cambodia—Rule and Response (1859-1905).* Ithaca, N.Y., 1969.

Osswald, Klaus-Dieter, Ulrich Köhler, and Werner Ruf. *Frankreichs Entwicklungshilfe: Politik auf lange Sicht.* Cologne, 1967.

Paraf, Pierre. *L'Ascension des peuples noirs: Le Réveil politique, social, et culturel de l'Afrique au XXe. siècle.* Paris, 1958.

Piques, Camille. *Les Carrières administratives dans les colonies françaises et les pays de protectorat.* Corbeil, Seine-et-Oise, 1904.

Pisani-Ferry, Fresnette. *Jules Ferry et le partage du monde.* Paris, 1962.

Prévaudeau, Albert. *Joost Van Vollenhoven.* Paris, 1953.

Priestly, Herbert I. *France Overseas: A Study of Modern Imperialism.* New York, 1938.

Réclus, Maurice. *Jules Ferry, 1832-1893.* Paris, 1947.

Regismanset, Charles. *Questions coloniales (1900-1912).* Paris, 1912.

───────. *Questions coloniales (1912-1923).* Paris, 1923.

Reinsch, Paul S. *Colonial Government: An Introduction to the Study of Colonial Institutions.* London, 1926.

Ringel, Albert. *Les Bureaux arabes et les cercles militaires de Gallieni.* Paris, 1903.

Roberts, Stephen H. *History of French Colonial Policy, 1870-1925.* London, 1929. 2 vols.

Robinson, Ronald, and John Gallagher. *Africa and the Victorians.* London, 1963.

Rondet-Saint, Maurice. *Dans notre empire noir.* Paris, 1929.

——————. *Un Voyage en AOF.* Paris, 1930.

Roupnel, Gaston. *Histoire de la campagne française.* Paris, n.d.

Rudin, Harry R. *Germans in the Cameroons, 1884-1914: A Case Study in Modern Imperialism.* London, 1938.

Saintoyant, Jules. *L'Affaire du Congo, 1905.* Paris, 1960.

Sarraut, Albert. *Grandeur et servitude coloniales.* Paris, 1931.

——————. *La Mise en valeur des colonies françaises.* Paris, 1923.

Sharp, Walter Rice. *The French Civil Service.* New York, 1932.

Sieberg, Herward. *Eugène Etienne und die französische Kolonialpolitik (1887-1904).* Cologne, 1968.

Simon, Marc. *Souvenirs de brousse, 1910-1912.* Rennes, 1962.

Siriex, Paul Henri. *Une Nouvelle Afrique, AOF, 1957.* Paris, 1957.

Skinner, Elliot P. *The Mossi of the Upper Volta: The Political Development of a Sudanese People.* Stanford, Calif., 1964.

Société des anciens élèves de l'Ecole Coloniale. *L'Ecole Coloniale et ses élèves, 1885-1905.* Paris, 1905.

Soustelle, Jacques. *Envers et contre tout.* Paris, 1947. 2 vols.

Southworth, Constant. *The French Colonial Venture.* London, 1931.

Spitz, Georges. *L'Ouest africain français, AOF et Togo.* Paris, 1947.

Suignard, Jean. *Une Grande administration indochinoise.* Paris, 1931.

Suret-Canale, Jean. *Afrique noire, occidentale et centrale:* vol. II, *L'Ere coloniale (1900-1945).* Paris, 1964.

Symonds, Richard. *The British and Their Successors.* London, 1966.

Talvas, Georges. *Madagascar depuis l'occupation française: Journal d'un administrateur.* Paris, 1939.

Tarde, André, and Henri Massis (under pseudonym of "Agathon"). *Les Jeunes gens d'aujourd'hui.* Paris, 1913.

Thiellement, André. *Azawar.* Paris, 1949.

Thomazi, A. *Marins bâtisseurs d'empire:* vol. II, *Afrique.* Paris, 1947.

Thornton, A. P. *Doctrines of Empire.* New York, 1965.

Trautmann, René. *Au pays de "Batoula": Noirs et blancs en Afrique.* Paris, 1922.

Üle, Carl Hermann, ed. *Die Entwicklung des öffentlichen Dienstes.* Cologne, 1961.

Union coloniale française. *Préparation aux carrières coloniales.* Paris, 1904.

Valmor, J. *Les Problèmes de la colonisation.* Paris, 1909.

Veistroffer, Albert. *Vingt ans dans la brousse: Souvenirs d'un ancien membre de la mission Savorgnan de Brazza dans l'ouest africain, 1883-1903.* Lille, 1931.

Vignon, Louis. *Un Programme de politique coloniale.* Paris, 1919.

Villamur, Roger. *Les Attributions judiciaires des administrateurs et chefs de poste en service à la côte d'Afrique.* Paris, 1902.

——————, and Léon Richaud. *Notre colonie de la Côte d'Ivoire.* Paris, 1903.

Wauthier, Claude. *L'Afrique des africains.* Paris, 1964.

Weischoff, H. A. *Colonial Policies in Africa.* Philadelphia, 1944.

Wilbois, J. *Le Cameroun: Les Indigènes, les colons, les missions, l'administration française.* Paris, 1934.

Younger, Kenneth. *The Public Service in New States: A Study in Some Trained Manpower Problems.* Oxford, 1960.

XXX (pseud.). *Réalités coloniales.* Paris, 1934.

Colonial Fiction

Arnaud, Robert (under pseudonym of Robert Randau). *Des Blancs dans la cité des noirs.* Paris, 1935.

——————. *Le Chef des porte-plumes.* Paris, 1926.

——————. *Le Grand patron.* Paris, 1925.

——————. *Les Meneurs d'hommes.* Paris, 1931.

Binger, Louis G. *Le Serment de l'explorateur.* Paris, 1904.

Crouzat, Théophile. *Azizah de Niamkoko.* Paris, 1959.

Delavignette, Robert. *La Paix nazaréenne.* Paris, 1943.

——————. *Les Paysans noirs.* Paris, 1931.

—————— (under pseudonym of Louis Faivre). *Toum.* Paris, 1926.

Gauthereau, Raymond. *Passage du feu.* Paris, 1958.

——————. *Les Survivants.* Paris, 1960.

Joseph, Gaston. *Koffi: Roman vrai d'un noir.* Paris, 1922.

Maran, René. *Batouala.* Paris, 1921.

Marquis-Sebie. *Cieux africains.* Paris, 1937.

Oyono, Ferdinand. *Houseboy.* Trans. by John Reed. London, 1966.

Renel, Charles. *L'Oncle d'Afrique.* Paris, 1926.

Valdi, François. *La Femme antilope.* Paris, 1928.

Vally, Georges. *Malaria.* Paris, 1944.

Articles

Adamoleku, Ladipo. "The French Tradition of Administrative Training in Africa: The Senegalese Experience," *Administration* (Nigeria) III, no. 2 (January 1969), 93-102.

——————. "Politics and Administration in West Africa: The Guinean Model," *Journal of Administration Overseas* VIII (October 1969), 235-242.

Alexandre, Pierre. "L'Organisation politique des Kotokoli du Nord Togo," *Cahiers d'études africaines* VI (1963), 228-274.

——————. "Le Problème des chefferies en Afrique noire française," *Notes et études documentaires* 2508 (February 1959), 2-24.

Anon. "Les Administrateurs de la France d'outre-mer," *L'Economie* 451 (July 1, 1954), 12-17.

——————. "Africanisation," *Le Bleu d'outre-mer* (April 1956).

——————. "L'Africanisation des cadres en Côte d'Ivoire," *Encyclopédie mensuelle d'outre-mer* 70 (June 1956).

——————. "L'Avenir du corps des administrateurs de la France d'outre-mer," *Latitudes* 2 (1957), 16-25.

——————. "L'Epuration," *Défense de l'occident* (January-February 1957), pp. 78-85.

——————. "Faillite de la colonisation?" *Colo* (December 1947), p. 7.

——————. "L'Institut des hautes études d'outre-mer à l'honneur," *Marchés tropicaux et méditerranéens* XIX (February 16, 1963), 313.

——————. "Le Péché de colonialisme: Lettre d'un ancien administrateur de la France d'outre-mer," *L'Afrique et l'Asie* 59 (1962), 45-53.

——————. "Le Problème de l'africanisation des cadres en Afrique équatoriale française," *Chroniques d'outre-mer* 25 (May 1956), 15-17.

——————. "Salaires, soldes et traitements au Sénégal," *Afrique documents,* no. 104 (1969), 212-285.

——————. "Sénégal, du contrôle des administrations," *Afrique nouvelle* (November 9-16, 1967).

Arlabosse, General. "Une Phase de la lutte contre Samory, 1890-1892: Souvenirs du Général Arlabosse," *Revue de l'histoire des colonies* XX (1932), 385-432.

Aron, Raymond. "La Quatrième République doit se réformer pour survivre," *Le Figaro* CXXIX (March 2-7, 1955).

——————. "Social Structure and the Ruling Class," *British Journal of Sociology* I, no. 1 (1950), 1-11.

——————. "Social Structure and the Ruling Class," *British Journal of Sociology* I, no. 2 (1950), 126-143.

Augagneur, Victor. "Le Recrutement des administrateurs coloniaux," *Annales coloniales* XIII (April 6, 1912).

Balandier, Georges. "La Situation coloniale: Approche théorique," *Cahiers internationaux de sociologie* XI (1951), 44-79.

Ballard, John. "The Porto Novo Incidents of 1923: Politics in the Colonial Era," ODU, University of Ifé, *Journal of African Studies* II (July 1965), 52-75.

Berge, Francois. "Le Sous-secrétariat et les sous-secrétaires d'états aux colonies: Histoire de l'émancipation de l'administration coloniale," *Revue française d'histoire d'outre-mer* XLVII (1960), 301-386.

Bernard, A. "Le Ecoles nationales d'administration en Afrique noire," *Coopération et développement,* no. 2 (August 1964), 28-35.

Besson, Maryvonne. "Une Ecole française pour les administrateurs africains," *Vie économique française* (March 4, 1960).

Betts, Raymond F. "The French Colonial Frontier," in Charles K. Warner, ed., *From the Ancien Régime to the Popular Front: Essays in the History of Modern France in Honor of Shepard B. Clough* (New York, 1969), pp. 127-143.

Blanchard, Marcel, ed. "Administrateurs d'Afrique noire," *Revue d'histoire des colonies* XL (1953), 377-430.

—————. "Correspondance de Félix Faure touchant les affaires coloniales," *Revue d'histoire des colonies* XLII (1955), 133-185.

Boisboissel, Yves de. "Un Grand pionnier: Faidherbe," *Cahiers Charles de Foucauld* XXIX (1953), 47-83.

Boucherie, General. "Les Bureaux arabes," *Revue de défense nationale* (July 1957), pp. 1052-1066.

Boussenot, Georges. "Que vont devenir les administrateurs de la France d'outre-mer?" *Revue de la communauté France-Eurafrique* XI (September 1959), 18-19.

Bouteille, Paul. "L'Ecole nationale de la France d'outre-mer," *Revue économique française* LXVIII (May 1955), 2-5.

Brierly, T. G. "The Evolution of Local Administration in French-Speaking West Africa," *Journal of Local Administration Overseas* V (January 1966), 56-71.

Briey, Pierre de. "The Administrations of the New States," *Civilisations* XIV (1964), 3-11.

Burke, Fred G. "Public Administration in Africa: The Legacy of Inherited Colonial Institutions," *Journal of Comparative Administration* I (November 1969), 345-378.

Bury, J. P. T. "Gambetta and Overseas Problems," *English Historical Review* LXXXII (April 1967), 277-295.

Chailley-Bert, Joseph. "Dix années de politiques coloniales," *Journal des débats* (August 16, 23, 29; September 3, 11; October 2, 4, 8, 1901).

—————. "Recrutement des fonctionnaires coloniaux," *Comptes rendus, Institut colonial international* (Paris, 1895), pp. 289-309.

Clignet, Rémi. "The Legacy of Assimilation in West African Educational Systems," *Comparative Educational Review* (February 1968), pp. 57-67.

Coanet, M. "Contribution à l'étude du rôle colonial de l'armée," *Revue militaire française* CIII (1933), 94-119; 354-367.

Cohen, William B. "A Century of Modern Administration: From Faidherbe to Senghor," *Civilisations* XX, no. 1 (1970), 40-49.

——————. "The Colonized as Child: British and French Colonial Rule," *African Historical Studies* III, no. 2 (1970), 427-431.

——————. "The Lure of Empire: Why Frenchmen Entered the Colonial Service," *Journal of Contemporary History* IV (January 1969), 103-116.

Compton, J. M. "Open Competition and the Indian Civil Service, 1854-1876," *English Historical Review* LXXXIII (April 1968), 265-284.

Cornevin, Robert. "Evolution des chefferies traditionnelles en Afrique noire française," *Penant* (1961), pp. 235-250; 379-388; 539-556.

Coudray, Lallier du. "Du rôle des administrateurs dans une colonie neuve," *Revue de Madagascar* V (June 1902), 507-533.

Crochet, B. "La Fonction publique outre-mer et l'africanisation des cadres," *Latitudes* 2 (1957), 6-15.

Crowder, Michael. "Colonial Rule in West Africa: Factor for Division or Unity?" *Civilisations* XIV (1964), 167-182.

——————. "Independence as a Goal in French West African Politics, 1944-1960," in William H. Lewis, ed., *French-Speaking Africa* (New York, 1965), pp. 15-41.

——————. "Indirect Rule—French and British Style," *Africa* XXXIV, no. 3 (July 1964), 197-205.

Cuau, Yves. "Les Nouveaux mandarins, une enquête sur l'ENA," *Figaro* CXLI (August 3-4, 1967).

Dalimier, Albert. "Une Brochure sur l'AOF," *Annales coloniales* XIII (May 14, 1912).

Dareste, Pierre. "Le Régime politique et administratif des colonies françaises," in *Organisation politique et administrative des colonies* (Brussels, 1936), pp. 59-92.

Delafosse, Maurice. "L'Ecole Coloniale," *Afrique française*, supplement, XXXIV (April 1914), 137-146.

——————. "Les Etats d'âme d'un colonial," *Afrique française* XIX (1909), 62-65, 102-104, 127-130, 162-165, 200-202, 240-241, 288-289, 311-313, 338-339, 373-375, 414-416.

Delavignette, Robert. "L'Administrateur territorial en Afrique noire française," *Revue des travaux de l'Académie des sciences morales et politiques* CXVIII (1965), 83-96.

——————. "L'Afrique occidentale française au travail," *Afrique française* XLII (1932), 403-407, 476-481, 528-537, 577-580.

——————. "Colo et chercheur," *Latitudes* (1963), pp. 5-9.

——————. "Les Colonies dans la Troisième République en 1939," *La Vie intellectuelle* XIII (July 1945), 62-79.

——————. "Connaissances des mentalités indigènes en AOF," *Congrès international et intercolonial de la société indigène* I (Paris, 1931), 553-566.

——————. "Décalages entre la colonisation et la connaissance," *Etudes Maghrébines—mélanges Charles André Julien* (Paris, 1964), pp. 1-12.

——————. "Le Discours de Gouverneur général Brévié," *Afrique francaise* XLIII (December 1932), 721-729.

——————. "L'Ecole Coloniale," in *De Vorming van den bestuursamtenaar voor overzeesche gewester in Nederland, Engeland, Frankrijk, Belgie en Italie* (Leiden, 1937), pp. 100-107.

——————. "Equipe Eurafricaine–place pour l'Allemagne?" *Esprit* VII (November 1938), 211-227.

——————. "L'Europe devant le problème colonial," *Union pour la vérité, bulletin,* XLVI (December 1938-January 1939), 61-67.

——————. "L'Evolution de la politique des puissances coloniales après 1945," *Revue économique et sociale* XVIII (September 1960), 11-22.

——————. "Lord Lugard et la politique africaine," *Africa* XXI (July 1951), 177-187.

——————. "L'Oeuvre de nos administrateurs d'outre-mer," *Tropiques, revue des troupes d'outre-mer* (July 1959), pp. 39-44.

——————. "La Politique de Marius Moutet," in *Léon Blum, chef de gouvernement* (Paris, 1967), pp. 391-394. [Cahiers de la Fondation nationale des sciences politiques, no. 155.]

——————. "Pour le paysan noir, pour l'esprit africain," *Esprit* IV (1935), 367-390.

——————. "Problèmes de la Communauté," *Revue de Paris* LXVI (October 1959), 36-47.

——————. "Tiers monde sans tiers état?" *Revue de Paris* LXXII (December 1965), 82-91.

——————. "La Vie de cercle au Soudan français," in André Siegfried *et al., La Mer et l'empire* (Paris, 1944), pp. 159-170.

Deschamps, Hubert. "Les Assemblées locales dans les territories d'outre-mer," *Politique étrangère* XIX (August-October 1954), 427-436.

——————. "Et maintenant, Lord Lugard?" *Africa* XXXIII (October 1963), 293-306.

——————. "La Vocation coloniale et le métier d'administrateur," *Afrique française,* supplement, XLI (September 1931), 497-500.

DeWitte, Baron Johan. "Trente-trois ans d'apostolat au Congo francais," *Revue des deux mondes* XCI (July 1, 1911), 150-184.

Diagne, Mokhtar. "La Sénégalisation des cadres," *L'Unité africaine* (April 17, 1962).

Diamond, Sigmund. "An Experiment in 'Feudalism': French Canada in the Seventeenth Century," *William and Mary Quarterly* XVIII (January 1961), 3-34.

Dobkin, Marlene. "Colonialism and the Legal Status of Women in Francophonic Africa," *Cahiers d'études africaines* VIII (1968), 390-405.

Donnet, Gaston. "Le Fonctionnaire colonial," *Revue politique et littéraire, Revue bleue,* 4th series, IX (June 4, 1898), 721-726.

Duggan, William R. "The New African Chiefs," *Review of Politics* XXVIII (July 1966), 350-358.

Emily, J. "La Corse et l'empire," *Le Monde colonial illustré* 188 (February 1939), 36-37.

Fortini, Napoléon. "L'Administration au Sénégal," *Revue administrative* 102 (November-December 1964), 644-649.

Friedrich, Carl J. "The Continental Tradition of Training Administrators in Law and Jurisprudence," *Journal of Modern History* XI (June 1939), 129-148.

Frochot, Michel. "Que ma joie demeure," *L'Observatoire colonial*, New Series, XII (June 1938), 4.

Froelich, Jean Claude. "De quelques anciens élèves de l'école qui se sont illustrés dans les sciences humaines," *Latitudes* (1963), pp. 10-16.

——————. "Delavignette et le Service africain," *Revue française d'histoire d'outre-mer* LIV (1967), 44-51.

Gain, Edmond. "L'Institut colonial de l'Université de Nancy," *Outre-mer* (1929), pp. 64-79.

Gautier, E. F. "French Colonial Policy in Theory and Practice: A Review," *Geographical Review* XXI (1931), 131-141.

Geismar, Léon. "Du rôle comparé des administrateurs coloniaux dans les possessions africaines de la France et de l'Angleterre," *Afrique française*, supplement, XLI (October 1931), 574-575.

Gentil, Pierre. "Le Tchad: Décolonisation et indépendance," *Comptes rendus, Académie des sciences d'outre-mer, séances des 3 et 17 janvier 1969*, XXIX (January 1969), 1-24.

Georges, Philippe. "L'Ecole nationale d'administration du Sénégal," *Penant* LXXIV (1964), 523-534.

Gifford, Prosser. "Indirect Rule: Touchstone or Tombstone for Colonial Policy," in Prosser Gifford and William Roger Louis, eds., *Britain and Germany in Africa* (New Haven, Conn., 1967), pp. 351-391.

Girault, Arthur. "Des conditions de recrutement des fonctionnaires coloniaux y compris ceux de l'ordre judiciaire et de la surveillance de leur action aux colonies," *Comptes rendus de l'Institut international colonial* XI (Brussels, 1908).

Glenisson, Jean. "Un Grand organisateur: Emile Gentil," *Cahiers Charles de Foucauld* XXXII (1953), 108-136.

Goelan, Jean Louis, "L'Afrique d'expression française et la francophonie," *Penant*, LXXIX (January-March 1969), 1-32; (April-June 1969), 209-242.

Gournay, Bernard. "Un Groupe dirigeant de la société française: Les Grands fonctionnaires," *Revue française de science politique* XIV (April 1962), 215-242.

Gourou, Pierre. "Gallieni," in Charles A. Julien, ed., *Les Techniciens de la colonisation* (Paris, 1946), pp. 93-111.

Hardy, Georges. "Adieux à l'Ecole nationale de la France d'outre-mer," *Marchés tropicaux et méditerranéens* XV (January 10, 1959), 53-56.

——————. "Les Carrières coloniales," *Le Domaine colonial français* IV (1930), 433-440.

——————. "La France d'aujourd'hui et le problème colonial," *La Nouvelle revue des jeunes* III (July 15, 1931), 17-34.

───────────. "Histoire coloniale et psychologie ethnique," *Revue de l'histoire des colonies françaises* XVIII (1925), 161-172.

───────────. "Un Revenant," *Afrique française* XLII (February 1932), 83-84.

───────────. "Le Rôle de l'administrateur reste de première importance, mais s'adapte aux conditions nouvelles," *Marchés coloniaux du monde* VIII (July 26, 1952), 2029-2032.

Hauser, H. "Colonies et Métropole," *Revue d'économie politique* LIII (1939), 487-507.

Hayter, Theresa. "French Aid to Africa: Its Scope and Achievements," *International Affairs* XLI (April 1965), 236-251.

Homet, Marcel. "La Vérité sur l'Afrique équatoriale française," *Esprit* II (March 1, 1934), 916-954.

Hugot, Pierre. "L'Ecole nationale de la France d'outre-mer," *La Nouvelle revue française d'outre-mer* IL (July 1957), 391-394.

Jaugeon, Renée. "Les Sociétés d'exploration du Congo et l'opinion française de 1870 à 1906," *Revue française d'histoire d'outre-mer* XLVIII (1961), 353-437.

Julien, Charles A. "Léon Blum et les pays d'outre-mer," in *Léon Blum, chef de gouvernement* (Paris, 1967), pp. 377-390.

Jumper, Roy. "Entrance examinations for the French Administrative Service," *Personnel Administration* XVIII (September 1, 1955), 31-37, 47.

Kesler, Jean François. "Les Anciens élèves de l'Ecole nationale d'administration," *Revue française de science politique* XIV (April 1962), 243-266.

Kiwanuka, M. Semakula. "Colonial Policies and Administrations in Africa: The Myths of the Contrasts," *African Historical Studies* III, no. 2 (1970), 295-315.

Knight, M. M. "French Colonial Policy: The Decline of 'Association,' " *Journal of Modern History* V (1933), 208-224.

Koerner, Francis. "L'Accession des malgaches à la citoyenneté française (1908-1940)," *Revue historique*, CCXLII (July-September 1969), 77-98.

Labouret, Henri. "A la recherche d'une politique coloniale," *Le Monde colonial illustré* LXXXII (June 1930), 134.

───────────. "Le Noir et l'homme blanc en Afrique," *Le Monde colonial illustré* LIV (July 1928), 147-148.

───────────. "Politique indigène en Afrique tropicale," *Afrique française* XLVIII (May 1938), 203-207; (June 1938), 267-270.

───────────, Robert Delavignette, and Albert Charton. "L'Afrique occidentale française, aujourd'hui-demain," *Le Monde colonial illustré* CXXIV (1933), 188-189.

Laffey, John F. "Roots of French Imperialism in the Nineteenth Century: The Case of Lyon," *French Historical Studies* VI (April 1969), 78-92.

Lampué, Pierre. "Le Régime municipal dans les états francophones," *Revue juridique et politique de l'indépendance et coopération* XXII (April-June 1968), 463-484.

Laubriet, P. "A la conquête des coeurs, par l'Ecole nationale de la France d'outre-mer," *Mer-Outre-Mer* I (June-July 1947), 8-9.

Laurentie, H. "Recent Developments in French Colonial Policy," in *Colonial Administration by European Powers* (London, 1947), pp. 1-19.

Lavroff, D. G. "Le Code sénégalais des obligations de l'administration," *Penant* LXXVI (January-March 1966), 1-13.

Leblond, Marius-Ary. "Les Officiers administrateurs," *Valeurs mobiles et valeurs stables* (1945), pp. 5-7.

Legris, Michel. "Esquisses centrafricaines," *Le Monde* XXIII (January 4, 1966).

Le Quesne, C. M. "French West Africa," *African Affairs* LXIV (April 1965), 78-90.

Le Vine, Victor T. "Political Elite Recruitment and Political Structure in French-Speaking Africa," *Cahiers d'études africaines* VIII (1968), 369-389.

Lewis, Martin Deming. "One Hundred Million Frenchmen: The 'Assimilation' Theory in French Colonial Policy," *Comparative Studies in Society and History* IV (January 1962), 129-153.

Lorin, Henri. "Bordeaux et la colonisation française," *Questions diplomatiques et coloniales* X (October 1, 1900), 385-402.

Luchaire, François. "Le Togo français: De la tutelle à l'autonomie," *Revue juridique et politique de l'Union Française* XI (1957), 1-46, 501-587.

—————. "Les Grandes tendances de l'Afrique noire," *Revue française de science politique* IX (September 1959).

Luethy, Herbert. "La République continue," *Preuvres* 89 (July 1958), 11-20.

Lyautey, Hubert. "Du rôle colonial de l'armée," *Revue des deux mondes* LXX (January 15, 1900), 308-328.

Machat, J. "L'Enseignement colonial dans les lycées et collèges," *Annales coloniales* IV (August 15, 1903), 241-247.

Marchand, A. H. "La Formation des cadres supérieurs de l'administration ivoirienne," *Penant* LXXIX (April-June 1969), 171-208; (July-September 1969), 333-361; (October-December), 443-529.

Margueritte, Victor. "De la justice," *Annales coloniales* XIII (June 1, 1912).

Martineau, A., ed. "La Campagne du Cayor en 1883," *Revue de l'histoire des colonies françaises* XXVI (November-December 1933), 251-292.

Masson, André. "L'Opinion française et les problèmes coloniaux à la fin du second empire," *Revue française d'histoire d'outre-mer* XLIX (1962), 366-437.

Masson, Paul. "Marseille et la colonisation française," *Questions diplomatiques et coloniales* X (1900), 129-141, 321-332.

Mazrui, Ali A. "Consent, Colonialism, and Society," *Political Studies* XI (February 1963), 36-55.

Méker, Maurice. "Administrateurs et techniciens," *Colo* LIII (January 1953), 17-19.

—————. "Cinq années d'évolution d'un cercle soudanais, Bougouni," *Colo* LII (April 1952), 6.

Ménier, Marie Antoinette. "Conceptions politiques et administratives de Brazza, 1885-1898," *Cahiers d'études africaines* VI (1966), 83-95.

Merlo, Jean. "Les Fonctionnaires africains et le mécontentement des masses rurales," *Le Mois en Afrique* 2 (February 1966), 60-68.

Morel, Victor. "L'Ecole Coloniale," in J. Charles-Roux *et al.*, eds., *Colonies et pays de protectorat, exposition universelle* (Paris, 1900), pp. 413-435.

Moutet, Marius. "The French Colonial Empire," in *General Directory of Exportation and of the World Commercial Fairs* (Paris, 1948), pp. 185-186.

Mus, Paul. "La Formation des cadres administratifs d'outre-mer: ENFOM ou ENA? " *La Revue administrative* 2 (March-April 1948), 16-23.

Newbury, Colin. "The Formation of the Government General of French West Africa," *Journal of African History,* I, no. 1 (1960), 111-128.

Noël, Pardon. "Administration contre colons: Nouvelles pièces d'un vieux procès," *Questions diplomatiques et coloniales* I (October 15, 1897), 321-336.

O'Brien, Donal Cruise. "Towards an 'Islamic Policy' in French West Africa, 1854-1914," *Journal of African History* VIII (1967), 303-316.

O'Reilly, Patrick. "Paul Feillet: Gouverneur de la Nouvelle Calédonie," *Revue d'histoire des colonies* XL (1953), 216-248.

Pajot, Lale. "L'Assistance technique française en matière administrative en faveur des états africains et malgaches," *Revue juridique et politique d'indépendance et coopération,* XXIII (April-June 1969), 253-274.

Pasquier, Roger. "Chronique de l'histoire coloniale: L'Afrique noire d'expression française," *Revue française d'histoire d'outre-mer* XLVIII (1961), 438-457; L (1963), 74-129, 382-535.

Perham, Margery, "A Re-statement of Indirect Rule," *Africa* VII (July 1934), 321-334.

Pignon, Léon. "L'Ecole Coloniale," *La Nouvelle revue des jeunes* III (July 15, 1931), 164-171.

Pillias, C. "Composition du corps des administrateurs des colonies," *BAPAC,* no. 1 (July 13, 1907), 1-2.

Prévaudeau, Albert. "La Carrière d'administrateur colonial: La Vocation coloniale," *La Grande France* VIII (1945), 8-9.

Quermonne, Jean Louis. "Esquisse d'une théorie juridique et politique de la décolonisation," *Revue juridique et politique de l'Union Française* XII (July-September 1958), 429-451.

Ramel, G. "L'Intégration des administrateurs de la France d'outre-mer," *Bulletin de l'Association générale des administrateurs civils* XII (March 1960), 2827-2835.

Reste, F. J. "Grand corps et grand commis—dans la France d'outre-mer," *Revue des deux mondes* (March 15, 1959), pp. 321-336.

Rey, Georges. "Réformes en Afrique noire," *Encyclopédie mensuelle d'outre-mer* 78 (February 1957), 49-50.

Richter, Melville. "Toqueville on Algeria," *Review of Politics* XXV (July 1963), 362-398.

Rio, Armand. "A l'Ecole Coloniale: L'Expansion de l'énergie française," *Je sais tout* 257 (May 1927), 124-127.

Robinson, Kenneth E. "French West Africa," *African Affairs* L (April 1951), 123-132.

——————. "Political Developments in French West Africa," in Calvin Stillman, ed., *Africa in the Modern World* (Chicago, 1955), pp. 140-181.

——————. "The Public Law of Overseas France Since the War," *Journal of Comparative Legislation* 32 (1952), 37-46.

Semidei, Manuela. "De l'Empire à la décolonisation à travers les manuels scolaires français," *Revue française de science politique* XVI (February 1966), 56-86.

Servoise, René. "Introduction aux problèmes de la République Francaise," *Politique étrangère* XIX (August-October 1954), 379-418.

Silvestre, J. "L'Ecole Coloniale de Paris," *Congrès colonial international de Paris, 1889* (Paris, 1889), pp. 327-338.

——————. "Le Recrutement des fonctionnaires de l'Indochine française," *Congrès colonial international de Paris, 1889* (Paris, 1889), pp. 231-247.

Simar, Théodore. "L'Enseignement colonial général et spécial," *Troisième Congrès international colonial* (Gand, 1922), pp. 3-11.

Skurnik, W, E. "France and Fragmentation in West Africa: 1945-1960," *Journal of African History* VIII (1967), 317-333.

Strayer, Joseph R. "Empires—Some Reflections on Roman and Modern Imperialism," *Comparative Studies in Society and History* IX (October 1966), 101-104.

Suret-Canale, Jean. "La Fin de la chefferie en Guinée," *Journal of African History* VII (1966), 459-493.

Sutter, Jean. "L'Evolution de la taille des polytechniciens, 1801-1954," *Populations* XIII (July-September 1958), 373-406.

Tarrade, Jean. "L'Administration coloniale en France à la fin de l'ancien régime, projets de réforme," *Revue historique* CCXXIX (1963), 103-122.

Tohngodo, Bruno. "Défaillance et insuffisances de l'administration publique des états d'Afrique noire et de Madagascar," *Développement et civilisations* 59 (March 1967), 13-31.

Torres, Paul. "La Formation des cadres de l'administration régionale en Afrique centrale," *International Review of Administrative Sciences* XXXV, no. 4 (1969), 302-314.

Valette, Jacques. "Note sur l'idée coloniale vers 1871," *Revue d'histoire moderne et contemporaine* XIV (April-June 1967), 158-172.

Vermont, René. "De l'Empire à la Communauté," *Preuves* 83 (January 1958), 16-26.

Vignes, K. "Etude sur la rivalité d'influence entre les puissances européennes en Afrique équatoriale et occidentale depuis l'acte général de Berlin jusqu'au seuil du XXème siècle," *Revue française d'histoire d'outre-mer* XLVIII (1961), 5-95.

Weinstein, Brian. "Félix Eboué and the Chiefs—Perceptions of Power in Early Oubangui-Chari," *Journal of African History* XI (1970), 107-126.

You, André. "L'Evolution administrative à Madagascar," *Outre-mer* II (1930), 406-417.

Zeldin, Théodore. "Higher Education in France, 1848-1940," *Journal of Contemporary History* II (1967), 53-80.

Zimmerman, Maurice. "Lyon et la colonisation française," *Questions diplomatiques et coloniales* IX (June 15, 1900), 705-719; X (July 1, 1900), 1-21.

Zucarelli, François. "Le Département sénégalais," *Revue juridique et politique d'indépendance et coopération* XXII (July-September 1968), 853-874.

Periodicals

Académie des sciences coloniales: Comptes rendus. 1922-1958.

Académie des sciences d'outre-mer: Comptes rendus. 1959-1970.

Afrique française. 1891-1939.

Annales coloniales.

Le Bleu d'outre-mer. 1949-1957.

Bulletin de l'Association professionnelle des administrateurs coloniaux. 1907-1937.

Bulletin de la Société des anciens élèves de l'Ecole Coloniale. 1901-1948.

Colo. 1942-1946.

Le Courrier colonial. 1907-1937.

Le Figaro littéraire. 1965.

Journal officiel de la Fédération des associations amicales et professionnelles des fonctionnaires et agents coloniaux. 1919-1940.

Latitudes. 1957-1963.

Le Libéral de l'Est. 1886.

La Libre parole. 1894.

Marchés coloniaux. 1948-1956.

Marchés coloniaux du monde. 1956-1958.

Marchés tropicaux et méditerranéens. 1958-1966.

Le Monde colonial illustré. 1923-1940.

L'Observatoire colonial. 1932-1938.

Presse coloniale. 1908-1938.

Questions diplomatiques et coloniales. 1897-1914.

Quinzaine coloniale. 1897-1938.

La Semaine coloniale.

Official Publications

Afrique équatoriale française. *Journal officiel.* 1911-1957.

Afrique occidentale française. *Discours prononcé par le haut commissaire de la République française devant le grand conseil de l'AOF à l'ouverture de la session: 3 Septembre 1949.* Dakar, 1949.

―――――. *Journal officiel.* 1904-1957.

Antonetti, R. *Discours par M. R. Antonetti, Gouverneur-général de l'AEF, à la séance d'ouverture du conseil du gouvernement. Session ordinaire de décembre 1933.* Brazzaville, 1933.

Boisson, Pierre. *Circulaire no. 517c. L'Esprit nouveau, 11 juillet 1941.* Dakar, 1941.

Brévié, Jules. *Circulaires de M. le Gouverneur général J. Brévié sur la politique indigène et l'administration indigène en Afrique occidentale française.* Gorée, 1935.

France. Armée. Etat major. *Les Armées françaises d'outre-mer, les grands soldats coloniaux.* Paris, 1931.

France. Commission du statut des fonctionnaires. *Rapport au conseil supérieur de statistique, rapport préliminaire.* Paris, 1908.

France. *Journal officiel de la République Française. Débats.* 1880-1970.

France. *Journal officiel de la République Française. Lois et décrets.* 1880-1960.

France. Ministère de la France d'outre-mer. *Bulletin hebdomadaire* [and various titles]. 1946-1957.

―――――. *Bulletin officiel de la France d'outre-mer.* 1946-1959.

―――――. *ENFOM.* Paris, 1947.

―――――. *ENFOM.* Paris, 1956.

―――――. *Pour un meilleur destin dans les territoires d'outre-mer, bilan d'un gouvernement, février 1955-janvier 1956.* Paris, 1956.

France. Ministère de la marine. *Bulletin officiel des colonies.* 1885-1893.

France. Ministère des colonies. *Bulletin hebdomadaire d'information.* Paris, 1944-1946.

―――――. *Bulletin officiel des colonies.* 1894-1945.

―――――. *Conférence africaine française–Brazzaville.* Paris, 1945.

―――――. *Recommandations aux fonctionnaires et agents désignés pour servir dans la France d'outre-mer.* Paris, 1935.

―――――. Agence économique des colonies. *Vous voulez aller aux colonies.* Paris, 1942.

―――――. Ecole Coloniale. *Rapport sur le fonctionnement de l'Ecole.* Paris, 1891-1938.

―――――. Gouvernement du Soudan. Service local. *Instructions à l'usage des commandants de régions et de cercles.* 2nd ed. Paris, 1897.

Great Britain. Foreign Office. *Miscellaneous Series: No. 520. Diplomatic and Consular Reports. Report on French Colonies.* London, 1900.

Guinea. (Territoire de la Guinée française). *Conférence des commandants de cercles. Conakry, 25, 26, et 27 juillet 1957.* Conakry, 1957.

Ponty, William. *Discours prononcés par M. Ponty, Gouverneur général de l'Afrique occidentale française, 1909.* Gorée, 1909.

Reste, Jules. *Circulaires sur la réorganisation du commandement indigène, 28 avril 1931.* Abidjan, 1931.

Roux, M. *Manuel à l'usage des administrateurs.* Paris, 1911.

Senegal. *Journal officiel.* 1856-1970.

Senegal. Ministère de l'information. *Sénégal magazine.* Dakar, 1960.

Senegal. Ministère de l'intérieur. *Communication sur la réforme administrative.* St. Louis, 1960.

Senegal. Ministère du plan et du développement. *Carte pour servir à l'aménagement du territoire.* Dakar, 1965.

Senegal. Secrétariat d'état au plan du développement. *Pour une politique cohérente en matière d'équipements administratifs.* Dakar, 1962.

Senegal. Service local. *Le Sénégal. Organisation politique, administrative, finances, travaux publics.* Paris, 1900.

Unpublished Works

Alexandre, Pierre, and Gibert Ancian. "Cours d'organisation politique et administratives des territoires relevant du ministère de la France d'outre-mer." Mimeographed copy, 1957.

Association des anciens élèves de l'Ecole nationale de la France d'outre-mer. "Annuaire." Mimeographed copy, 1949.

Bikanda, Jean. "Grandeur et servitude administratives outre-mer: L'Administrateur français." Unpublished mémoire of the Ecole nationale de la France d'outre-mer, 1957-1958.

Blondiaux, P. "Cinquante années d'administration française à Melfi (1903-1952)." Unpublished mémoire, Centre de hautes études administratives sur l'Afrique et l'Asie modernes. 1952.

Bournazel, Alain. "L'Officier colonial, 1919-1939." Unpublished mémoire, Institut d'études politiques, 1967.

Coleman, James. "The Legal Aspects of Staff Problems in Tropical and Subtropical Countries." Mimeographed copy of working paper, 32nd study session of the International Institute of Differing Civilizations, Munich, 1960.

Coste, Jean. "Problèmes et perspectives de l'administration du Sénégal." Unpublished dissertation, Université de Bordeaux, Faculté de droit et des sciences économiques, 1965.

Delavignette, Robert. "Le Recrutement de l'administration. Administration technique et administration générale. Africanisation des cadres." Mimeographed copy of lecture given at Table Ronde of Association française de science politique, March 1959.

———. "Voyons clair au continent noir." 1936.

Deschamps, Hubert. "La Communauté française: Evolution politique et juridique." Mimeographed copy of course given at the Institut d'étude politique, 1960-1961.

———————. "Les Empires coloniaux et les nationalités d'outre-mer." Mimeographed copy of course given at University of Paris, 1947-1948.

———————. "La France d'outre-mer et la Communauté, évolution politique et juridique." Mimeographed copy of course given at the Institut d'étude politique, 1958-1959.

Devèze, M. "L'Empire colonial français en 1914: Organisation politique et administrative." Mimeographed copy of course given at the University of Paris, 1948.

Diamant, Alfred. "European Models of Bureaucracy and Development." Unpublished paper given at meeting of the Comparative Administrative Group, University of Maryland, 1963.

Ecole Coloniale. *Documents Divers, 1885-1914.* 7 vols.

Eisenstadt, S. N. "Continuity of Modernization and Development of Administration." Unpublished paper given at meeting of the Comparative Administrative Group, University of Michigan, 1964.

Froelich, Jean Claude. "L'Organisation politique et administrative de l'Afrique noire." Mimeographed copy of lecture given at the Centre militaire d'information et de spécialisation pour l'outre-mer, 1959.

Garner, Reuben. "Watchdogs of Empire: The French Colonial Inspection Service in Action, 1815-1913." Unpublished Ph.D. dissertation, Rochester University, 1970.

Garreau, P. "Evolution administrative d'un cercle Voltaïque." Unpublished mémoire, Centre de hautes études administratives sur l'Afrique et l'Asie modernes, 1956.

Gentil, Pierre. "Tchad: Décolonisation, indépendance." Unpublished mémoire, Centre de hautes études administratives sur l'Afrique et l'Asie modernes, 1965.

Girault, Arthur. "L'Evolution de l'administration des colonies depuis 1815 jusqu'à nos jours." Mimeographed copy of lectures given at the Ecole Coloniale, 1908-1909.

Grivot, René. "Problèmes d'Afrique noire: Le Beau métier d'administrateur colonial; Essai de psychologie du commandement en brousse." Mimeographed copy, n.d.

Hervé, M. "Le District de Kouango." Unpublished mémoire, Centre de hautes études administratives sur l'Afrique et l'Asie modernes, 1950.

Jumper, Roy. "The Recruitment and Training of Civil Administrators for Overseas France: A Case Study in French Bureaucracy." Unpublished Ph.D. dissertation, Duke University, 1955.

Kair, M. "Organisation administrative des colonies." Mimeographed copy of lectures given at the Ecole Coloniale, 1922-1923.

Lebègue, Robert. "Cours de géographie économique coloniale et d'administration coloniale." Mimeographed copy of course given at the Institut national d'agronomie de la France d'outre-mer, 1938.

Liebenow, Gus. "The Dilemmas of Development: Makonde." Unpublished manuscript.

Marty, Paul. "La Politique indigène du Gouverneur général Ponty." Typed copy in Archives nationales, Section outre-mer.

Masson, Paul. "Recrutement et formation des administrateurs coloniaux à l'étranger, 1885-1938." Unpublished mémoire, Ecole nationale de la France d'outre-mer, 1943.

Mournat, E. "Comment on cherche et on trouve une place aux colonies." Mimeographed copy, 1937; available at the *Bibliothèque nationale.*

Nolde, E. "De la carrière d'administrateur des colonies." Mimeographed copy of lecture given at the Ecole nationale de la France d'outre-mer, 1942.

Richardson, Sam. "Decolonization and the District Officer." Unpublished paper given at meeting of the Comparative Administrative Group, Boston University, 1963.

Ronen, Dov. "Political Development in a West African Country: The Case of Dahomey." Unpublished Ph.D. dissertation, Indiana University, 1969.

Spiegler, James S. "Aspects of Nationalist Thought Among French-Speaking Africans, 1921-1939." Unpublished dissertation, Nuffield College, 1968.

Villandre, Jean-Jacques. "Les Chefferies traditionnelles en Afrique occidentale française." Unpublished thèse de doctorat, Paris, 1950.

Viollier, Bernard. "La Participation à la vie politique et administrative des indigènes de Gold Coast et de la Côte d'Ivoire." Unpublished mémoire of the Ecole nationale de la France d'outre-mer, 1946.

Weinstein, Brian. "Governor General Félix Eboué–A Short Biography." Unpublished manuscript.

Zucarelli, François. "Du canton à l'arrondissement sénégalais." Unpublished mémoire for the Diplôme d'études supérieures de droit public, Dakar, 1965.

Index

Administrators: functions, 8, 11-12, 67-69; social origins, 55, 74, 90, 92, 152-153
Africanization, 138, 154-157, 156 n. 45, 185, 187-188, 194, 195 n. 5
"Agathon." *See* Massis, Henri; Tarde, André
Agents (*agents des affaires indigènes et civils*): entry into Corps of Colonial Administrators, 27-29, 97-98; recruitment of, 22-23; and technicians, 137-138, 169; training at *Ecole Coloniale,* 31-32, 85, 97-98
Agriculture, 12, 67, 112
Alexandre, Pierre, 95, 181, 203
Algeria, 7-8, 11, 11 n. 7, 161, 165-166, 183, 187, 192
Angoulvant, 80, 128
Aniaba, "Prince," 38 n. 5
Annet, Armand, 169
Anthropology, 46
Arboussier, Henri d', 82
Aristocracy, 55
Arnaud, Robert, 52, 116
Assimilation, 45-46, 117, 133, 142, 167, 177, 179, 204
Association, 47-49, 72-79, 117, 118, 133
Atlantic Charter, 167
Augagneur, Victor, 31
Aymonier, Etienne, 45
Azan, Paul, 161

Ballay, Victor, 53
Bandung Conference, 154, 192
Barthelemy, Georges, 110
Baudelaire, Charles, 53
Berlet, Albert, 209
Bernard, Albert, 107
Bert, Paul, 37
Besnard, René, 210
Binger, Louis, 74-76
Bléhaut, Henri, 145, 170
Boisson, Pierre, 132, 141, 158-160, 169
Borgnis-Desbordes, Gustave, 62
Boulanger, Ernest, 209
Bourges, Yvon, 197
Bouteille, Paul, 151
Boutmy, Emile, 25
Brazza, Savorgnan de, 53, 60, 71, 82, 105

Brazzaville Conference, 149, 166-170, 167 *n. 22,* 178, 180
Brévié, Jules, 115, 117, 127, 130-131, 161, 163, 170
British administration: and Colonial Office personnel, 59; and economic development, 113, 204; and independence, 191, 195; and indirect rule, 72-73; permanence in district, 124; and politics, 199-200; prestige of, 25; and recruitment and training, 7, 38, 48-49; and secretariats-general, 61
Bugeaud, Thomas, 8
Bureaux arabes, 8

Cameron, Governor, 131
Cameroons, 84, 86, 93, 102, 177, 179
Candace, Gratien, 58
Carde, Jules, 100, 111, 120, 130
Career motives, 51-55, 104-107, 141-142, 145-146
Carrère, Frédéric, 14
Cartier, Jacques, 105
Casamance, 194
Cayla, Léon, 169
Central African Republic, 197, 200
Centre de hautes etudes administratives sur l'Afrique et l'Asie modernes (CHEAM), 147-148
Chad, 32, 82, 123, 174-175, 178, 186, 195, 197, 206
Chailley-Bert, Joseph, 37-38, 48
Champlain, Samuel de, 105
Chappedelaine, Louis de, 210
Chautemps, André, 209
Chiefs, role of, 11, 12, 72-79, 114-119, 140, 163, 165, 180-182, 198, 202-203. *See also* Indirect rule
Citizenship of colonial subjects, 161-162, 170
Clémental, Etienne, 31, 58, 209
Cochin-China, 14, 37
Coleman, James, 199
Collège des stagiares, 37-39, 37 *n. 1,* 45
Commandants d'arrondissements, 11
Concours, 43, 153
Congo, 16, 30-31, 60, 62, 70, 77, 80-82, 110-111, 183
Coppet, Marcel de, 118, 131, 137
Cornevin, Robert, 95
Cornwall, Sir George, 15
Cosnier, Henri, 110, 123
Coste-Floret, Paul, 174-175
Cultural relations, 132, 203-205

Dahomey, 81, 114, 118, 123, 131, 137, 140, 196, 201, 216
Dampierre d'Hornoy, Charles de, 209
Daladier, Edouard, 210
Dalimier, Albert, 210
Dariac, 210
Death rate, 23
Debré, Michel, 195
Decentralized administration, 57-67, 175
Decolonization, 188-193, 213
Decrais, Albert, 209
Dédougou, 80
Defferre, Gaston, 186, 188. See also *Loi-cadre* Defferre
Delafosse, Maurice, 49, 64, 67-68, 79, 86, 94, 129

Delavignette, Robert; on Africanization, 156; attitude toward Africans, 100-102, 116; colonial commission member, 139; on decentralization, 57, 64; on Delafosse, 49; director of ENFOM, 45 n. 28, 99-104, 143-148, 151; and economic development, 100, 113; high commissioner to the Cameroons, 148; and reforms of 1946, 177-178; on relations with colonies, 134, 171, 204; on role of administrators, 121-122, 127-128, 146, 148; on rule through chiefs, 74, 179; use of interpreters, 127
Delcassé, Théophile, 20-21, 75, 209
Demaison, André, 52
Deschamps, Hubert, 24, 108-109, 113, 120, 133-135, 139, 142, 147, 155
Dien Bien Phu, 183
Diori, Hamani, 95
Diseases, 23
Dislère, Paul, 44-45
Doucet, Robert, 61
Doumergue, Gaston, 120-121, 209, 210
Dupuy, Charles, 20
Dutch administration, 6-7, 38, 38 n. 3, 176

Eboué, Félix, 78, 124, 148, 159, 163-165, 167, 179
Ecole cambodgienne, 38, 45
Ecole Coloniale: administration of, 44-45, 86-90, 98-104; admission to, 41-43; 84-91; founding of, 37-38; geographic origins of students, 43-44, 89, 106; language training, 46, 48; "native section," 38-41; opposition to, 25-26, 30, 41-42; social origins of students, 55, 90, 92; students' entry into colonial service, 25-26, 29-32, 36, 84-85, 93-98, 104-108
Ecole nationale d'administration (ENA), 41, 151-152, 154-155, 203
Ecole nationale de la France d'outre-mer (ENFOM); administration of, 143-152, 212; admission to, 145-146, 151-153; and German occupation, 143-144; social origins of students, 152-153
Economic aid, 190, 191; loans, 110-111; Sarraut plan, 109-110
Economy: budget, 69; contributions to France, 109-111, 159, 165; development of, 11-12, 67-68, 100, 109-113, 137-138, 166-167, 173, 204-206
Elites: attitudes toward the French, 116, 131-132, 140, 189, 205; French distrust of, 40-41, 134, 140-142, 165, 180-181, 192-193; French policy toward, 114, 128-129, 131-132
ENA. See *Ecole nationale d'administration*
ENFOM. See *Ecole nationale de la France d'outre-mer*
Ethnology, 93-95, 127, 147
Etienne, Eugène, 15 n. 23, 19-21, 37-41, 74, 209
Ewé, 184

Fabry, Jean, 210
Faidherbe, Louis, 9-16, 11 n. 7, 38 n. 6, 108, 206
Faure, Félix, 19-21, 37-38, 209
Fonds d'investissements economiques et sociales (FIDES), 173
Forced labor, 69-70, 111-113, 118-119, 137, 170, 173, 176
Fourichon, Martin, 209
French Community, 190-191
French West Indies, 43-44, 47
Freycinet, Charles de, 19
Froelich, Jean-Claude, 141
Futa Djallon, 76

Gabon, 14, 16, 196
Gallieni, Joseph: administrative system, 108-109; on decentralization, 64-65;

influence on career choice, 53, 105; inspection system, 63; language policy, 126; ministry of colonies favored by, 20; rule through chiefs, 75, 78; in Senegal, 16; and tax burden, 69
Gambetta, Léon, 19
Garnier, Francis, 53
Gaulle, Charles de, 145, 158-159, 163, 165-166, 190-191, 194
Gentil, Pierre, 183, 184 n. 87
German administration, 33, 48, 61
Ghana, 202. *See also* Gold Coast
Gicquet, Albert, 209
Gide, André, 111, 139
Gold Coast, 112, 159, 184, 188. *See also* Ghana
Goldie, Sir George, 73
Gourdon, Henri, 98
Grand Popo, 21
Griaule, Marcel, 147
Groupe d'etudes politiques de l'Afrique et de Madagascar (GEPAM), 153-154
Gueye, Lamine. *See* Lamine-Gueye law
Guieyesse, Pierre, 209
Guillain, Antoine, 209
Guinea, 75-76, 78, 81-82, 117-118, 123, 126, 131, 182, 187, 190-191, 198-199, 203-205, 217
Guy, Camille, 132

Hadj Omar, El, 75
Hailey, Lord, 141
Haileybury, 7
Hardy, Georges, 24, 87-90, 92-98, 102
Hazoumé, Paul, 101
Heredia, José Maria de, 53
Herriot, Edouard, 171
Hesse, André, 210
Holle, Paul, 14
Houphouet-Boigny, Félix, 183
Hugot, Pierre, 117

IHEOM. See *Institut des hautes études d'outre-mer*
India (British), 6-7, 40, 73, 131, 133
Indigénat. *See* Justice
Indirect rule, 7, 72-73. *See also* Chiefs, role of
Indochina, 21, 38-40, 45 n. 31, 47, 86, 91, 129, 132, 179, 184, 187, 192
Inspection system, 59-60, 63-64, 139-140
Institut des hautes etudes d'outre-mer (IHEOM), 156-157, 157 n. 47
Institut international d'administration publique (IIAP), 157, 203
Isambert, René, 124
Ivory Coast, 32, 69, 74, 80, 82, 94, 111-112, 118-119, 123, 126, 131, 159, 174, 187, 191, 195, 197, 204, 206, 217

Jamais, Emile, 209
Jauréguiberry, Jean, 11, 14-15, 209
Joseph, Gaston, 87
Jouvenel, Henry de, 210
Justice, 68-69, 68 n. 43, 119-120, 159, 172-173

Kat Angelino, A. D. A. de, 176
Kipling, Rudyard, 52-53

Labé, 75, 78
Labouret, Henri, 93-95, 113, 115, 134, 178
Lamine-Guèye law, 170
Lamoureux, Lucien, 210
Lanessan, Jean Marie de, 72
Languages, knowledge of, 39, 46, 48, 82, 103, 126-127, 147, 151
Lapie, P. O., 142
Laurentie, Henri, 181
Laval, Pierre, 210
Lebon, André, 42, 209
Lebon, Gustave, 40, 48
Lebon, Maurice, 209
Lebrun, Albert, 209, 210
Leconte de Lisle, Charles, 53
Legal studies, 34-35, 45, 97, 102-104, 150
Legris, Michel, 200
Leroy-Beaulieu, Paul, 18, 38, 62
Lévy-Bruhl, Lucien, 102, 139
Leygues, Georges, 209
Loi-cadre Defferre, 185-187, 212-213
Loti, Pierre, 52
Louango, 21
Louveau, Emile, 158
Luethy, Herbert, 171
Lugard, Sir Frederick, 73, 116, 133
Lyautey, Hubert: administrative system, 108; disciple of Gallieni, 65; and *Ecole Coloniale,* 30; influence of, 105, 121, 178; motive for going overseas, 52

Madagascar, 63, 69, 75, 76-77, 81-82, 86, 103, 119, 129, 137-138, 150, 159, 169, 191, 203-204, 216
Maghreb, 204
Maginot, André, 115, 210
Mairey, Jean, 144 *n. 8*
Mali, 191, 197-198, 203
Mandel, Georges, 98, 126-127, 135, 210
Manoury, Maurice, 210
Massis, Henri, 53
Maunier, René, 161-162
Maupoil, Bernard, 95
Mauritania, 32, 59, 204, 217
Maurois, André, 52-53
Messimy, Adolphe, 58-59, 77, 209
Messmer, Pierre, 197
Metropolitan civil service, 27, 170
Military officers, 26-27, 146, 160
Military troops, colonial, 109, 113-114, 116, 118
Milliès-Lacroix, Raphaël, 56, 209
Ministry of colonies: contact with other imperial powers, 60-61; control over empire, 57-60, 80, 135-137, 178-179; established, 21; need for, 17-20; personnel in, 58-59, 134-137, 160-161
Mitterrand, François, 183, 189-190
Mollet, Guy, 154
Morel, Jean, 209, 210
Moutet, Marius, 102, 135-138, 171, 210
Mus, Paul, 148-152, 148 *n. 18*

277

Napoleon, Prince, 18
Napoleon III, 18
Nationalism, 132, 142, 158, 192-193
New Caledonia, 16, 21
Nietzsche, Friedrich, 53
Niger, 32, 59, 100, 115, 126, 200-201, 217

Ogoué, 21
Olivier, Marcel, 117, 138
Organisation commune africaine et malgache (OCAM), 203
Oubangui, 77, 174, 180
Oubangui-Tchad, 62

Paraf, Pierre, 187
Parliament and the colonial administration, 19, 21, 41-42, 51, 69, 109-110, 138-139, 170-171, 194
Pavie, Auguste, 38, 105
Péguy, Charles, 53
Perier, Léon, 87, 210
Piétri, François, 210
Platon, Admiral, 170
Pleven, René, 146, 165-167
Poincaré, Henri, 53
Political integration, 203-204
Political representation, 129-132, 159, 167-168, 173-174, 176, 182, 185-186
Pompidou, Georges, 204
Ponty, William Merlaud, 62, 68-69, 75, 122
Popular Front, 118, 137-139, 147, 159
Porte, Jean de la, 209
Porto Novo, 21, 38
Pothau, Louis, 209
Psichari, Ernest, 53

Ramadier, Jean, 187
Randau, Robert, 52
Rassemblement démocratique africain (RDA), 183
Regismanset, Charles, 55
Reste, Jules F., 53, 71
Réunion, 47
Rey, Georges, 187
Reynaud, Maurice, 210
Reynaud, Paul, 210
Richelieu, Cardinal, 18
Rimbaud, Arthur, 53, 105
Rollin, Louis, 210
Roosevelt, Franklin D., 192
Roume, Ernest, 61, 63, 68-69
Rousseau, Armand, 209
Roussin, Albert, 209
Roupnel, Gaston, 101
Rouvier, Maurice, 41
Royal Academy of Delft, 7, 38

Sainteny, Jean, 197
Salaries, 21, 24, 45 *n. 31,* 138 *n. 124,* 195, 201
Samory, 75

Sarraut, Albert, 109-110, 125, 129, 210
Secretariats-general, 27, 61-62
Senegal, 8-11, 13-14, 38 *n. 6,* 73, 81-82, 93, 111, 118, 120, 123, 126, 131-132, 147, 159, 182-183, 186, 191, 194-195, 197-202, 204-205, 217
Senghor, Léopold, 101, 142, 189, 201-202, 204
Simon, Henry, 210
Socialist students, 154 *n. 39*
Somaliland, 107, 190
Soustelle, Jacques, 147, 160
Steeg, Théodore, 210
Stern, Jacques, 210
Stevenson, Robert Louis, 105
Sudan (Anglo-Egyptian): Political Service, 74 *n. 63*
Sudan (French), 67, 75-76, 111-112, 119, 122, 124, 131, 180, 191, 217

Tanganyika, 124, 131, 141
Tarde, André, 53
Taxation, 69-71, 111, 187, 206 *n. 47*
Technical assistance, 195-196, 196 *n. 7*
Technicians, 112, 173
Teitgen, Pierre Henri, 184-185
Tevoedjre, Albert, 158
Togo, 84, 86, 181, 184, 196-197
Tolstoy, Leo, 53
Toqué, Emile, 30
Tovalou-Houenou, Kojo, 140
Trouillot, Georges, 209

Uganda, 202
Union africaine et malgache (UAM), 203
United Nations, 154, 184, 188, 197
Upper Volta, 77, 82, 100, 158, 158 *n. 2,* 182, 217

Van Vollenhoven, Joost: career, 52, 61, 65; in central administration, 46 *n. 32*; on chiefs, 77-79; and decentralization, 65, 67; and Eboué, 163; on *Ecole Coloniale,* 51 *n. 45*; on elites, 114; influence of, 64-65, 65 *n. 36*, 121; on leniency toward maladministration, 81 *n. 100*; on ministry of colonies, 59, 60; resignation as governor-general, 65 *n. 35*; rotation of desk officers, 62
Vichy regime, 126, 143-146, 158-163, 169-170
Vieillard, Gilbert, 95, 106-107
Vignon, Louis, 41, 48-49
Vincennes colonial exposition, 105-106